AND SUDDENLY THEY'RE GONE

What Parents Need To Know About The Empty Nest

Patricia S. Olson

With a Foreword by
Thomas E. Colley, Ph.D.

Tiffany Press
Boulder

Publisher: Tiffany Press, P.O. Box 62,
Jamestown, Colorado 80455-0062

Cover, Illustrations: Power Graphics, Inc., Louisville, Kentucky

Copyright © 1993 by Patricia S. Olson

Library of Congress Catalog Card Number 92-61770

ISBN 0-9634523-0-4

All Rights Reserved

Printed in the United States of America

No part of this work may be reproduced or transmitted in any form by any means, electronic or mechanical, including photocopying and recording or by any informational retrieval system, except for the quotation of brief passages in criticism, without advance permission in writing from the publisher.

To Glenn and Tiffany
my two wonderful and loving children whose encouragement to write this book was echoed in a thumbs up "Go for it, Mom!"

CONTENTS

Foreword	vii
Acknowledgments	ix
Prologue	xi
Introduction	1
1 / The Joy of It All	5
2 / The Other Side of the Coin: Postpartum	13
3 / How Are the Kids Feeling?	28
4 / Siblings: How Do Things Shake Out?	48
5 / Do Fathers Feel the Same as Mothers?	62
6 / Additional Stress for the Single Parent	74
7 / What the Women's Movement Didn't Tell Us	94
8 / Letting Go: Laying the Foundation	100
9 / Letting Go: Practical Application	120
10 / Myths of Midlife	140
11 / Parents Forced into Self-examination	148
12 / Setting New Directions	173
13 / Alone at Last...But Are We Happy?	182
14 / When the Nest Fills...Again	202
15 / Variations of the Theme: Marriage, Military, and Moving Out	210
Conclusion	227
Bibliography	232
Index	235

FOREWORD

We prepare them to leave the nest. We prepare ourselves for their leaving — but we are never really ready for the effects in our lives or theirs. That is what this fine study is all about.

This is a very insightful book which will prove of great value to any parent anticipating or experiencing the process of having a child leave home at age eighteen. It will also be of value to mental health professionals, college counselors, ministers, and those who study human life cycles.

Although primarily a mother's book, the perspective is broad enough to include everyone involved in the letting go process and many fathers will find it enlightening — I did.

Patricia Olson has judiciously pursued her topic and the thorough presentation is the result of many careful interviews with parents and children and discussions with knowledgeable professionals. Her very perceptive analysis is clear and down-to-earth. I am sure it will be quite helpful to many parents. And it would be appropriate for young adult children to give a parent who has difficulty with the separation process.

My role with regard to this work has been that of an editor/commentator. Based upon my years of experience counseling in a variety of family problems, I have provided feedback to the authenticity of Ms. Olson's ideas and presentations in every chapter. Her exploration of the subject is rich and meaningful and has a fullness often not found in more professional studies of circumstances such as this. I can highly recommend its psychological integrity.

The mixed feelings of both loss and growth which parent and child experience are described by Ms. Olson in such a manner that the reader will surely feel, "I knew all of this, but now I know it better." In Gestalt psychology there is a term called "closure" which refers to the bringing of experience into a meaningful whole. This book will provide a feeling of closure for those who have gone through the "and suddenly they're gone" experience.

Thomas E. Colley, Ph.D.
Louisville, Kentucky

ACKNOWLEDGMENTS

I could not have written this book without the thoughts, wise consultation, and advice of psychologist Tom Colley. He brought critical insights and professional expertise to a book imbued with psychological detail.

Writing a book is a consuming, oftentimes lonely, endeavor. Intuitively, some friends are there at the right moment to provide unspoken support or, fortunately, computer know-how and accessories. I was fortunate to have three such friends: Judith McCandless, Grady Clay, and John Hunter. They took me to the movies, gave me hugs, re-inked my ribbons. I will never forget them.

How fortunate I was to have found my way to Louisville, Kentucky, and the vast network of friends and neighbors I knew there. Many helped bring this book to fruition by correcting not only spelling and grammar but also by helping me clarify my thoughts on paper: Jane Wehner, Gerry Toner, Carol Toner, Martha Henning, Judy Ryce, Eddie Middleton, Allen Share, John Hines, and those I quoted on the back cover. Others, who gave me practical suggestions along the way, include Lilialyce Akers, Alanna Nash, Lucy Freibert, and out-of-towners, Gaynor Ellis and Manisha Roy. Louisville Literati and Jane Pickering nurtured my ongoing need to read, read, read, as did Maria Picard. Annie Lawes nurtured my spiritual growth. Peela Rao and Eat Group nurtured my stomach. Sandy Hart and Calista Morrill nurtured my wanderlust and love of the mountains. Mike Power and Mike Schmidt contributed design expertise. John Conely was just there. And Steven Channell made me laugh when he sent a postcard saying, "...and I knew her *before* Phil Donahue, Oprah Winfrey, and David Letterman."

I also want to thank Keith Auerbach, M.D., David Dolen, M.D., Lee Epstein, Ph.D., Ann Block, Betty Ann Miller, Lovick Miller, Ph.D., and Wendy Fidao for scheduling interview time. Their professional, therapy-oriented insights helped provide a framework for many of the book's comments and conclusions. In addition, Drs. Auerbach and Dolen read the final text and gave substantive psychiatric critique.

Daily walks with my loving golden retriever, Misty, invariably ended up on Frankfort Avenue at the Crescent Hill Branch of the Louisville Free Public Library. There, Betty Mann and her co-workers ordered dozens of books for me, found information, and provided a supportive environment that is too often taken for granted. No request was turned down, no question left unanswered. Betty's patience and polite encouragement reinforced my long-standing opinion that libraries are wonderful institutions.

I have been blessed to have a loving family. Their support and encouragement sustained me over the years it took to bring this book into publication. I'm glad the journey is over.

Finally, I want to thank those parents and children who so generously shared their time with me and revealed their feelings so that we all might learn.

PROLOGUE

For about two weeks, I was passing on all these bits of wisdom — a last-ditch effort to influence the son who was leaving my life. Glenn would silently look up with pain and roll his eyes, or snicker a little smile of indulgence. After all, he had only a few more days to put up with me.

I had started thinking about his leaving home a year earlier as we went around visiting colleges. I began to realize that I could take some control of my life: move where I wanted, do what I wanted — feel free for the first time in a long while. Probably the first time ever. Oh, of course, daughter Tiffany would still have two years of high school left, and there would be plenty of college expenses, but the end was definitely drawing near. What was I going to do?

The more I thought about it, the more scared I got. No wonder mothers often had another child when the youngest trotted off to grade school. Just as these women's lives were about to open to new possibilities, the process could be effectively delayed with more mothering responsibilities. I felt like using some delaying tactics myself. There was absolutely no doubt that being a mother was fulfilling and gave me a sense of purpose. But what happened when the children left home and that sense of purpose, as well as a piece of me, walked out the door?

I spent a lot of time just thinking, getting used to the idea of moving, of making some new choices. Because I had a life of my own and my activities did not revolve totally around children, I figured that the adjustment to Glenn's leaving would be fairly smooth. I didn't worry too much about how his departure would affect me. As it turned out, I was in for a surprise.

As Glenn and his father drove away, the car packed to the gills, I was a bevy of mixed emotions: thrilled that the time of expectation was drawing to a close, for Glenn looked forward to going to Brown University; glad that the loading of the car had gone smoothly, for Glenn's father and I did not always get along even though we had been divorced for years; and wondering how this was really going to hit me, for I could feel a slight discomfort in the pit of my stomach. I turned, walked back across the front yard, and climbed the porch steps.

Once inside, I didn't know exactly how to feel in the emptiness of the house. I knew that I would have preferred that Tiffany were home, but she had had plans of her own and had already said her goodbyes. I was all alone. It was still early in the morning, but going back to bed was out of the question. I had to be busy, so the solution was automatic: Glenn's room.

Glenn's room was in a constant state of chaos during his teenage years, and off-limits to me. We had agreed, however, that it was his responsibility to leave the room clean at departure time if I were to stay out. Remaining true to form to the very end, he had made no attempt to clean or straighten anything. In fact, the room was in shambles. I began the attack.

Over the next few hours, and even most of the next day, I sorted and cleaned, taking boxes of trash to the garbage can. I found everything, much of it in the depths of his walk-in closet. Dozens of empty beer cans and bottles left discarded in brown grocery bags. Shopping bags with price stickers and cellophane wrappers that had once held new shirts. A final solution to the missing extension cord mystery — a mystery involving four cords and many years. Forgotten posters of favorite rock stars. School papers written in the wee hours of the morning. Pictures and love letters of an old girlfriend. All kinds of miscellaneous paraphernalia. And lots (and lots) of girly magazines, many of them six, eight years old.

I found the magazines in the narrow space between the bed and the wall about lunch time. Feeling the need for a break and being rather curious, I gathered up about ten or twelve and headed downstairs. The sun on the back porch was inviting, so I carefully placed the magazines next to the faded blue butterfly chair and went back into the house to pour myself a glass of white wine. A big one.

I saw pictures and poses I had never seen before, and had to chuckle to think of all the years that Glenn had been looking at some of the same magazines over and over again. Most of the old ones, I knew, had been retrieved years ago from our apartment Dumpster where he had discovered a free and dependable supply of discards. Once he even brought me "something you might be interested in, Mom." It was a magazine for women, full of pictures of nude men. How I had laughed. But now, here I was, sitting on the back porch sipping wine, looking at pornographic magazines, and mourning the loss of my son. What an ironic twist. I got up and went back to cleaning his room.

* * * * *

Glenn's leaving wrenched me. I felt as though someone had swooped down and plucked out a piece of me, leaving this gaping hole with nothing to fill it up. Amazingly, my career seemed pretty insignificant and I began looking at most careers as just jobs: something that made a few people very wealthy or something that allowed the vast majority to pay their bills each month, but not something that truly seemed to give significance to life, not in the vast scheme of things. The purpose of life seemed to lie with other people, in helping someone else, or in sharing the simple things. Or at least I thought so.

The house became a big empty shell. A presence was missing and it cried out to me each time I passed the dining room where he had spent so many hours sitting at the table reading the newspaper, eating, or doing his homework. His chair was empty, like a death in the family. Oh, I knew he'd be home again. He'd even been gone for two-month periods in summers past. But somehow I knew that this time it was different. I was shocked at the finality of it all. Going away to school was symbolic of the end: Glenn didn't need me anymore. Sure I had a financial obligation, but he really didn't need me. Inside I ached.

INTRODUCTION

When my son left home for college, I was surprised at my anguish. I was forty-one. On the surface, I was very happy for him and was sharing his excitement. As I began to explore my other feelings and look for possible explanations to my many questions, I was again surprised to discover how little literature existed on the leave-taking process, how rarely parents talked of their true feelings. Reams of how-to material have been written on how to raise a two-year-old, for instance, but not on how to prepare both parent and child for the inevitable separation.

My need to understand my own feelings, coupled with the need to fill the void left in my life by Glenn's departure, eventually resulted in the idea for writing this book. By conducting well over one hundred interviews with parents spanning a twenty-year midlife spectrum, with children both old and adolescent, and with professionals, and by using what research material was available, I found my answers about the separation process — information and healing insights now to be shared with other parents.

Insight, however, does not always make for ease. Relationships are intricate and mysterious, at times. Many aspects of interaction between people are unconscious and, in that sense, uncontrollable. Intellectual knowledge and laundry lists of *do*s and *don't*s do not prevent pain or minimize failure — and I do not want to appear to have oversimplified the complexities of the parent-child relationship.

In limiting the scope of the book, I have confined my research socioeconomically to middle- and upper-class families. The issues facing impoverished and many lower- or working-class families are simply too complex and diverse. Although a few minority individuals were interviewed, their numbers were not significant enough to determine whether different trends were present. I have also limited research to voluntary separations, as opposed to involuntary separations such as death. Much has been written about death, in general, and particularly the death of a child in the family. I have not dealt with the separation process that occurs at the time of a marital split or divorce, when a child runs away, or if a young adult is incarcerated or leaves home because of a drug or alcohol abuse situation. Nor have I investigated the myriad of forces at work when children leave a home environment of physical or sexual abuse.

Further, I have placed primary focus on the separation process as it relates to college-bound children. This emphasis is apparent throughout the book and accounts for using the designation *eighteen-year-olds* as symbolic of the age when children leave home. However, my research did show that many feelings relating to the voluntary separation process affect parents similiarly, regardless of the type of separation or when it occurs. In that sense, then, the book has relevance to parents whose children leave home due to marriage, military service, or moving out, and quotes from these parents are intermingled throughout. What specific differences I could determine, based on limited interviews, are briefly outlined in a separate chapter.

One difficulty I encountered was what, exactly, to call the daughter or son so often talked about in this book. There are a variety of possible phrases such as young person, young adult, fledgling adult, neo-adult, emerging adult; some of these work well descriptively while others seem contrived or miss the mark. Over the years, the term *kids* has gained an air of familiarity — as in, "Where are you kids going tonight?" — that has increased its everyday usage and made it more acceptable for printed material. This is fortunate.

Often I simply settled on the word *child* although it was not a happy choice. Technically, the word covers all aspects and ages of childhood, beginning at birth and encompassing a lifetime. Most frequently, we think of a child as someone quite young; yet in this book the word usually represents the eighteen-year-old who is simultaneously experiencing departure from youth and preparation for adulthood — a person who falls somewhere between being a child and being an adult — and often vacillates back and forth in thoughts and actions. Sadly, this in-between word does not exist in the English language. I can only hope that the reader sympathizes with the problem and adjusts the concept of the word *child* to fit the situation being described.

Another term that is somewhat problematic is *working mothers*. Certainly, all mothers work. In addition, a great many earn an income outside of the home. For convenience, the term refers to that group of mothers who do earn an independent income from employment.

Except in the sections specifically talking about the marriage unit or single parents, comments of both married and single parents are interwoven throughout without necessarily referencing their marital status. The names of the parents and children interviewed are pseudonyms and facts which might reveal their identity have been changed to protect their anonymity.

There is a wide spectrum of parental reactions to the leave-taking process. On the far ends are those few parents who either see the departure as having no meaningful significance or have an extreme reaction because the departure aggravates psychological problems. For other parents, children leaving home is *a piece of cake* which requires only minor adjustments.

The vast majority, however, lie somewhere in between. For these parents, the separation signifies parental lives in transition. Midlife issues are confronted and changes made as parenthood begins to recede in importance. The negotiation of this midlife transition is carefully examined in this work.

The main aim of the book, however, is to help parents in the letting go process — to show that successful parenting means preparing children to parent themselves. Too frequently, parents forget that the goal is to work themselves out of a job by allowing children to become responsible for their own lives. This is not an easy task for either the parent or the child. In fact, it is often fraught with confusion, reluctance, and failure. This is why those parents interviewed often spoke of their fears and doubts about parenting, not because there was an emphasis on the negative, but rather because people tend to talk about their concerns. But by learning of the problems, thoughts, and feelings of parents during the *unhitching* process, the reader will, I feel, gain new perspective and discover ways of turning the leave-taking into a positive experience.

For it is only by letting go successfully that parents and children gain mutual respect for each other.

CHAPTER 1

THE JOY OF IT ALL

I felt great when I left home...really great.

FEELINGS OF EXCITEMENT

children moving on It's a story told over and over again, year after year; almost all people, at some point, leave their parents' home. The departure may occur for a variety of reasons: going away to boarding school or college, getting married, joining the military, or moving out to be on one's own. Emotions surrounding the leave-taking are charged, but usually the most prevalent feeling is a combination of excitement and joy. For the newly-emancipated child, the idea of parents no longer *looking over your shoulder* is exhilarating. There is an overwhelming sense of freedom and relief.

While some young adults admit to being scared or apprehensive, and some exhibit an air of ambivalence, generally there is eager anticipation of the new experiences that being on their own will bring. Yet as they move forward, there is also the expectation that home and family will stay the same, will always be there.

parents left behind While the offspring look forward to new lives that they can actively create and define for themselves, many parents do the same. The postlaunch has begun: feelings of relief and freedom bring a sense of getting on with a new phase of life. Those parents who are aware of the dynamics of separation, who have some understanding of how their lives will be affected and who have, over the years, prepared both themselves and their children for the launch will be better able to share in the feelings of excitement and pride.

"I felt wonderful for her," said Karl about his daughter. "Her leaving was not a loss to me...the children's maturation process does not infringe on my happiness. She's at an age to do things. That does not diminish me. I was not sad about her leaving because it was so good for her."

Many parents acknowledge that separation represents a transition from childhood to adulthood, a crucial shift from a relationship of parent and child into a relationship between two adults. The grace with which parents *let go* and give up well-ingrained parenting habits may affect both the child's ongoing maturity as well as long-term personal growth. Unfortunately, parents sometimes lose touch with the aspects of disengagement that make it a good experience when their own sentiments and personal needs get in the way.

The more parents are able to view separation in a positive manner, the healthier both children and parents will feel. Most importantly, parents must realize that leaving is an inevitable part of a child's growing up and represents the fulfillment of what should be the ultimate goal of parents: to work themselves out of a job.

"I felt neat," Daphne reflected about her child's leaving. "It was good for her and she wanted to leave. I didn't feel that my whole reason for being had been cut out from under me. I felt that we were moving into the next step."

IMPORTANT STEP TO ADULT LIFE

growing up Leaving home does signify an important step in a person's life — it is part of growing up. While a daughter or son lives at home, full adulthood remains at arm's length. Moving away and becoming independent (which may or may not occur simultaneously) are milestones that mark entry into adult life.

"As much trouble as Aaron has given us," said Aaron's mother, "we both missed him more than we realized. But that's part of being a parent. If you think your kids are going to stay with you...if you want them to stay with you all their lives, then something's missing up there," she laughed, pointing to her head. "You want them to be on their own. You hope that they're capable of being on their own. Aaron loves us and misses us and is happy doing what he's doing. And we feel the same way."

Parents know that the child's leaving home is the culmination of an eighteen-year pilgrimage through life together. Whether gradually or suddenly, lives change and paths separate. As identities become more distinct, the child's future seems less predictable in the eyes of the parents.

parents' pride Underlying the immediate upheaval is an immense sense of pride. Pride that the child is going off on her or his own. Pride that the child has arrived at this point in life safely, in spite of the risks of alcohol, driving, drugs, pregnancy, AIDS, and teenage suicide. Pride in who the child is — the inner self of the child. Pride in the accomplishments that the child may have attained: good grades, sports excellence, elected offices, social networks, job interests, fine health, and general well-being. Pride in the nice things that friends and family have to say about the situation. Pride in the successful job of being a parent.

child's hard work For so many young adults going off to college, the leave-taking represents years of study, fretting over competitive college entrance exams, the tedious completion of college applications, and a concentrated effort to find the school representing the right fit. After the many months of waiting for the results, it's wonderful and heartwarming to see a child's eyes light up with the excitement of finally knowing where the next year will be spent, finally feeling the release of a huge weight, and finally breathing a sigh of relief. Not only does leaving home effectively shut the door on high school, it becomes symbolic of the new journey ahead — a path to be forged almost entirely by the son or daughter alone.

One parent, whose daughter had headed off to an Ivy League university, expressed it this way: "I was excited for her because I think that college is just a marvelous experience...that's when the world opened up for me, and I was sure it was going to open up for her. She was ready to go."

IMPROVEMENT IN FAMILY DYNAMICS

time together Over a period of time both preceding and following the separation, a shift in family dynamics occurs. Much of this shift is generated by the parents in a desire to have meaningful *last-time* memories — the last quiet talk, the last time doing a favorite thing, the last visit to a special place. Even though the children are already feeling emancipated, they may be more receptive to overtures of togetherness and play along with their parents' whims and notions, possibly accepting a togetherness which may seem a little contrived or phony. Each may gain a new appreciation of the other which is heightened by the knowledge that the end of one era and the beginning of another is near.

Although not the end of the relationship, the curtain is falling on the relationship as it has existed in the past. It's not unusual for a family to decide to go on one last vacation together. Extra time may be spent shopping and getting ready. Favorite foods are cooked a final time. Even though children may have left home in the past during summer months, most parents realize that this time is different. This realization may not occur to their children. But parents know: things will never be quite the same again.

As children feel more content and at peace with the way life is going, they may find it easier to be nice to other members of the family. A certain mellowing occurs. Ongoing conflicts or nagging criticisms no longer have to be fought and pursued with the same intensity. Grudges may even disappear. A mental and sometimes physical housecleaning is in process. School-required books may be passed on to the next brother or sister. Undone chores may actually be completed. Often there is a striving for a climate of love.

clearing the air Many parents feel that now is the time to clear the air, to deal with unfinished business. There's no point in entering this new phase of the parent-child relationship with excess baggage in the form of unresolved issues. Although apologies may be due from both sides, more often the parents want forgiveness and acceptance for those situations in the past which didn't work out, for times when they showed a lack of understanding, for mistakes made. Parents who have gone through their own personal crises along the way, whether it be divorce, death of a loved one, unemployment, disenchantment with parenthood, or periods devoted to *finding oneself*, need to find relief for errors of the past.

By acknowledging that times may have been rough for the child, or that things weren't always easy, parents help to open the door to a new dialogue of a more adult nature. If the parent can admit to weaknesses or errors in judgment, how much easier for the child to do the same and say, "I'm sorry I gave you such a hard time." One parent called the summer between high school and college a period of peacemaking and forgiveness. Parents who acknowledge the uniqueness of this period and use it to reacquaint themselves with their children seem to be better equipped to let go and enjoy the leave-taking.

a positive transition Perhaps the most dramatic change that occurs within the family structure is the shift of the parent and child to an adult-adult relationship. The transition is slow in evolving and often does not receive sufficient attention until after the child has left and begins to return home for visits. When the parent does not actively participate in making this transition, the child may have to force the issue by demanding respect as an adult.

The wise parent who chooses to be an active participant in this shift not only reaps the appreciation of the child but also gains new depth and meaning in this unique relationship. A daughter or son can then seek out advice without fear of ridicule, make decisions without fear of criticism, and admit mistakes without fear of retribution. The reward for the hard work involved in making this transition — and it is hard work — will be an ongoing and loving relationship that can last a lifetime. Healthy adult-adult respect also helps to define a role model for evolving relationships between siblings and other members of the family.

LETTING GO

detachment from child There are many aspects of this important role of parents in letting go during the separation process. One factor seems to be a parent's ability to *enjoy* the child's presence in a separate and somewhat detached manner. The willingness to view one's offspring as a unique individual with certain personality traits, idiosyncracies, strengths, and weaknesses allows a parent to delight in the child as his or her life takes on new direction.

All parents see parts of themselves in their children; but the way these characteristics blend together and the manner in which the child chooses to exercise her or his own free will results in a separate and distinct person. Parents who truly enjoy this differentness can step back, look at their child and marvel, "Wow! Isn't that a super person?" This ability does not preclude missing the child after the departure, but rather reinforces a desire to deal with the separation itself from a perspective of joyfulness, not sadness.

confidence in child If a child's ability to cope in the world is a measure of the parents' success, then most parents can allow themselves to sit back and relax. Young adults are often more ready, more responsible, and more mature than parents give them credit for being. Somehow, parents seem to forget that they, too, left home, coped with life, and met the challenge.

John, whose seventeen-year-old son had decided to attend boarding school thus delaying his entry into college for a year, reflected: "I was surprised at the amount of his maturity in the whole process. I didn't give him credit for being nearly as mature as he was. His *coming of age* came on much faster than I thought it would." By the end of the school year, John had to admit that his son's decision had been a good one, that perhaps father didn't always know best.

As John found out, giving up the parenting habit isn't always easy, but it is part of a positive separation process. Over the years, parenting becomes a conditioned response, one often very difficult to put aside. The inclination is to continue telling children what to do and how to do it. Parents have a hard time remembering that most young adults know the difference between right and wrong even though their actions do not always seem to reflect this fact.

Yet, ultimately, a child has to make decisions alone and have confidence in his or her own judgments. By gaining confidence in their children, parents don't have to spend as much time talking and being in control; they can (and must) spend more time listening, more time relating to their child as they would relate to a friend and adult. The fact that a parent hasn't discovered this changing relationship before the child leaves may indicate that the child or the parent, or both, are not ready for the separation. Although many parents have difficulty adjusting to their child's maturity and independence, parents need to relate to their child's growth and development as a rich experience.

There's something to be said for the adage that a person rises or sinks to the level of someone else's expectation. Studies have shown that children perform better in the classroom when the teacher expects them to do well; grades decline when the teacher expects less. By exhibiting confidence in children's ability to make decisions and figure out where they're going in life, by giving children the freedom to make mistakes or change their minds, parents can relieve themselves of some of the parenting responsibility.

PARENTAL FEELINGS: RELIEF AND FREEDOM

welcome relief Relief comes in other forms as well. Many parents readily admit to feelings of relief at having a child leave home, particularly when all the children are gone. Not infrequently, parents may also experience feelings of guilt when they realize that they are happy that the child no longer lives at home. While in large families the departure of one child may not seem to affect family life much, for the average-sized family definite changes are noticeable. The smaller the family, the more impact an absent child may make. The phone doesn't ring as much. There aren't as many simultaneous activities to coordinate. Meals are simplified. Life may seem easier.

In those cases where the child who is leaving has been a source of anxiety to the parents, for such diverse reasons as teenage unhappiness, inability to live by family rules, problems in school, or involvement with drugs or alcohol, the relief may be even greater. "I miss her," said one parent, "but, God, I'm at peace! I was so angry with her during some of her high school escapades."

When the child has gone, most parents worry less and begin to feel unencumbered of the ultimate and overwhelming responsibility for the child's life. The old saying, "Out of sight, out of mind," gradually takes over and parents may discover time and new energy for tackling their own lives. For some parents, the worrying may have been as simple as whether a procrastinating child completed a school assignment on time; for others, worry may have meant nerve-wracking curfew violations. When a child lives at home and isn't home by two o'clock in the morning, it's natural to worry and keep an ear cocked for the car pulling into the driveway.

Once the young adult lives in another state, or even a few miles away, the reminders to worry greatly diminish. Parents can let go. As many parents discover, it's less stressful to have a general concern about someone at a distance than to have ongoing daily worries about specific activities, manners, and responsibilities.

wonderful freedom The greatest sense of freedom is sometimes felt by those parents who no longer have any children in the nest. These parents are now free to proceed with the next phase of their lives; many are ready and eager to do so. Regardless of what that phase brings, there is a firm awareness that the active role of parenting is over. For many, this results in feelings of joy.

"I felt wonderful. I began to think differently about myself as a person," Jeanne exclaimed as she described how she had lost weight, renewed her interest in clothes, and begun to think of herself as a more sexual being after both of her children finally left home. Her eyes sparkled as she talked. "It's fun and I don't think that I have any clothes left from that time. I think that all those years I was aware of being a mother first and now it's fun for me to be a woman first."

No longer do parents have to rush home from work or meetings. No longer do they have to plan ahead; last-minute plans and spontaneity can be welcomed and enjoyed. No longer do they have to think of the children first.

Another parent described the strong feelings of freedom and release that he and his wife had felt: "There was a great exhilaration in our relationship. Sex was much more spontaneous and fun. Our total relationship was more open. We were able to scream at each other better. We were able to make love anywhere we wanted, anytime we wanted. We were able to dress any way we wanted. Things stayed where we put them. The house was cleaner. The noise level was much lower. The cars stayed clean, the garage uncluttered." All of these factors lead to a new sense of privacy and rediscovered togetherness for many couples.

People are usually not surprised that the child is eager and joyous to be leaving and, in many ways, the parents can and should share all of that joy. But sometimes the parting feels like a mixed blessing.

CHAPTER 2

THE OTHER SIDE OF THE COIN: POSTPARTUM

I wasn't expecting it...but the empty room looked like an empty nest.

FEELINGS OF LOSS

surprise at the void After the joy comes the pain. In spite of all the mental preparation done in anticipation of the leave-taking process, in spite of the fact that parents know many years in advance that children will inevitably leave, and in spite of wanting to be in control of their feelings, most parents are surprised at the void.

"Terrible," "devastated," "empty," "shattering," and "traumatic" were just some of the words used by parents to describe their immediate reactions to the separation. "I was shocked at how much I was affected," one father related. "I was not really prepared." He then described how he cried for the first time in years when his children left. "It was as though they'd died and gone away...were no longer in existence."

It was not unusual for some mothers to cry when being interviewed as though reliving that very moment — even though the leave-taking had occurred years earlier. More than one tearful mother refused to continue talking unless the tape recorder was turned off while she regained her composure. Associated with those tears was perhaps a certain embarrassment that one could still be so affected, an embarrassment that those vulnerable feelings were still so close to the surface and could be recaptured so vividly.

"At the time I knew Thanksgiving was not that far away," said one mother through her tears. "I felt so silly. But that didn't make the hurt go away, and look, here I am...I can't believe I'm crying."

accepting unpleasant feelings All feelings are legitimate — by virtue of the very fact that they exist. There are no right or wrong feelings. Sometimes feelings are ambivalent. Sometimes they are conflicting. Sometimes they are negative. If parents are to move into a new stage of life and continue their own growth as people, they often must deal with a whole range of unpleasant feelings which relate directly to the parent-child separation and its attendant feelings of loss.

PSYCHOLOGICAL ASPECTS OF SEPARATION

pain One of the hardest problems for people to deal with in life is that of separation. Whether due to death, divorce, or a child leaving home, a separation represents a loss and inherent in this loss are feelings of pain. Yet, somehow, parents are surprised at these feelings; consciously, they don't put a child's leaving home in the same category as death, divorce, or abandonment. Subconsciously, however, they may react as though experiencing the same gut-wrenching blow. While parents may be affected differently by their children's growth into independence, separation hits especially hard those parents who see their primary parenting role coming to an end, those parents who haven't seen themselves in any other role, those parents who recognize that life will never be the same. Yet the psychological health of parent and child alike demands the end of a dependency relationship, the end of the family as it has existed.

One mother's comment tied together both her sense of surprise and also an acceptance of the change brought about by her daughter's departure: "When she was gone on summer trips, I would almost forget about her, so I thought I would get over it fast. But now I realize she isn't coming home, at least not on a permanent basis."

lack of understanding Some parents, particularly mothers, have difficulty in understanding the sense of loss, frustration, and emptiness that may arise when children leave home, even though the parents' lives have been full — with careers, friends, and other activities. However, because most parents allow their offspring to take up so much of their conscious and unconscious concerns, the space that the absent child leaves in a parent's life at the time of separation may be enormous indeed. Parents may not think that they are focused on their children, but children make constant demands around which day-to-day life tends to revolve. Even when a teenager learns to drive and no longer requires as much parental attention and chauffeuring, parents continue to be very aware of and influenced by the adolescent's comings and goings.

Knowing something intellectually can be very different from knowing something emotionally. Feelings of loss and pain do not conveniently follow the rules of logic. How an individual parent reacts to loss depends on the person, her or his personality structure, and how the person views the world. Underlying all of this is perhaps the fact that the parent-child relationship is basically not an intellectual bond so much as it is a primal one.

In an effort to avoid the pain, parents resort to a variety of coping strategies: repression ("...it doesn't bother me that he is leaving"); rationalization or trying to make sense of the loss ("...I know that she wants to stay close to home, but the local colleges don't offer the right courses"); denial or pretending ("...this is just a temporary absence, things will really be the same when he gets back home"); bargaining ("...if I can just be the perfect mother, she won't want to leave right away"); withdrawal or distancing ("...I don't know what happened before he left, we were fighting all the time; it was a relief to see him go"); anger or resentment, sometimes tinged with ambivalence ("...it was time for her to leave and yet I feel so awful that it makes me mad...it's not the way it was supposed to be"); projection onto others ("...I seem to be picking on her brother all the time...I know her mother really misses her"); action ("...I had to do something so I cleaned his room from top to bottom"); redirecting negative feelings inwardly ("...I don't know what's the matter with me but I feel so depressed all the time"); alcoholism ("...ever since my children left, I just can't help myself"); and, finally, replacement ("...I had all this time on my hands, so I took flying lessons, which I've always wanted to do").

Whether or not the parent uses one of these methods of coping, eventually the loss has to be integrated into everyday life; there needs to be an acceptance of and reconciliation with the fact that *this is the way it is*.

partial loss of self When a person loses something or someone who is valued, be it a cherished object, a treasured family pet, or a beloved human being, lost too is a part of the self. There's a loss of something personal, almost like an amputation. There's a feeling of being somewhat less, of being not quite the same person. Although the parent may feel joyful knowing that the child is getting on with his or her life, when the child actually leaves, a piece of the parent leaves also. This generally holds true even when the child has been a source of irritation.

Many parents suffer one of their biggest losses in life as their child grows away from them. Loss (or impending loss) may often compel an individual to make new plans, pursue new goals, develop new associations. Human nature seeks to replace a lost object with something new, but rarely is this void filled with a new child. As parents reconcile themselves to the loss, they can face the truth: the departure signals the beginning of the end of the child's being in the nest.

loss of roles It is a death of a sort: the death of the role that the child has played in the home and family, the death of the role that the parent has played out over and over again for eighteen years, and the death of the parent-child relationship in the traditional sense. Interestingly, these feelings may persist even though there are other children living at home for whom parenting is still required. In cases where no children remain at home, the recognition that the parenting phase of life is complete is more intense and final. An important chapter in an adult's life closes, a chapter that not every parent wants to admit is over.

Mourning the child's rite of passage should not be unexpected, as Jane discovered. In spite of motherly vows not to get emotional, her tears flowed freely. "I was dreading saying goodbye. I really didn't want to cry, but I did. I didn't want her to see me cry. She was astounded, I think, that I was so emotional. I cried for two days...all the way back home. We went to see some friends in Boston, and I couldn't even enjoy being with them. I just kept crying." Jane chuckled softly as she recalled the events and went on to explain her feelings of devastation: "Why? The loss, of course. A forever loss, in a way. I'm so happy for her...but I feel so...it's a whole empty part. It used to be her and now it's not."

loss of unconditional love Understanding the reason that parents, particularly mothers, cling so desperately to the old relationship is difficult. Psychiatrist Dr. David Dolen, a specialist in child therapy, speaks of this aspect of the mother-child relationship in terms of unconditional love:

> There are only two times in life that one can have unconditional love, or experience it in any way. One is as a child: if we are fortunate we can get unconditional love from a parent. It does not matter what we do. Even if we end up in prison, that parent is going to care about us. The parent may not agree with what we did but the love is, for the most part, unconditional. Two, the only other time we can experience

it is to have a child. The child will not give us unconditional love, but we can give it as a parent. I think that, particularly for the mothers who've had that unconditional love for their child, the loss is so great because they've been fortunate enough to have it two times. But, no more. That's a really painful thing to lose. There's some sense of "this will never be quite the same again." It really is a significant loss for that parent.

To the parent, the child is more than just a loving and caring relationship; she or he represents a total commitment, one of the greatest loves available. Few relationships match the enduring fiber of that between parent and child. The seeming threat of losing this love is disturbing indeed.

Certainly the love is still there when a child leaves, but as the everyday contact drops off, often precipitously, there is an overwheming sense that this ongoing relationship is evaporating. In dealing with this loss, parents may also be forced into examining that period of time when they left home, or perhaps reliving childhood feelings of emotional abandonment. Dr. Dolen goes on to note: "The loss of a child builds on the time when we left home; there's a cumulative affect. You then deal with the part of your own separation that maybe you haven't dealt with well before."

end of child-bearing years   A last or only child leaving home can have a personal and profound impact on mothers. Most are forced to face the fact that their child-bearing years are over, or nearly so; their biological clocks are running out. For medical reasons (such as a hysterectomy) some women have had to accept this loss earlier in their lives and numerous other women have chosen voluntary sterilization as a form of birth control. Nonetheless, this *end* may pose a psychological hurdle for many mothers, particularly when they realize, perhaps with resentment, that male reproductive capabilities do not follow the same timetable. The loss is theirs alone.

MOURNING THE PAST

nostalgia   When the young adult leaves, thoughts linger and tears are shed for the memories of the child's youth, the child who no longer exists. Parents reflect on all the special times of the past: birthday parties, caressing baby-soft cheeks, tight hugs of a two-year-old, skinned knees, nursery school, adorable smiles, fun vacations, pictures drawn with crayons, pictures frozen in time by a camera, kindergarten, grade school events, ballet lessons, Little

League, first dates, learning to drive the family car, and many, many more. A time of nostalgia, reminiscences contribute to the sense of loss.

Although these reflections may be shared over the next few weeks or months with a spouse or another family member, more often the parent quietly retreats to the solitude of the departed child's room, thinking both of events that involved all the family members as well as those times shared with only the son or daughter. Because the departing child's room may be dismantled for other uses, such as an office or bedroom for a sister or brother, quite often such personal reflection consists of a psychological reverie which is unrelated to the child's bedroom itself. The process may seem self-indulgent or somewhat masochistic but, as part of the grieving, it represents a cleansing that is necessary. During this period, the unpleasant memories are usually left at rest; the loving and humorous ones are revived and revisited.

The intensity of this mourning was clearly illustrated by a couple interviewed on the Florida beach as they were fishing. They considered themselves semiretired and clearly enjoyed spending time together. First, Irene told the story of their daughter who had been extremely attached to a baby blanket throughout her entire life. "Jake, that's my husband, and I had often joked about her walking down the aisle with this blanket! We lived in upper New York state and had to drive her to school in Ohio. After we got back the next day I went into her bedroom to clean up and saw the blanket neatly folded on the rocking chair. That blanket brought back so many memories of her being little and growing up. Now it looked so alone. I sat down on the bed and cried for half an hour because I missed her so much and felt so empty."

After pulling some seaweed off his hook, Jake walked over. Almost immediately he asked his wife: "Have you told the story about how you cried when you saw the blanket?" Obviously, the blanket symbolized not only past memories, but also the actual loss that both mother and father felt with the departure of their daughter.

missing the companionship How much a parent misses a son or daughter may well relate to which parenting phase felt most comfortable. Not all mothers and fathers are equally good parents during all stages of a child's development. While some parents totally identify with the dependency stage of infants or young children and don't want them to grow up into individuals over whom control cannot be so easily exerted, many parents are at the opposite end of the spectrum. This group of parents hits its stride when children become more adultlike and their personalities become more distinct. These parents look on their offspring more as equals and less as *my children*.

The interview with Mary Lou illustrated this aspect of parenting styles nicely. Her three children had all been home for the holidays and were now going on their separate ways: one to London for a modeling assignment, one to California where he was taking up residency as an artist, and the last to college in Illinois. Mary Lou already missed the sharing and great conversations during the Christmas meals. "The problem for me is that I enjoy them so much as adults that I really miss them when they're not around. I like the adult, the person to person relationship with them. That's why I wasn't all that turned on when they couldn't talk much...from birth to age three. But when they learned language and could respond...as adults I guess I've gotten hooked on them."

Children perceived as equals may be integrated into a parent's life in a variety of ways: as a friend, as someone to share activities, common interests, or sports with, as someone to talk with, as someone to seek advice from, as someone to share other friends with, or as a catalyst for intellectual stimulation. When this child leaves, the parent may miss the companionship acutely. The more the parent likes the child as a person, the more the absence of the child may be felt.

child no longer the same person Parents may also shed tears in anticipation that the person who so recently left won't come back home the same. Other influences will now shape this person's life, influences over which parents have little or no control. Parents may wonder if their values, philosophies, and life styles, so ingrained into their son or daughter during youth, will hold up under these new pressures. While the adolescent child may begin examining and shedding some parts of the family value system while living at home, the young adult who has moved away generally reevaluates the parents' personal and cultural tenets in a harsher and more intense fashion, keeping some aspects while discarding others. Identities seem to separate with the physical distance that lies between parent and child.

Parental involvement in the child's personal growth shrinks from daily contact to vacation visits and perhaps phone calls; parental involvement becomes more passive than active. Adjustment to this passive role may be difficult for parents because then they must usually relinquish participation in the future development and transition of their daughters or sons unless specifically invited. This situation distresses many parents — in spite of the fact that previous attempts at involvement in their teenager's life may have provoked a great deal of conflict, argument, and hostility within the home setting.

Parents must also face the possibility that they might not like the newly-evolved daughter or son. This can be a little frightening.

parents no longer held in awe Even more frightening than the thought of the parent not liking the child is the distinct possibility that the changing child won't like the parent as much as she or he did while still within the family setting. By leaving home, the child gains a different perspective: parents can be perceived more objectively as separate and distinct individuals; their strengths and weaknesses, more clearly evaluated. Parents are stripped of that protective, idealized, *camouflaging* parent role.

Some of the awe that children have for their parents begins to recede during the early teen years, to be replaced with honest appreciation for their parents' vocations, place in the community, dedication to supporting the family, personal values, artistic sense, and other qualities. Simultaneously, that childlike awe may also be replaced with a more critical eye to the parent's irritating habits, personal quirks, foibles, and particularly those personality characteristics or individual values which differ from the child's. Even those traits in which the child mimics the parent may meet with condemnation.

These reassessments occur continually throughout adolescence but, once again, there is that heightened objectivity gained by physical separation. "Being away," said one daughter, "allows you to see the good and bad points of your parents...to be more objective." Being human, it's easier for parents to deal with the positive evaluations than with the negative ones.

During this adolescent period, the relationship gradually changes from one of a vertical nature to one of a horizontal nature, from one of parenting to one of mutual recognition. Many parents, however, don't really want a relationship of equals with their children. The more insecure parents are as individuals, the harder it is for them to accept criticism. If other areas of their lives don't seem to be going well, they need their children's praise to reinforce weakened egos. Parents want to be in control. They want to be seen as perfect. They want to be idolized in the same way that a toddler idolizes its parents. They want to cling to the old relationship of uncritical love. They don't want to feel scared.

How ironic, perhaps, that the *fruits* of an independent child (such independence being the thrust of parenthood) are the very things which can cause parents concern. From this point forward, the child filters almost everything through a critical consciousness — often disapproving of or dismissing actions and suggestions of parents.

FEAR OF THE FUTURE

avoiding discussion Fear of the future and the effect that the leave-taking will have on parent and child, as well as their relationship together, produces a certain amount of stress for everyone involved, but particularly for the parents. Unfortunately, this stress is often not discussed. Most parents feel that they must absorb all fear, sadness, and stress by themselves. They don't want to make the child feel guilty for leaving. They don't want the child to worry about them or their feelings. They don't want the child to see their tears of concern and sadness. They don't want the child to have any negative feelings. Consequently, fears tend to be pushed under the rug and ignored; there is rarely open dialogue between parent and child.

different patterns of feelings For some parents, these stressful feelings are intense for a short period of time, a week or less; for others, the feelings seem like a low, dull pain that persists at length. In some cases a parent's anxiety may even occur in advance of the actual separation and once the child is physically gone, the stress stops.
    A mother of two children felt that she had experienced the same reaction each fall when they left for school: "It's now six times that I've been through this. The way I've identified what is going on is that I become overemotional and unreasonable. I become angry about things that I don't normally become angry about...weepy...and then I realize that it's at a totally different level, almost as if my physical reactions tell my mind what's going on. I did become smart enough to tell my children what was going on and for them to ignore the fact that I was having this little tantrum while going through the whole realization that they were leaving again. Each time I feel like a mother hen losing a chick, a wrenching feeling. But the day after they've left, it is gone, healed somehow."

worry about the child Fears involving aspects of the child's life after the leave-taking encompass a wide range. Parents frequently mentioned:

* the child's physical safety
* survival in a general sense
* ability to cope in different and new circumstances
* unattended sickness or injury

* exposure to and use or abuse of marijuana, alcohol, or other drugs
* ability to make decisions, particularly the *right* decisions
* involvement with sex
* ability to manage financially
* the lack of restrictions now on college campuses (many parents remember the days of curfews, no members of the opposite sex in dormitory rooms, and sign-out sheets)
* the child's lack of a *security blanket*, especially in times of problem or crisis
* ability to take care of the details of life that one or the other parent has traditionally done (such as laundry, eating right, etc.)
* the fact that the child seems *so far away* not only physically, but mentally as well
* the fact that the child may not want to return home for vacations once discovering the joys of freedom
* the fact that the child may never again live nearby

These fears may be communicated to the child in a negative manner by either verbal statements or nonverbal messages. Either way, the child is given a vote of no confidence. Unfortunately, many parents have considerable doubt that their child can make it. If parents are not careful, this belief in failure becomes self-fulfilling.

The last item on the list may be less of a fear and more a statement of fact. Career opportunities may preclude a child from returning when college is complete. In assessing the direction her children were headed, a very realistic mother put it this way: "The thing that would crush me is their coming back. I just don't think that there's that much of a future here for young people." Another, whose son had difficulty in making the decision to leave, said: "Chances are great that he will never come back here to live. He will have to go north to some big church to get the kind of job that he wants. Perhaps that's why he clung as long as he did."

personal challenge to the parent Stress arising from parents' concern about their own futures comes from many sources. Both fathers and mothers may experience that huge emptiness in the house and in their lives after the children are gone. Both may feel forced to reexamine all facets of their lives: career, aging, mortality, ongoing relationships, direction, and priorities, as well as life without children. Neither is immune to stress from multiple sources and the many concerns parents face are discussed in later chapters.

When the child seeks to establish a unique identity, the family unit can also come under attack. Part of the strength of the family is that no one questions its individual members, no one challenges the members' interactions, no one questions its specialness. Howard Halpern in his book, *Cutting Loose,* terms this the "myth of the family." If this myth is scrutinized by the adolescent child, not only may individual family members be threatened but the marriage, itself, may come into question. Parents may be challenged about the quality of the relationship that they have with each other, as well as the quality of their individual lives.

defining the new relationship While parents adjust to the loss of the parent-child relationship, so also must they define and cultivate the adult-adult relationship. Setting off for this uncharted territory, parents often experience a great deal of anxiety and stress. Fearful of not making an easy transition, parents may worry over the possibility of failure: almost everyone seems to know people who did not make that shift in the relationship with their parents. This phenomenon is best illustrated when statements are made such as, "Well, we make it a habit to go back home to visit the folks for the holidays, but no more than that." Or, "We're only going to stay a couple of days; that's about all we can handle." Or, "I couldn't wait to get back to school, my folks were driving me crazy." The idea of their own children feeling the same way scares many parents — and rightfully so.

As much as they want to avoid this result, parents' natural inclination is often to resist the adult-adult transition, to resist giving up control over their children's lives, goals, and timetables; sometimes parents just don't know how. Yet, when parents continue to treat children in the same old patterns, many children rebel.

Children are very aware of the many personal changes occurring in their lives, most of them internal. When parents continue to *push the same old buttons*, children may hate the way they act when around their parents. Because parents feel a need to finish their parenting and tie the results in a nice neat package, living with the upheavals and uncertainties that all young adults face is difficult. Not only does this new and detached role feel vague and uncomfortable for many parents, the emerging relationship takes persistent effort and not all parents are equipped to handle the task.

feelings of rejection One of the most powerful feelings that some parents experience is rejection or abandonment. Just as the mother (or father) may resist losing unconditional love, parents of either sex may resist losing control over their children. The child's desire to escape from home, the center of child-rearing love and care, may be seen as a direct attack on the worth and sense of adequacy of the parent. The more insecure the parent, the more the parent's identity is wrapped up in and is an extension of the child and, hence, the more intense the feelings of fear and abandonment.

Parents who question their ability to parent often become overprotective. Constant attention given to children and their needs is used as proof by the parents that they are doing the best they can, that they should be appreciated. Parents hope that by engendering this appreciation in their children, the feelings of abandonment can be delayed or avoided. Rarely does this smothering work.

In an effort to postpone the departure, parents not infrequently resort to tactics which will coerce their children into staying home. Denial of financial support (often previously agreed to), making children feel guilty about leaving, convincing children that they are not *ready* to be on their own yet, attention-getting sickness, efforts to become *tight* with the child, emotional blackmail, and other *excuses* are all used by parents to delay the parting and avoid the pain. Sometimes these attempts work on a temporary basis, but usually bad feelings between parent and child intensify, the situation becomes worse, and the departure inevitably occurs on schedule.

A parent who has succeeded in keeping a child nearby may be surprised to learn that this child can create just as much isolation and separation as the child who moves out of town. Three miles can be as distant as three hundred miles, but parents are then deprived of being able to rationalize and use lack of physical proximity as an excuse to deny the child's desire to separate. These parents may be faced squarely with the fact that their children are avoiding them.

unexpected anger One of the most unexpected emotions that can arise from the inevitable leave-taking is anger. Parents may be angry that the child has to leave and cause them pain, or angry that they are feeling so powerless over their reactions. Sometimes this anger is turned inwardly; other times, not. The problem is that parents have no legitimate or reasonable target at which to direct their anger, making it difficult to resolve without lashing out at the child or redirecting frustrations toward another family member. This behavior fits a pattern, though, in which people create hostility in order to keep themselves apart and in order to avoid the pain of separating from intimate relationships. The anger does not negate the strong feelings of attachment; rather, it disguises them. Unfortunately, when partings are riddled with anger, people have a difficult time reestablishing lines of communication and real understanding.

All of these emotions — sadness, pain, loss, anxiety, rejection, anger, and fear — can impede viewing the parent-child separation as a natural, healthy, and positive experience in the life cycle. Avoiding some of these feelings is almost impossible but, when combined with feelings of joy and acceptance, parents can meet the challenge, as the following Profile reflects.

PROFILE

Separating from his son two years ago was poignant for Ray Shafer, a partner in a national accounting firm. He had been the primary nurturer for his two children, Mark and Laurie, since he and his wife split up ten years ago. Although he subsequently remarried, most of the parenting responsibilities fell on his shoulders. His recounting of Mark's leaving home revealed emotions of joy and sadness, sage philosophy, and elements of personal growth.

"I was real glad to see Mark grow up, and leaving is a part of growing up. I was glad to see him go away. He's not that self-confident so I told him to go at least two hours away. He hated it the first three months...he was really homesick. He was in love with his girlfriend here. But I always made it a point to encourage them to grow up. I tried not to tell them how lousy it was to be a teenager.

"I drove him to college. He was scared and felt just thrown in. I cried when I left. We hugged each other. (And, wouldn't you know, I forgot my wallet and I had to go back so it was all very anticlimatic.) I was going along crying. Really that was the most intense feeling that I've had about him...right when I left. I usually don't cry much, but I get choked up a lot. I was very sad. I felt a loss...felt like a bridge had burned. I felt like it wouldn't be the same. I wanted to get the hell on down the road. I felt like something had happened...a change had come about.

"I had a very introspective trip back. I thought a lot about him...and us. It was good. I was thinking about our lives together, what had gone on, what a nice, good kid he was, how lucky I was. It really makes you appreciate somebody...to lose them, depart, move on in your relationship to another level. I had a lot of good feeling about it.

"I fantasized about things that I wanted to do with him to let him know how close I really felt towards him. When I left I told him that I loved him which I don't think I'd ever really done before, at least not in recent history. I just wanted to get real close...closer. It's easy now to tell him I love him and he'll say it back to me, too.

"I also began to think about all the places that I didn't do as good a job as I should have. I would do a lot more things with him if I had it to do over again. I would take him with me...anywhere...the hardware store...out to lunch on Saturday...down to the lake. He's the first kid. I didn't know that they were going to be gone. I didn't realize what it was like on the other end, that you can't ever get that time back again. There were a lot of things...every now and then something will pop up and I'll think...I wish I could do that with Mark. He'll get married, get a job and that makes it a little worse when you think about it because that's one more step beyond the possibility of ever trying to recoup these things. It's not the same now. It will never be the same. It's just that I miss him. We call a lot, two or three times a week. We're pretty open when we talk.

"When you've got a kid who's healthy, normal, doesn't have any problems, not in a wheel chair...really, that's enough for me. That kind of thinking dawned on me, also. All I want is for him to survive and be happy. I began to worry about automobile accidents...because I wasn't there.

"Was I a good parent? Yeah, but I've been too hard on him, though. I did feel guilty about those times that I lost my temper and raised hell. Luckily my second wife has been a good influence in that area. But I still have the same flash points, still get mad at the same things.

"It's been hard controlling my temper and feelings, and yet wanting to tell him what to do and how to organize things and how to run his own life. I see him doing things that I don't like in myself and I want to tell him. Maybe the reason it was so hard was knowing that he's up and out pretty soon and I'm not going to have any more opportunity to do this and I'd better get my licks in now so he'll be the better off for it.

"When Laurie leaves I've even thought about having another child. It makes one think of those things. We have a big house. It's going to be pretty quiet. Plus, with all this new-found skill at being a parent in retrospect...Mark and Laurie are all for it. I think about it. I'd be a better father, a lot better. I don't want to lose touch with being young and I sort of identify having a child around with one way to do that, one way to keep from aging and closing in. I used to know people forty-six and I thought they were old as anything...and now, here I am thinking how nice it would be to have an infant!" Ray paused with a burst of laughter and obviously enjoyed laughing at himself and his preconceived notions. "I don't want to lose touch with what is important to people in their thirties, late twenties. I'd be a great father. It'd be fun to raise somebody, fun to have Laurie and Mark involved in this family. I know they'd like it. But there are some obvious minuses: loss of freedom and time. My wife and I are both busy.

"I would take more vacations with the kids if I could start over.

As a single parent, when I went on vacation, the kids visited their mother or grandparents. But that's my fantasy of what a family should be like. Maybe a family's not any better if it vacations together.

"As kids grow older, they don't want to hang around you as much. Does that hurt me? Oh, sure. Makes me mad. I turn my hurt into anger. Nobody likes to feel like they're being assessed for a better deal. That's hard to accept. There's a one-way thing from parents to kids and I can never...there's no justification for me to expect anything from my kids. I cannot have expectations of any kind because if I do, I'm going to be disappointed. I know it's normal for parents to expect things when they've worked hard, fixed dinner, etc., and every now and then I slip into that trip and get mad and hurt. It happens more now as the kids get older because they're only home for short periods of time. I want more of their time. I'm looking forward to watching them in college, seeing what they're going to do...fascinated by the whole thing. I feel a sense of fascination, particularly watching their bodies grow. I've gotten a kick out of that.

"Regardless, the important thing at the end of life is just getting there and doing the best job that you can. The purpose in life is not to raise kids, but it's more fun having them than not. After all, you just borrow your kids for a while. I realize now that they're not yours, they're God's and you have a chance to be with them for a few years and then they move on. That philosophy makes you concentrate on your kids."

CHAPTER 3

HOW ARE THE KIDS FEELING?

> *Did you hear the story about the kid who was leaving for college? All summer he refused to do any chores...a real slob. Finally, in desperation his mother lamented, "I'm putting up with stuff from you I never would with a husband!"*
>
> *Her son smiled and then he laughed. "Yeah, but you can't divorce a kid, can you?"*

FEELING GREAT

excitement   Overwhelmingly, kids feel great when they leave. Perhaps the teenager in the joke seems arrogant; more surely he feels invincible. While home is still his base, his mental presence has already moved on. Not only will his parent tolerate him a few weeks longer, but he expects most things to come his way. He may feel that the world will respond like putty in his hands.

By far the majority of young people leaving home are more than ready to embrace college and begin their new lives. In their eyes everything that has occurred thus far is a culmination of events and efforts pointed in one direction: freedom and independence. High school graduation is momentous and provides a sense of moving forward; leaving home represents a threshold. Whereas parents may feel trauma or loss, eighteen-year-olds' comments reflect that it is, quite simply, the natural thing to do.

- * "I felt good...I felt real good. I was glad to get away from home, real happy about it, and eager to start a new life somewhere else."
- * "I wanted to get away. I chose a school that was far away from home. I loved all the freedom...I enjoyed that a whole

lot. I had such a good time at school that I was never really worried about homesickness."
* "I was doing absolutely what I wanted to do. I was excited about this new experience. All in all, it felt great."

These quotes are similar to the advice given by an older brother as his sister went off to college, "Just be happy with yourself, and everything else will fall into place."[1]

Certainly, there are a few young people who will experience negative feelings at leaving home. They may suffer from prolonged homesickness, from an intense longing for a boyfriend or girlfriend, or because they have unhappily selected the wrong school. But these children are decidedly in the minority. Most are excited by the prospects of discovery and new insights.

on their own Anticipating being on one's own is not actually being there. As prepared as a teen may feel, there is still a moment of realization, a moment when that aloneness is all too clear — overwhelming, and yet grand.

One young woman spoke with infinite understanding about this moment. Upon graduation from high school she had, in the British tradition of taking a year off, left the States to spend time abroad before attending college. Under the watchful eye of relatives part of the time, her realization of being on her own was, nevertheless, absolute.

"We went to this country pub to sing carols on Christmas Eve and I stood there in the midst of it all trying to sing but I got choked up. Even though I was surrounded by all those people, I remember thinking...here I am, this is me, this is my life...and feeling very...by myself...but it was a good feeling. It's like there was a mental click in my brain saying...you're it, you're the one. Life revolves around what you do and not what your family does. I didn't realize what was happening at the time; it was more hindsight."

Another young man spoke of his recollection of that moment of the mental click. "My brother drove me down to school. We put my trunk in the room and it's like...adios, that's it. I suddenly realized...here I am...no transportation to speak of...no going home for four months. I can't back out even if I want to...just a total separation...for the first time. I got used to it real quick, but there was that point where I suddenly realized it."

What these young people recognize is that they have to get used to organizing their own lives, to being in charge. In some sense they are all alone; there is no one else running the show. They are not an extension of their family any more; they can mold their lives as they choose. Life becomes a very personal challenge.

independence Although most children experience a growing sense of independence throughout high school, true freedom begins the moment they walk out of the house or their parents drop them off at the college dormitory. They have finally escaped the rules set down by their parents. They have finally escaped the sometimes smothering parental protection that they have lived under for so many years. No wonder they are relieved. Usually by this time, young people have developed some sense of their own will, some sense of direction, and some sense of what they want to do.

The constraints of home act as inhibitors to this self-development and only physical distance can curtail some parents' insistence about imposing their ideas on their children's lives. As kids look for their own answers, *advice* that is given over the phone is easier to ignore, particularly given the typical attitude that, as one college sophomore expressed it, "You know everything better than your parents do." Spoken like a true teenager — one for whom wisdom is as yet a tight-budded flower. If advice is needed, many teens would rather consult their peers or an adult friend to avoid appearing dependent on their parents.

Freshmen can go to many extremes to isolate themselves from their parents and exercise control over their lives. In spite of the frustration she had felt, one mother spoke philosophically of her experience when her son left home. "Todd took a phone to school but he didn't get it hooked up for two or three months. I had absolutely no way of getting in touch with him. Can you imagine? I knew that he would wait a while to call so after the first week I was amused, but certainly not surprised. After the second week I was feeling rather irritated. By the end of the third week I was both worried and mad.

"Finally, he called. Obviously, he wanted this new life to be on his own terms and keeping his parents out for a time was part of the deal. He just had to do it his way. I survived." She laughed — but with a touch of bittersweet.

Because becoming independent takes so much time and energy, children may go for periods without making contact with their parents or without even missing or thinking about home. Often, "No news is good news." Children are preoccupied with their own lives. Said one son, "It was refreshing to have so many choices and make my own decisions. I missed my parents but it was time to develop my own self. During my sophomore year, I didn't even fly home for Thanksgiving."

This new sense of power over their lives is not always used in constructive ways and it's not unusual for freshmen to overindulge in small or large doses. Many experiment and do things that they would never have dreamed of experiencing at home, including excessive alcohol, drugs, wild all-night escapades, and, for many, their first sexual encounters. Eventually most settle back down. Those who don't may have academic and personal problems.

The financial situation of each young adult may vary greatly — from large allowances or independent wealth to scholarships, work programs, or barely making ends meet. Some children have been fully emancipated (i.e., gainfully employed and living self-sufficiently) by their parents in order to establish independent financial status and thus be eligible for appropriate educational loans and grants.

There usually is a financial aspect to the independence equation and independence may be more perceived than real if parents are footing most of the bills. Out from under a parent's watchful eye, however, student expenditures seem uniquely free of parental judgment. Said one sophomore, "Sure I went to the same concert three times in a row. So what? It was my money." The wisdom of such folly — and folly it seemed when he ran out of money later in the semester — appeared to do little to negate his strong feelings of fiscal independence.

NEW PERSON

children in a different light   After leaving home, children feel changed, almost like a *new person*. Part escape, part fabrication, and part reality, the image of a slate wiped clean in a brand new environment is appealing. Certainly, newly-emancipated teenagers do change, but not as dramatically as they anticipate. Slowly these young adults awaken to the disparity between illusion and fact; they have misjudged how easily modifications can be made to a personality. Yet intuitively, most know that without risk and experimentation one cannot grow. They do see themselves in a different light, and having the space away from all the knowns of family, friends, and home makes change easier and liberating.

The new-person component in the child's life is special and unique. Like giving birth, there are elements of joy and pain, ups and downs. Too many unmet expectations can bring thoughts of failure. Escaping parental quirks and habits by the adoption of opposite behaviors can prove unproductive and sometimes self-defeating. Escaping the past and its reputations or embarrassing memories, however, can be wonderfully freeing. Nicknames can be shed. A new image created. Only upon returning home will the vision of a former image return to visit.

"I remember when I went to school four years ago," Hank related, "I had an idea in my mind that I wanted to be a different person. I had this feeling...here's a chance to go someplace where nobody knows me and I can be just about anything I want to be, put up a whole new identity, whatever. I was going to be more outgoing. Of course, that didn't work out because you just turn out being exactly what you are anyway." Hank paused to laugh.

"After four years people at school know me as well as the people at home. It all shines through eventually but there's some history at home that, whether it's good or bad, no one knows so you do have a little bit different identity at school. Counting on being a new person is not a very wise move; it doesn't work. I couldn't pull off making a big change in my personality. I don't think I had a clearcut image of what to present...but just to be something different. That's one of the reasons I went away to school in the first place. I wanted to break away and change at a faster pace than I would at home...which is a good idea. After four years I'm broader and I have some hindsight. It's good to evaluate your life and say here's what is good and here's what is bad, and to take the good with you and leave the bad. But I realize it's much more of an ongoing process. You can't force it."

parents in the dark Although they do not totally transform, these young adults do shift from the daughter or son their parents remember. If parents do not perceive this evolution or unconsciously resist it, a subtle resentment can permeate the atmosphere when child and parent are together.

"At home they don't know me as I am at school," said a twenty-year-old student. "Sometimes I wish that they could just see me without my knowing that they're there...with my friends...feeling more comfortable than I do when I'm at home." When children feel trapped in the old role, home becomes awkward indeed. Hence the expression sometimes voiced by children and adults alike, "You can't go back."

Julie had similar feelings. "The hardest thing for me," she said, "was going back and forth from home to school; it wasn't adjusting at school so much. It was coming back and living at home. My parents treated me the same way but I felt changed. It's hard to let them know that you've changed because it's more internal, I guess." Fortunately, her parents came to understand — as many parents eventually do — the change that she had undergone. "It took a while," Julie concluded, "to get them to realize that it's not *that* way, anymore."

Regardless of whether the outward appearance and actions of the child manifest that inner independence and transition which has taken root, these young adults feel the essence of being apart, both physically and emotionally, from their parents. When children return home for visits, parents are often kept in the dark about the new person, even though the student may enjoy sharing that new self with friends. "The exciting part is to come home and open myself up to my friends," said one freshman, "so that they can see deeper...more than they saw before." His parents were not to be privy to his trek into adulthood — except at a distance.

Not all parents fail to see the emerging person. Many will openly embrace the new changes. "I'm closer to Mother now," said one twenty-year-old. "She wants me to talk to her more about what's going on in my head because she's aware of all these things having changed."

Other parents are aware of these changes but consciously resist them. Some parents manifest bewilderment or erupt in anger or constant argument. Still others will react as though kids living their own lives is a personal affront to them as parents. When these reactions occur, the gulf between parent and child usually widens.

parents' weekend   Parental visits to college usually heighten children's awareness of the old-person/new-person duality. Parents naturally want to see and get to know the environment where their child spends so much time — the campus which usually comes with the hefty price tag. On the other hand, parents need to be aware of some of the feelings that their child may be having about such a visit.

Said one college junior: "It's awkward, I think. I've never liked it very much. It's still a little bit hard for me to put the two lifestyles together. My parents don't know my friends, don't know what I've been doing at school. My friends don't know much about my home life. And then they're all thrown together." Another's feelings about her parents were even stronger: "When they come to visit me at school, that is so weird. It's like they're invading this other world and the two worlds clash. It is a relief when they're gone."

Pain outweighs pleasure in this daughter's mind. In a sense, parents have a right to invite themselves for *their* weekend, but sensitive parents will listen for hesitation or lack of enthusiasm in their child's voice before automatically assuming that both parties are equally excited about the visit. This is not to say that parents should not set foot on campus, but simply that they should be attuned to the honest feelings of their son or daughter.

changing outlook As young adults begin to escape parental control, they are in a position to begin facing their parents on equal footing. Despite past or ongoing hostilities, evaluations of parents can begin to soften with love and understanding. The inability of parents to perform at the *perfect-parent* level can be forgiven and young adults can begin to see and respect their parents as people with admirable traits, valuable ideas to share, and, perhaps, wisdom — but people who are also fallible.

This understanding is slow to develop, but gradually children may see themselves free to clear the air of past times of unhappiness, differences, conflicts, or condemnations. As life in the real world hits them face to face, most children slowly (often, ever so slowly) gain a confidence that allows them to put their lives in order and overcome the emotional baggage inherited from their parents. As children come to know themselves, they can let their parents be who they are. When the external separation of college is echoed by a guilt-free internal separation of child from parent, the maturation process is truly under way.

Maturation is elusive. Looking into the thoughts of children reveals some of that process often kept from parents. "I talk to my mom and my sister more than before I went away," said one young woman, "because I feel more confident in my feelings, more expressive of them. I feel closer to my dad. I came home from a party and we just talked until two o'clock in the morning. It was really neat...very special.

"When you go away, you do so much learning and growing from being with people and forming relationships, having some of them blow up in your face, and having others just be wonderful...so maybe that's why I felt more ready to talk to them. Sometimes they treat me like their child, but I know I've proven myself."

Dealing with parents is an important aspect of growth for children. "Until we learn to relate as adults to our parents, we remain forever vulnerable to habits of adolescent overreaction," says Michael Nichols in his book, *Turning Forty in the Eighties*. "Until people stop running from their parents they have trouble getting close — and staying close — to anyone else." In some sense, those young adults who run from their parents can be as emotionally dependent as those who stay home.

Ultimately, children must take responsibility if they want to achieve a functioning adult-adult relationship with their parents. "Parents may represent the most important unfinished business of our lives," Nichols continues. "These relationships are the source of all subsequent relationships. Once we begin to resolve how we feel about our parents...we can start to relate to others."[2]

In the end, parents should take to heart the advice given by one parent. "In spite of everything...the breaking away...the conflicts...the distance...I should have known better than to worry. They still loved me!"

waking up For some children this transition of leaving parental control is uneventful; for others it is not. Although many children will make the break during college, others will find it a much lengthier process.

In his book, *Giant Steps*, basketball star Kareem Abdul-Jabbar relates his own personal experience breaking away from his mother. For many years, escape from her control meant avoiding her. Only at age thirty-three, and with the help of his second wife, was he finally able to reconcile with his parents and feel comfortable being an adult in their presence. His insights chronicle part of that journey:

> I was so well trained that I had internalized my Mom's (sic) nervousness, given up my independence for her peace of mind. My mother wanted to protect me from what she saw as dangers in the street, but in the process she wasn't giving me the time or space to find the facts for myself. It was as if she didn't trust my judgment, wouldn't handle the fact that I could fend for myself. And, of course, the less I actually faced, the less I was prepared for. In her earnestness she made it, despite my size, hard for me to grow. [Senior year in high school]
>
> I was in and out of the house, a new man in my old boy's room, about to head off into the world without her. She didn't want to lose what little of me she still had, but she would not be disobeyed. I was twenty-two and no longer listening. It was a difficult summer. [After graduating from college]
>
> My parents had been shut out to the point where my occasional visit to them was abrupt and uncomfortable....[I had to]...insist that...everybody else allow me to make my own decisions and live by my own lights.[3] [Age thirty]

Abdul-Jabbar's experience is not unique. A middle-aged daughter reminisced about her breaking away and how long the process actually took: "I went through my teenage rebellion at age thirty-two. Can you believe that? Thirty-two! My dad and I fought like cats and dogs, much to the family's dismay. Finally, he stopped telling me what to do. Things are okay now. I wish it hadn't taken me so long...but better late than never."

When teens or young adults do not complete this breaking away phase in a timely fashion, it merely gets delayed. Although in some cases independent adulthood is postponed indefinitely, and in others it is very rocky, eventually most offspring do wake up and take responsibility for their lives.

PANGS OF ADJUSTMENT

fears and anxiety Going to college is facing the unknown alone. Kids can't help but wonder: "Will I make it?" "What will I end up doing with my life?" "Will I make the right decisions?" They may worry about academics, finances, making new friends, liking their roommates, fitting in, and being accepted.

They may worry about the pressure of having career goals and what life will bring. They may worry about being cut off from family in an uncaring environment. They may be apprehensive about changes in their personal identities. Some children may intuitively understand that, regardless of whether or when they come home again, they are leaving their childhood behind. In short, they are frightened.

Some young adults resolve these anxieties by theoretically eliminating them — the young person remains at home. Others make the emotional break from home in an angry, negative manner — they effectively close off the emotional ties to family. Neither way allows a healthy resolution of the young person's profound attachment to caring parents.[4]

The fears of the child are usually not as concrete or profound as those of the parents. The fears are, however, complex in the sense that they are surrounded by ambivalence. Many kids will feel a gut-level anxiety that they cannot specifically identify. This does not mean that they are unhappy to be leaving, but because children are often hesitant about communicating feelings of insecurity, parents who are aware of the anxieties can be supportive.

Each child knows that college classes will be harder than high school and that more will be expected academically. Students who were somewhat poor performers may set new goals for themselves which are more consistent with their potential or which will allow them to fulfill career aspirations. Students who did exceptionally well and gained entry into a top college may hope that they can maintain that excellence in a more competitive environment. Others hope that they can just get by. Regardless of the students perspective, academics often contribute to stress.

Most students seem to understand that being scared is an emotion that often accompanies the undertaking of something new. "I was pretty scared before I left. I wasn't sure how I was going to adjust. It was pretty easy though," related Sandy after the end of her first semester. Paul had similar thoughts: "My school was really big and I was a little scared of the academics. I guess I was apprehensive about everything."

For other students, fear and adjustment take on larger proportions. "I was really scared," said Bonnie. "The first few days I was depressed that things weren't happening quite the way I had envisioned them. I was tired of high school and excited about college even though I was worried at first. I was looking forward to meeting a lot of new people and finding people that I could connect with. When that didn't happen, I was really down for a while...but you have to adjust."

moments of frustration Even for the most optimistic of teens, frustrations arise to remind them of the vagaries of life. Only this time, problems are faced alone; there are no parents to step in and take control. Nor do children want or need their parents to intrude. Success at negotiating these situations breeds confidence, character, and, ultimately, composure. Failures also have lessons to teach.

Just the mechanics of getting to school can be complicated. Packing is time consuming and can be exhausting. For those who travel hundreds of miles to reach their destinations, the trip can be physically tiring. Some make the trip alone. Not all trips proceed smoothly, as one freshman related.

"I left for school at five in the morning. I had all my belongings packed up for the eight-hour drive. As I went along...first of all I realized I'd left all of my hanging clothes in the closet. The night before I'd hidden my suitcases in the garage so they wouldn't get stolen out of the car...and I realized I'd left them where I'd hidden them. Then I finally realized that I'd left all of my money in my wallet on the table. I was about four hours into the trip and couldn't see turning around to go back, so I got to school and had absolutely nothing that I needed. I was there a day early and didn't know anybody so I was pretty miserable for the first two or three days. The whole thing seems pretty funny now, but it sure wasn't then. In spite of the snafu, I felt incredibly independent being away from home."

For another freshman problems arose a day or two later. "My frustrations started off with getting my schedule straightened out which definitely was messed up. Man, I hated it. It was like....it was like a Monty Python sketch or something: send me here and send me there and send me here and who do I see...like I couldn't reach someone who was in control and say 'what's up?' like I could in high school. You can't find anybody in control, and if you can, you can't get an appointment.

"I was so frustrated one time. I was in the university hall, where the bursar is, and I started talking to this lady...I don't even know who she was but she was listening to me...and I unloaded on her and she helped me out some, but the big realization was that...man...no one can help you; you've got to figure it out yourself. I've had to come to the conclusion that I know what I want more than anyone else." Out of feelings of frustration the flower of wisdom begins to unfold, teaching one of life's more valuable lessons.

life more difficult While they expect life to be different in a positive way, children are often unprepared when that differentness seems obtrusive or burdensome. Yet much of what they took for granted or was done for them will change or disappear. Life will seem harder. Adjustments to responsibility and decision-making drain energy — energy that is not always offset by the inherent rewards that accompany these life changes.

Mourning the ease of the past is common. Students often want life to be, "...like it was before," according to one freshman. Not only does this desire affect some of the trivia of daily life, but particularly it shows up in the formation of friendships — for peer relationships generally play an important role in most teenagers' lives. This was the case for Scott.

"You expect to go off and make a lot of friends but it's a lot harder than what you expected. Not so much that you miss home as you miss friends that you had there...easy to make, fun to keep. And you didn't have to go through the ritual of introducing yourself to them, etc. It's harder to find that group of people that you connect with."

Bonnie echoed similar thoughts. "It's not harder for me to meet friends at college," she said, "it's just harder for me to really like them and get close to them. In a lot of ways I compare them to high school friends and I have too many expectations of them and the way they're supposed to be. I want to be able to get along with them really well, even though I didn't always get along with my high school friends. I think that if I met some of my old friends in college I actually wouldn't like them. I think you can like different kinds of people in high school because you're secure in the home environment. In college you're more picky."

What both Scott and Bonnie are articulating is the added role that college friendships play as a substitute family. High school friends can be taken in small doses; in college, friends have to fulfill a more intimate need — and that takes time.

MISSING HOME

surprise! Ironically, many children are surprised to find that they miss home to the degree that they do. Such feelings do not readily surface during conversation; children have to be asked directly in order to reach these emotions. With its long-standing, familiar comforts, home is easy to take for granted, as are parents, brothers, and sisters. Once asked, however, the honesty of those girls and boys interviewed was touching:

* "I remember thinking at the last minute...wow, I haven't been paying attention to the fact that I'm actually going to be taking off. I sort of took it lightly. It wasn't until the day I left and got to school that I realized...even though I didn't want to admit it when I left...family was what I missed. I definitely missed them more than I thought I would. Friends I knew I was going to miss, but family I took for granted. I was a little bit younger than I thought."
* "Ma Bell got a lot of business out of me. Finally I was told not to telephone so much...to cut down on the expense."
* "I think that a lot of people go away eager to start the new life, and then are shocked to find that they miss the life they had before they left."
* "Surprisingly, I did miss home. When I went off on other trips it wasn't on a permanent basis. Now it's more reality. It will never be the same again. I'm pretty much out of the house...just come back for vacations and that sort of thing. That was unsettling at first. I didn't expect to miss it. I expected to go off and be a college man. I'd never experienced homesickness before."
* "I missed my parents a lot. That's what was really hard...it was just hard."

Today's long distance telephone service, usually paid by the parents, helps to reduce the impact of a separation that would seem more traumatic if simply reduced to written correspondance. Kids are able to apprise their parents of college life; parents feel more in touch with their child's transition. This communication grows out of a need of both parents and child and eases them into the postseparation phase. High phone bills are common and reflect how much kids miss home.

emotional gap More than missing the physical presence of home, children miss the emotional support that home and parents represent. That this support is still needed (and wanted) for emotional security, for advice, or as a buffer from the harshness of everyday life sometimes surprises a teenager. Said one teen of his parents, "It's nice to know that they're always there."

There are times when life back home doesn't look nearly as bad as it used to and, certainly, parents are often easier to appreciate from a distance. Praise for family togetherness is more forthcoming once it is no longer expected. The security, comfortableness, and nourishment of home are easier to measure when judged against dormitory life.

A simple "It's good being home," spoken by a child, may not be a casual statement; it may reflect a previously unrecognized depth. Parents, understanding this real meaning, may gain insight into their child. In the end, home not only means missing family and feeling loved, it also symbolizes the freedom to act like a kid, roll on the floor with the dog, be taken care of when sick, and feel uniquely sheltered — times not likely to come again.

Slowly young people may come to realize that as their youth slips away, they appreciate it more — and the greater the appreciation, the further its carefreeness escapes their grasp. This is one of the hard parts of growing up — no wonder it comes as a surprise. Yet perhaps the desire to recapture those feelings of security is the reason that most children like to come home, no matter what their age. To many (and in spite of family conflicts), home represents an oasis of love, a place to restock and replenish on the path of life.

The emotional gap may run deeper for children of divorced parents, as child psychologist Dr. Tom Colley explains:

> When kids leave home at this point in their lives, many of the ones from split homes not only miss home, per se, but they also reconfront and mourn the loss of the original two-parent home that may have broken up years previously. They actually want to reestablish that original home structure — as a way of clinging to the security of the past. Many children and teenagers never totally accept emotionally that they no longer have two parents living together.

less control Sometimes children at college feel that they have less control over their lives or that some of the freedoms gained are offset by those lost. This was the case with Peter: "I had a lot less control over my environment. There's no such thing as privacy. That was hard for me to deal with...and not having a car. You can't escape. You live in a house and you have the freedom to change your environment.

"You just can't do what you like to do at college," he continued. "I might have even ended up with a net loss of freedom. The campus environment is a small one; home seems like a real sanctuary. It was strange adjusting, harder than I thought. It was more difficult to detach myself from home. I did miss family and friends and the comforts of home more than I thought I would. The dorms seemed unfriendly, the school big. What I felt was parents as comfort level...a buffer. You don't have to worry about impressions and stuff like that. It's hard to call that dorm room home because home has a lot of physical connotations and I refuse to make the connection. Sometimes it seems more like a prison."

Peter had underestimated the pull that home would have on his freshman year. Less control and less security were sacrifices that he was forced to confront.

fact or myth? Some people might argue that missing home is a myth — either they didn't miss home or they know someone who didn't. This may well be the case. For example, children may suspect that their parents wanted them to leave. "I know a lot of people who have the impression that their parents were glad to see them go, to get them out of the house," said Dan, a college senior. "I don't know if that's just a front they're putting up or what. I've always felt lucky that I didn't get that feeling. A lot of it may not be true. It could just be that people like to talk badly about their parents or something. But some of it may be true...kind of a relief. More boys seem to say it; they go home mostly to see their friends."

Clearly, some young adults may deny missing home simply to seem overly independent or to disguise more intimate feelings, as Dan guessed. Other children may be extra critical of home and family because they are emotionally troubled in some way or because the family unit is dysfunctional.

In other instances, young adults don't like coming home because they are treated as dependent children — not independent individuals — by their parents. When this happens with regularity, meeting on *neutral* ground for vacations, such as the grandparents' house, can help to alleviate the situation.

And sometimes, young adults can use their indifference to home as a tool for manipulation. One mother related the frequent disagreements which occurred with her son over the Christmas holidays. In a grandstand play to get his way, her son retaliated that he would leave and go back to school early. Not to be outmaneuvered, his mother responded, "Well, if that's what you have to do, that's what you have to do." She turned and left the room.

"My gosh, that was a hard thing to say to him. I had this sinking feeling of being a failure as a mother if he couldn't even last at home through the whole vacation. But what really happened was that I called his bluff. He never mentioned leaving early again. I guess home wasn't so bad, after all."

AMBIVALENCE

independence versus dependence A major dilemma that kids often face is when to do something on their own versus when to ask for help. In short, they have mixed needs. On the one hand they want to be mothered, but on the other they don't. On the one hand they want to grow up, but on the other they don't. A successful compromise ultimately leads to successful interdependent living — maintaining independent status while recognizing the need to be taken care of once in a while.

Said one student, "It didn't really bother me to leave my family. I missed them...they're comfortable and safe. I didn't feel lost yet I needed their guidance. I need my parents to help me out, but I don't need them to always be there looking over my shoulder. It's like I want their help and then I don't."

Children do look forward to being home — but often with mixed feelings. They are more apt to be busy catching up socially with the friends and lives they left behind. A child may look forward to coming home for a visit and yet, at the same time, be anxious to leave again, if that seems possible. A five-day visit is often preferable to a longer three-week stay. Speaking frankly, some students admit that home seems boring.

One son laughingly described his contradictory feelings on the first trip back home: "I had a girlfriend when I left and I wanted to come back because of her. Once I arrived, I wanted to leave the day after I got home. That was funny. When I was actually driving home, I felt like I wanted to be driving back, even though I missed my family. I just wanted to be independent as fast as I could."

emotional conflict Melinda was a shy introspective young woman, whose emotional conflicts were illustrated by her ambivalence. Her parents, well-off financially and well-intentioned, flew to Chicago many times the first fall to help ease her homesickness. Although their visits perked her up, with a few months of hindsight Melinda eventually realized that such frequent meetings only made the problem worse. "Each time after I saw them, I had to settle in all over again. It was hard. I hate to say it, but their visits were a mistake. I wish they hadn't stepped in. I wish they'd stayed home and just let me adjust."

Even when she missed her parents, Melinda's feelings were contradictory and difficult to reconcile: "You think that you miss your parents and that when you come home you're going to get along great because you got along great on the phone, but it's not like that. The first night that I came home for the holidays...already I was getting very impatient with them." The fact that she had been homesick made little practical difference when relating to her parents one-on-one and engaging in her struggle for independence.

Yet in many ways she wasn't ready to be an adult. "Sometimes my family treats me a little differently, but I don't want to feel that I've changed that much. I don't like it because mainly I don't want to grow up, I think. I'd like to just go back to high school and stay there. I want to be treated like I'm not growing up. I want to be babied and not have responsibilities. I never wanted to get older. It's more secure here at home and I like my high school friends better and my teachers better, and we knew everybody. I know I'm romanticizing but I can't help it.

"I was so ready to *love* college. It was a hard adjustment...I'd never been away from home so that was a big deal. But there was no way that I could come back home because it wouldn't be the same. Looking back, high school wasn't as bad as I thought, and I liked it a lot...it was so easy and now I have to deal with all this new stuff." At this, Melinda could not help laughing at herself.

"I wish somebody had made me go off and do something on my own...because there are a lot of things that you choose not to do in a new place if you're not happy. It's important to be able to adjust fairly quickly so you can get out and like your school."

the room left behind Many children will leave a room meticulously picked up — antiseptic looking or unrecognizably neat. Others will leave their distinctive stamp of messiness. What does the messy room say? Children may be saying that a neat room is too final, too much of a separation. They may be laying claim one last time to the now-disappearing role of child by seeming to say, "I'm still a kid — if you want me to pick it up, parent me and make me do it."

They may want to leave loose ends, ravelings that still mark their presence; they don't want to close the door on their past. They may want their way of life to stay the same—even though they are no longer there. They seem to be saying to their parents, "You may not have me around anymore, but you still have my mess. I haven't really abandoned home."

When mothers clean and straighten, some of that familiarity and comfortableness is lost — and kids want to come home to the same smells and spaces that they left. Some children lose their rooms — to siblings, guests, one of the parents, or even a renter. Belongings may be packed away. Though ill-advised, some parents even throw out their child's possessions.

Children's intuition may also tell them that they are less a part of home and all that it represents. They may even lose their sense of belonging and fitting into the family structure. Because their bedrooms are such an integral part of their identities growing up, changes to that room can seem alienating.

feeling guilty Even though children enjoy leaving home, they also feel guilty. These feelings of guilt may arise for a number of reasons, some of which are:

* the child is the last to go, deserting a single parent or leaving parents all alone
* parents don't want the child to leave
* parents feel that the child is ungrateful for all of their sacrifices
* parents feel that they are being abandoned

Even if not discussed openly, these messages can easily be picked up by children. In a metaphor reminiscent of the empty nest, one son said of his family, "I was jumping out. I felt that I was deserting them."

The last daughter of six children felt the same: "I did feel guilty in a way, because everybody always said to me, 'Oh, my gosh, your poor parents. They're going to be so sorry to have you leave.' Sometimes at school I'd start to have a really good time...and then I'd feel a little guilty that I wasn't missing home any more...and then I'd feel bad...which was silly."

In an effort to lessen her mother's emptiness, one daughter planned ahead and was very creative. "I left notes and quotes (twenty-five in all) around the house for Mother to discover...for example, under the fourth plate in the stack, among the towels, etc. Perhaps I was being egotistical." But as an only child, she obviously suspected the void that she would leave. The impact of her leaving on her father seemed to cause her less concern.

Another child expressed his thoughts home in a letter to his single-parent mother:

Dear Mom,
   I don't have time to write, but I have something to tell you. I love you and always will. Don't you ever forget that. I'll never forget everything you've done for me. Mark my words. When I become successful I'm going to take care of you better than anyone has before because you deserve it. I love you so much.
Always, John
P.S. Don't send me money you deserve and need.

Ironically, some children are even made to feel guilty for missing home. As an adult talked of her long-ago separation from home, she related how her feelings of grief at missing home were dismissed by her parents. "My mother said, 'You shouldn't feel that way.' So much for my feelings!"

Ambivalence persists throughout the leave-taking process — before, during, and after. Slowly, it fades.

PROFILE

The thoughts of a daughter, Rachael, and a few comments of her older brother, Doug, comprise this Profile. Rachael had always had a warm and loving family relationship, but insights into that specialness did not become evident until after she had left home. Her brother was also aware of family support, as well as his continuing need to expand his horizons. All of these feelings came through in their letters or notes on cards commemorating special occasions.

LETTERS FROM RACHAEL (Excerpts)

October, Freshman Year "I have matured a lot. I have more confidence in myself. One has to — thrown into such an independent state — you cannot survive unless you look out for only yourself at all times. With this new maturity I'm experiencing a different level of feelings towards you and Dad, my parents. I feel equal — you make me feel equal. I feel I can talk to you about anything and can relate to your actions and thoughts. It has taken eighteen years for me to experience this.

"I agree with your saying that one's self-directedness comes from within, yet I would not deny either you or Dad of the credit. You put us two children in an environment that allowed us freedom, yet structure to follow and be our own person. You directed us when we needed it, but also gave us space to grow. You implanted those seeds of striving for goals and succeeding in life. You've given us every advantage and possibility to do so. Granted, it is we who must take these advantages and work to produce a product, but your input cannot be denied. You've been the best parents."

November, Freshman Year "The more I talk with different kids, the more I realize what best parents you have been. I can't understand some of the ways some kids are brought up. Obviously I am biased — but I think you did a magnificent, praiseworthy job. You succeeded in making us independent (o.k., I'm still a little attached). I can only hope my children (??) will be raised in the same fashion — and will respond in the same manner.

"On that note I really must run. I love you—"

Spring, Freshman Year "Thank you for raising your children in such a secure, motivating environment. The end products of all your hard work are certainly two beautiful adults!"

December, Sophomore Year "I basically feel good about myself. I've grown up a lot, which I didn't think was possible. I realize now, though, that I'll never stop growing up...it's never ending.

"I'm glad you've supported me through the semester. I don't know if you realize how much it helps. I'd say you two have done a *splendiferous* job in raising me. What an outcome! And we did it together. Thank you.

"I'm very excited about being home in January. It will be wonderful to actually spend some time with my parents. It's been a long time — my fault. So I guess you're stuck with my scampering feet for a month — sorry. No more fun for you two...your daughter is back!"

Spring, Sophomore Year "I can't thank you enough for the support you have given me this year, especially. Whether you know it or not, you have given me a lot of advice this year. Your input has helped quite a bit. Thank you.

"I'm very much looking forward to spending time with you this summer. (Yea!)"

LETTERS FROM DOUG (Excerpts)

As a way of introduction to Doug's correspondence, his mother spoke of the following event: "In high school, Doug and I had our differences of opinion. He just seemed to be rejecting me entirely, but he was able to continue on good terms with his dad.

"After being away at school for six weeks or so, he came home in October with a red rose to thank me, and to offer amends for the rugged high school years. So when I decided to attend the same university while he was still a senior there, I had his full approval, encouragement, and blessing...as a fellow student enriching one's brain and partaking of the wonders that academic life offers."

October, Junior Year "My main purpose in writing though was to thank you both for all the support. While I feel I became essentially independent when I entered college, I've always felt I can lean on my parents when times got tough. It's a good feeling."

September, Senior Year **(after taking a year off)** "I thank you both for allowing me to partake in these different things which I have done. I sure have learned a lot in this past year about myself and the crazy world out there."

Spring, Senior Year "Happy Mother's Day. I hope that you enjoy yourself on this special day. Thank you for everything you have done to get me to where I am. It still appears as if I will graduate. I look forward to seeing everyone here. It should be a time to remember."

Fall, after graduation "I hope my trip with Kristen across the continent will not worry you. Do not worry. It will be a good year.
"A tree needs branches for nourishment and shape. Although I may not appear as a tree, I think the more branches the better."

1. As quoted in a letter, "The Children Are Gone," by Deborah F. Reese, *The New York Times*, December 11, 1985, p. C13.
2. New York: W. W. Norton & Company, 1986, pp. 197 and 250.
3. New York: Bantam Books, 1983, pp. 111, 195-6, and 281.
4. Maggie Scarf, *Intimate Partners* (New York: Random House, 1987) p. 292.

CHAPTER 4

SIBLINGS:
HOW DO THINGS SHAKE OUT?

I told them, "Someday when you're all away, you'll learn to appreciate each other." That's what I had to make myself think when all this stuff was going on.

OUT FROM UNDER

sibling dynamics In the midst of raising kids, parents often despair: happy, loving sibling relationships seem a distant goal. Ever a complex issue, many books have been written on the dynamics between siblings, the influence of birth order within the family structure, and the rivalries which ensue. The scope of this chapter is not to examine any of these in depth, but rather to concentrate on the reactions that siblings have when a sister or brother leaves home and how other family members view those reactions.

When the oldest child leaves, younger siblings have rarely, if ever, known a life without the older person around. Their very being, as well as the dimensions of their world, have been shaped to some extent by that sibling. The smaller the family, the greater the influence that the older sibling has usually had. Sometimes the impact has been so strong that the younger siblings' self-identities are poorly defined. Thus, as each succeeding child in the family departs, siblings have a chance to redefine their own boundaries and separateness. They may not consciously be aware of this redefinition; they rarely discuss it in concrete terms. The process seems to be more internal, as change so often is.

In today's typical two-child family, the effect of the older child on the younger is enormous. Said one parent, "I guess I knew that he influenced her a lot, often negatively with all his bullying and their constant fighting, but I never really stopped to think much about the fact that her life...her space...was completely colored by him. He was always there. What a drag! It must have done her a world of good to be out from under that."

Perhaps for this reason, most comments about sibling reaction to the separation process are positive. Relations between family members left behind often improve. Even though there may be feelings of longing for the departed brother or sister, siblings and their parents seem to understand that the break is healthy.

"She said it was weird," commented one teen of his sister. "She missed me...but think of her position. It's just all of a sudden a new environment. She's never known a world without me at home...all the good and bad things that go with it. I think that it would be good for her...even though it's weird adjusting...so I wouldn't expect her to miss me to a great extent."

Many aspects of sibling disengagement cannot be isolated from the natural maturation process of the younger siblings who would grow and change even if the older sibling did not leave. Certainly, the separation provides an impetus; how much is not always clear, as one mother realized while talking about her younger son. Her daughter had left for college some months earlier. "Roy competes with her. His self-image is not great. He cares a whole lot about what she feels about him, so it's probably a relief not to be under that pressure. But he also relied on her to give him strokes, too.

"Now he can develop his own style, his own personality, without having to worry quite as much as when she was home. He likes being more important. He's blossomed just like I knew he would. They weren't close. But he's only fifteen so some of these changes may be due more to his age and not to her leaving."

an empty space "When my brother left, it was a weird feeling," said Shelley. "There was kind of an empty space...especially when I needed to talk to him at one point. I was thinking about what I wanted to do with my life and he wasn't around. I was mad about that." Shelley paused to laugh at herself.

"Telephone calls are weird, even now. When he calls from far away it's like getting a letter; it's not like speaking to him because he's not really here with me. The greatest time was when he just appeared at the door."

Having grown up in a family of three boys, Charlie also felt an emptiness; now, he was the only sibling at home. "When my oldest brother left it didn't affect me. I was the little bratty brother and he was going to college and that was it. But I got a lot closer to my other brother because he had no one else. We've got some strong ties together now. It was fun. The fighting with each other stopped...most of it...which was nice.

"So when he left I was real disappointed. I wanted him to stay. I didn't know what it was going to be like all alone. Mom's mostly at work and I'm stuck here all by myself, so I didn't know what to expect. I was a little scared."

The special bonds that some siblings have with each other can be quite strong for any number of reasons — close friendship, common interests, mutual need, hero worship, competition, protection. A younger sibling may especially look to the older for advice, as Shelley had with her brother. The seeming loss of this relationship leaves a noticeable gap which, although usually anticipated, is not easily filled.

Siblings may show extra concern when a younger sister or brother leaves first — particularly if that person is the *baby* of the family. They may worry about the sibling's immaturity or ability to cope alone; they may feel an ego loss that comes from no longer being needed, no longer being looked up to, no longer having all the answers.

Young sisters and brothers can miss the sense of security that an older sibling gives. If they have shared the same bedroom, sleeping alone may seem frightening. In some cases an older sibling may have been a parental figure, particularly with very young siblings, or the figure-largesse bestowing gifts that make a youngster feel important and loved. Adding to the emptiness, little children may not immediately understand that an absent sibling will return.

"My six-year-old cried," said one mother. "He really missed Alice...who was like a second mother to him because I worked. He worried about whether he would see her again. At first he got upset when Alice called, but it's okay now and he looks forward to the phone calls and the vacations."

Sometimes siblings have a real comraderie. Said one father of his four sons, "They always played together and shared their toys. They all were in the band and went to camp. They did Little League together and were in the same Boy Scout troop. They had arguments but not a lot of sibling rivalry. When the first one went off to the Army, the other boys were very disturbed. By the time the last one was left alone, he was really bored without his brothers and all of their friends around."

relief that they're gone Yet in many ways, significant or trivial, siblings are usually glad that brother or sister has left home. They may finally know the freedom of having a bedroom all to themselves. They may acquire other privileges heretofore reserved solely for the eldest. They may talk of the things that they no longer have to contend with: full-blast music, waiting in line for the bathroom, someone barging into his or her room, selfish antics, sharing the car, fighting over which television program to watch, interrupted telephone calls.

Parental comments often revealed the speed with which younger siblings adjust — and then sometimes have to readjust. "They didn't waste any time taking his room over when he left," said one father, "but they worried that they were going to have to give it back when he came home."

"He loved taking her stereo set," related another parent, laughing. "He took it immediately...and when she got home at Christmas, she retrieved it immediately. I mean...she got home at midnight and by twelve fifteen that stereo was back in her room."

Sometimes an emptier house is the main attraction. "Our house has a small TV room which wasn't big enough for both her friends and my friends so we were always in competition for that," said one teenager after her older sister left. "Now I get it pretty much to myself. It's a relief not to have to deal with her friends...especially when my boyfriend comes over and we want to be alone."

Younger children have grown up having to accommodate the older ones, perhaps without giving it too much thought. When the older sibling leaves, the younger ones may subtly acknowledge or openly express — for the first time — what they have had to tolerate for years. Often they have had to put up with a lot.

"I did not miss her at all," said Emma's brother. "She just gave me a big headache. It was nice not to have to hear her whining...to get into the bathroom...to have the phone free." Emma was a first born.

First borns tend to be self-centered. They don't just walk into a room, they often command a presence. When they have been the instigators within the family, their absence usually brings a sigh of relief and a much-needed harmony that is refreshing. Said one parent about the oldest leaving, "There was not as much arguing. He was the agitator...very disruptive. The rest of the kids got along better. They've grown up more. He was constantly sticking one of them or making trouble so it was real different with him gone...very quiet...but we got used to it!" It was easier for the siblings to get along with each other and their parents when the friction caused by the first born had disappeared.

The oldest is not always the provocative one. "When Penny left it was very quiet," said a mother of four. Penny was her second child. "There was always conflict between Penny and the other three. She and her older brother got into it physically! One time Ken punched a hole in the wall rather than hit her...she could be an agitator. He had more friends in because she wasn't there. Life certainly was more peaceful."

In addition to a lessening of fighting and tension, sometimes teenagers have directly injected a bad influence into the family — drugs, alcohol, wild partying, irritating or foul language, bad or illegal habits — that not only the parents are happy to see removed from the household, but the siblings as well.

"It was good for Willie to be alone," said one mother. "His brother had been a bad influence...always in trouble or flunking out. Willie is studying more. He failed last year but he's getting better grades now that his brother is gone. Whether that's the reason, I don't know; maybe he just needed a little tender loving care."

Often the initial break acts as a catalyst. The family begins to confront those issues which have long been ignored: the concessions and accommodations which they had to make because of the child; the inconvenience and inconsiderateness which they experienced and chose to ignore; the child's obnoxiousness which frequently marred daily life. By the time the child returns, these negatives may be either forgiven and forgotten or more in focus for families willing to voice their dissatisfactions at inappropriate or selfish behavior.

A father spoke of the openly-articulated tension arising between his daughter and a visiting son during the holidays. Previously, they had always gotten along. "They had a fight this Christmas. He had to sleep on a hideaway and he disturbed her each night when he came home late. They ended up getting in an argument over it. 'Can't you be a little quieter when you come in?' she asked.

"Everybody in the family always knows that this is going to happen when he comes back home...so we have to get mentally prepared before he arrives. We all dread it in a way. It's a different world when he's here. We usually hold our breath until he leaves but this time it didn't work that way. She was tired of having to put up with him."

If parents were uptight raising the oldest child, the next siblings may experience a freedom that comes with more relaxed parents. "They got looser, more relaxed after the first left," said one son, "and with each next child. They were encouraging to me for the things I wanted to do, without making a big deal about it. They were telling me they were proud of me without pushing me."

Sometimes siblings are glad that a brother or sister is leaving, but not for a selfish reason; rather, they realize that leaving is the right step toward independence. "I was happy for him," said a teen whose brother had left for the military. "He was going to get away from Mom and Dad and be independent. He was getting on with his life...it was all laid out for him...and he was going to make it financially on his own. I admired that. I guess you could say that I was envious."

finally "top dog" "When Dick left for college, I was sort of relieved. All of us have been competitive and it just left me top dog, I suppose." Gary grinned. Obviously, being the most important child at home was a role that he enjoyed. "I got a lot more attention, that's for sure. I liked it."

When an older child has excelled and been an achiever — in sports, academics, or some other field — a younger sibling may feel relieved to no longer have to contend with that competition or reputation. The sibling-to-sibling comparisons tend to lessen and perhaps disappear. The younger sibling's self-confidence may improve once out from under the shadow of the older sister or brother. Opportunities to develop previously-untapped skills may arise, as happened in one family where a daughter dominated conversation. "She was a talker," explained her mother. "After she left the others were at a loss for what to say — as if they were waiting for her to come in and say something. Gradually they came out of it."

Parents often recognize the importance of this shift for the siblings. Instead of the world revolving around the oldest, the spotlight shifts to the next in line. "Number two daughter came to the fore more," remarked one parent. "She finally had her turn to be on top of the heap."

Some parents go out of their way to make the next sibling seem special, perhaps to compensate for the many years of playing second fiddle. "For the first year he was thrilled to death that she was not around," commented Marge, mother of two. "He got his favorite foods, which was fun...and if I fixed one when his sister came home and she complained, I told her to adapt! He got more of my time. He also got her double bed, which really upset her at first. She didn't like it. It was like being relegated to visitor status."

Just as older brothers and sisters may feel a loss when they are no longer idolized by younger siblings, new *top dogs* may feel resentful when they lose this position to a sibling returning home for the holidays. Having been in the recognition spotlight, they hate to feel so easily deposed.

ambivalence Ambivalent feelings turn up frequently during the separation process; the attitudes of siblings are no exception. Siblings may miss the departed brother or sister, yet simultaneously experience opposite feelings. Ambivalence may manifest itself as simple indifference, sometimes disguising jealousies, mutual dislike, or avoidance of other issues.

"I was disappointed to see her go but..." said one sister, her voice fading off. "I wondered how it would be. Really, I was not affected. We did not do much together...we're pretty different people." After she thought about what she had said, she worried that her comments might sound a little calloused. Ambivalence can be perplexing.

The greater the difference in personalities and interests, the less siblings may miss each other. This distance in sibling relationships was repeatedly revealed in parental comments — as if parents were mindful of the fact that siblings are born into a family, not chosen because they will be friends.

* "He's just different...very independent, very conservative...so they didn't really miss him. The kids weren't really close. They kind of went their own separate ways."
* "She was quiet so it didn't make a whole lot of difference when she left. She didn't have a lot in common with her sisters."
* "They missed him but they weren't that close to him. He never hung out with them. They didn't always approve of the things he did. They mentioned how quiet the house was. We all joked about that, in fact...he's a whirlwind. They didn't like his leaving but it was very cathartic."
* "They missed Tom the least because he was a loner."
* "She was so busy at school with her activities that there was no time to miss her sister. I don't think that there were any pangs."

In the same way that college students may have mixed feelings about returning home, siblings may also have conflicting feelings about the person returning. "Everybody missed him while he was gone and wanted him home again," related one father as he discussed sibling reaction. "When he came back and had been here about a week, then everybody was hating him again and wanted him to leave. So they missed him when he was gone but hated him when he was back. They all got on each other's nerves and were back to their fighting ways. It was really quite funny."

Sometimes, however, outward ambivalence is a facade for much deeper feeling. "It bothered her that he left one day before her birthday. She didn't say much...she holds everything in. But there was a lot of feeling...you could tell. She was angered but she couldn't talk about him except to say, 'He wanted to do it, so I'm not worrying about him any more.' She really cared. She was upset more than anyone."

extra responsibility Along with the benefits which often accrue to the child left behind, additional responsibilities may also arise. "Sometimes he is nervous about being home alone," said a parent. "He's the only sibling now and that's a responsibility. He has to fill that void and that's not easy for him."

Not only may parents expect a greater sense of maturity on the sibling's part, but the departing teenager may have such expectations, as well. For younger siblings, the message may clearly be that they are going to have to act older, take care of mom or dad, look after the house, or assume some particular chore previously performed by the now-absent child.

"I expect him to take care of our parents," said one son whose parents were in their late fifties and in poor health. "Maybe that's a lot to ask of him but I really expect it. He's kind of resentful at times. I think it's forcing him to grow up some."

Conceivably, the sibling may consider these unasked-for duties the *detriments* of being the oldest child at home. Even those rewards which are pleasurable, such as sole car privileges, may mean securing a job in order to pay for gasoline. Suddenly, a leisurely pace of life may demand more maturity. While the older brother or sister remained at home, there was little incentive to assume additional responsibility; the older sibling acted as a buffer to protect the younger ones. Now that buffer is gone.

the last child . . . a special closeness Older siblings often notice the closeness that can develop between parents and the last child remaining at home. Usually that child is the youngest, but not necessarily. "I've noticed a change," remarked an older brother speaking of his single-parent mother and sister. "There's sort of a duo scheme to things instead of a trio scheme to things."

Sometimes this special relationship causes envy or jealousy; sometimes it reflects the fact that parents are out from under a budget crunch. They have more money, nicer things, and fancier vacations to share with the last child. Regardless of whether or not older siblings feel left out, an improved relationship often gets their attention. "I enjoy seeing them become friends," commented a sibling. "They're closer. They did not always get along." Said another, "My mom's really going to miss him. They do a lot together."

LARGE FAMILIES

less impact . . . or more? Large families generally do not feel the absence of one child as much as small families do. One departure may not make a noticeable dent in an already hectic atmosphere, unless that son or daughter has played a particular role in the family which is sorely missed. As each succeeding child leaves, the departure is usually taken in stride; both parents and siblings have had practice with the issues of relationship realignments.

"With all these kids," said Ian, referring to his family, "there always was one person who was a leader and when that person took off there was a readjustment in the hierarchy of the family. The next oldest always took over and that was the person you looked up to. Whether you admitted it or not, that was the person who was the most wise of all the kids...the person who had the most power."

As the size of a large family gets noticeably smaller, the change may seem significant. Siblings have often organized their activities around sisters and brothers — someone is almost always available. Their departure, therefore, leaves a void not only in terms of the family, but also in terms of the sibling's social life. The house seems particularly empty after years of neighborhood kids, schoolmates, boyfriends, and girlfriends.

"When the others take off, it's not the old gang," said youngest sibling, Jennifer. "You feel like the family unit has been broken up. It's traumatic for everyone in the family. For me, there was always somebody to play with; they were my entertainment." Undoubtedly Jennifer was the most traumatized; she felt very alone.

"It was hardest for the youngest to see everyone go off," observed one mother. Her comments about her youngest son echoed the aloneness experienced by Jennifer. "I think that the most painful thing for him was the change; the family had taken on a different shape. During holidays he noticed it if everyone didn't come home. When we were all together, he felt wonderful."

In large families, because of the diversity of personalities to choose from, there is a good chance that one sibling may bond with another — and particularly miss that sibling when she or he leaves. There is also the chance that the kids left behind may fight more because their previous patterns of interaction have been disrupted. To some extent, how much a sibling misses a brother or sister depends upon their age spread and whether or not there are any siblings within that age span. If the age difference is greater than five or six years, then the departure may not make a great impression unless there is no older sister or brother left at home, unless the siblings shared an intimate bond, or unless the older was clearly a parental figure.

appreciation of times together Once the large family has scattered, reconvening in the same location at the same time can become doubly difficult. Some families go years before all members are able to gather for a particular holiday or event. These times become very special.

"We were used to being together," commented one sibling, "and now it doesn't always happen. You have to really cherish the times when it does, especially with a big family...because there are times when we're all just so far away. Once we had someone in India and Yugoslavia at the same time. When you're back home together, it's a really nice feeling. I love it."

As each succeeding child turns adult the age difference that may have separated one sibling from another is gradually neutralized. "There is a change," said another. "It's very much on an incredibly equal basis. Socially, we do things together. We're all adults now, no longer kids. We're our own people."

ADULT RELATIONSHIPS IN THE MAKING

a beginning The same pattern of growth which allows many kids to establish an adult relationship with each parent also leads them to restructure their relationship with each sibling. Unresolved rivalries or rifts can contaminate not only their ongoing lives but future relationships, as well. According to experts, this restructuring often does not happen until siblings are in their late twenties, but first steps may begin much earlier.

Sometimes an awakening occurs before a sibling's actual departure. "We fought a lot," said one brother, "but we became better friends her last year of high school. I realized that I better start being nice...and she did too. It was our last year together.

"Now when she's home we go places together...she doesn't mind if I hang out with her friends. I'm much more talkative and interesting than I was before...not as boisterous. We've realized that we have more in common...we both like to write."

For some siblings, making a transition comes in gradual steps after the initial departure. Phone conversations may establish a means of communication which eventually facilitates person-to-person closeness back home. Said one brother, "She and I had more meaningful conversations when we were apart...so now we communicate a lot better when we're both back for vacation."

The fabric of sibling relationships also begins to change simply because siblings, as individuals, grow up. They mature. As the age gap between them becomes less important, siblings feel less compelled to maintain a protective distance. "When I was younger," said one sibling, "I had to work very hard to be my own self and not just a little sister. Now it's not such a big deal."

Growing up does not always mean growing together: separation may accentuate differences, as well as likenesses, between any two siblings. Gradually, this awareness may either draw them together or cause them to move apart.

getting along better   Perhaps one of the most surprising and rewarding emotional changes that may occur is the development of improved relations between siblings. Where fights and chilly cold wars may have prevailed in the past, parents may gratefully see genuine affection and friendship evolve. Not that all annoyances disappear, but the prevailing atmosphere may become one of support and caring. A parent who observes this transformation may delight that a secret dream has come true.

Said one mother who had witnessed such a change, "Why at that point you could just die, couldn't you, and know that everything would be okay?" The gleam on her face was contagious — and she radiated joy knowing that her children had turned noncaring attitudes into geniune concern for each other. They would be friends for life.

If parents are sometimes surprised to see this new development, siblings may be even more surprised to experience it. "Weird thing is," said Matthew about his leaving home, "it's bettered our relationship. We don't get on each other's nerves as much. I think that we both realize that we appreciate each other's company. I did miss her. It was weird. We began to move our relationship from child brother-sister to adult brother-sister...which was incomprehensible to me as a kid."

Of course, one of the reasons that siblings get along better is simply that they don't have to spend as much time together and putting forth an effort is easier to sustain for short periods. "I went and visited her at school for the weekend," said Ronda. "It was the best we've ever gotten along. It was really neat.

"Now when she comes home we get along really well. We want to get along and we both make an effort, so it happens. We don't argue about the little things. I figure she's only here for a short while so I can put up with anything. By the end of a week and a half it begins to wear thin, though. If she had to spend the whole summer, we might get back into our old ways. So far we haven't really been put to the test."

The change in sibling relationships may reside more with the person who has gone away and less with other family members. That person may not only feel more accepted by the siblings but is more accepting, as well. There is more of a sharing of common experiences, more of an awareness that each sibling passes through similar life passages.

Some former trouble-makers begin to repair the negative influence imposed upon a sibling. Willie's brother, mentioned earlier in the chapter, took a step in that direction after joining the military. "Now he calls home," said his mother, "and tells Willie, 'You better be getting good grades in school and you better not be giving Mom any trouble.' He's acting like a father figure. He looks out for Willie. Now that he has some money, he even wants to enroll Willie in some karate classes and pay for them." Clearly, Willie's brother had grown up.

growing apart Given the space to experience separateness, some siblings come to the realization that they will never be close. While this may be a disturbing conclusion to certain individuals, others will conclude that being different is okay. As siblings continue to grow apart, these differences may be accentuated and delineated. Finally (and this may take years), siblings may come to understand that they don't really like each other very much.

But during the teenage years, such a conclusion is perhaps premature. Siblings may cling to the hope that time will rectify the discomfort that they bring to each other. "Right now we don't have much to talk about," said one sibling. "There's not much in common. It's sort of a sad thing. My cousin says that after I go away to college it will probably get better. I hope so."

Other siblings may come to terms with the situation through gradual acceptance of a certain distance. "We're just so different that I don't like him. We get along okay; it's not that. I think that we'll always be distant."

As an interesting phenomenon of the times, some young adults are faced with the situation of having a half-sibling that they may never live with or know very well. For example, if a teen's noncustodial father marries a younger woman, they may have children. Said one twenty-year-old about such a situation, "I haven't quite come to grips with my new half-sister or whether we'll ever be friends. It makes me feel weird to think about it."

PROFILE

Emily was sixteen when her brother Matthew left for college two years ago. They fought often growing up, rarely getting along. Matthew was a self-centered first born. Emily learned to retreat to her bedroom to avoid dealing with him. Because mutual caring seemed very remote, they were both surprised when their relationship took a turn for the better. Matthew's surprise was registered earlier in the chapter.

"I wasn't there to see him off because I had to work. When I got home, he was actually gone. His room was just totally different...everything that he wanted to have with him was gone...and that made me feel bad. I felt so lonely. Before I left I had given him a big hug and wished him best but it just wasn't the same. I wished that I had been there.

"I thought that I was going to be glad when he was gone because all the time growing up we didn't get along very well. I thought that it would give me more space...without his coming around and invading it. We wouldn't have to fight over the TV or who ate how many Poptarts or whatever. Before he left I was looking forward to it; but afterwards, the house felt empty. There was just me and Mom...I knew I was going to miss him.

"Because he is two years older than I am, all of my life he was always there. When older brother was finally gone, it was time for little sister to grow up...although I don't feel that I'm too much different now than I was then.

"I never went to him for advice but he would say little subtleties and I would really think about them. For instance, I had a party...this was several years ago...when Mom was out of town. When I mentioned it to Matthew, he told me that it was a bad idea and that I shouldn't do it. At that age, since we were fighting...especially after he told me not to...I felt rebellious and wanted to do it anyway. Things did get out of hand but in the end Matthew saved me. After that, things that he said meant a lot to me because he knew what he was talking about. He wasn't just saying it to get on my nerves. I knew he was saying it for a reason.

"We did start to get along a few months before he left. It wasn't a drastic change. He wasn't all of a sudden nice to me...it came gradually. I think that he grew up a bit. He had always picked on me because I was younger and because, I guess, there was nothing better to do. He started to outgrow his bully stage and accept me for what I was. He invited me to do something with him...which was a first. So the fact that we got along better before he left did make it more difficult.

"After he left I had more time to get to know my mom because it was just the two of us. Since he wasn't there to talk to, I would talk to her more, spend more time with her. We got closer. Matthew made her mad a lot when he was around. She got uptight because he was a slob. She might be uptight with me about something, but she didn't have that constant aggravation. It made things a lot calmer around the house...which also brought us closer together.

"I did especially miss him at certain times. When both of us were bored, we enjoyed playing games; but when I was bored after he left, there was no one around to play a game with. If I was home alone, there was no one to talk to.

"That first Thanksgiving I was real excited to be able to spend time with him. We went to my grandparents. The mountains were the perfect place to be with somebody that you have missed. When I saw him, I think that was the first hug I ever got from him on his own accord. We took many hikes together and talked about a lot of things and it was really great. I think that those were probably the best couple of days I've ever had with him. We didn't feel obligated to be with each other but we wanted to be together. He seemed glad to be spending time with me.

"We're pretty close now...his being away helped that. It makes me feel good because when we were growing up and fighting I *never* thought it would happen. I never thought I'd see the day when we would not fight. Now I think we'll always be friends."

CHAPTER 5

DO FATHERS FEEL
THE SAME AS MOTHERS?

I guess we feel pretty much the same...only she lets it show and I don't.

HARD TO TELL

mothers more emotional Whether fathers feel as much of a sense of loss as mothers is difficult to determine. In fact, how some fathers really feel may be the sixty-four-thousand-dollar question. As a whole, mothers seem to suffer more when a child leaves — perhaps because they have usually been the primary parent. They are more expressive of their feelings and more willing to acknowledge their emotional attachment or need for a child. Doing so is not a sign of weakness or even a sign of more emotional commitment to the youth. This is the way mothers are expected to act.

fathers less aware of feelings Just the contrary, showing emotions is not the way fathers are expected to act. Mainstream American fathers have grown up as little boys told not to cry, never to act like sissies, and always to be strong. Showing sentiment is a sign of weakness. Attachment to or dependence on people is taboo. After years of such conditioning, the ability to hide, camouflage, or deny emotions is automatic for large numbers of men. Thus thwarted, certain emotional responses gradually become hidden.

These men constitute many of today's midlife fathers — fathers who have not assumed a nurturing role in the home. For them, acknowledging a need for children, especially sons, as part of an emotional support system is contrary to the male image — some might even call it the macho-male image. Feelings lie beneath a well-constructed barrier of protection and often contradict the image being projected to others. What feelings fathers do experience may be disguised simply as concern for the child's financial or career aspirations.

These fathers frequently cannot say to their children, "I love you," or "I'm going to miss you," and may even convey opposite messages of hostility or indifference. Fearful that the emotional door may open to uncontrollable feelings, some fathers do not face the reality that their child is leaving. Worse yet, having been cut off for so long in a kind of emotional void, some fathers do not experience separation feelings.

The emotional filtering that so many fathers experience has a subsequent affect on their children. Comments Dr. Tom Colley:

> Married males tend to delegate the emotional and affectional aspects of child rearing to their wives. When the children leave, fathers may hurt as much as the other parent but they don't expect to have to deal with it. Often these fathers don't recognize a child's separation as something that really bothers them. If they do, they are much more apt to realize it after the fact, whereas women are conscious of their feelings before the children leave.
>
> Unfortunately, though, there are still vast numbers of fathers today who don't reveal how they feel and are afraid to show physical affection. They're unaware of the emotional needs of their children. Consequently, the children don't even know that their fathers will miss them. This can be quite disturbing to a teenager or young adult. Fathers may experience pain in their own caves, but that doesn't help the child much.

As if to reinforce this conclusion, the thoughts of a young adult — conveyed during a high school reunion party — echoed those of Dr. Colley: "My dad has a hard time expressing emotions. He comes from an Italian family and the men in the family turn their emotions inward. For him it actually led to physical problems: he got an ulcer. I guess you could say that he was emotionally deprived. When the first son left home he really felt hurt because he thought Dad didn't miss him. But what it really boiled down to was that my father couldn't communicate those feelings. He couldn't say how much he cared."

A father's awareness of his feelings can, in some ways, resemble the tip of an iceberg. So little is acknowledged compared to the magnitude of what exists. In practical terms this usually translates into a distance between father and child. Such was the case with Sid, a father of four. When his wife returned to school to complete her Ph.D., he became very active in meeting his children's daily needs for a number of years. In spite of this involvement in their lives, he later recognized that he had been aloof in an emotional sense. Sid quite candidly admitted that when the children left, "She was more affected, more emotional. She was more dependent on the kids' emotional input. I was more distant."

Like Sid, Eric was another father who also had a difficult time getting in touch with and describing his feelings after his daughter left home. At first he discussed whether she was well enough prepared to function on her own. Then he mentioned the fact that she could be hard to get along with at times; eliminating those minor irritations from his life was nice. When pressed about his feelings, Eric quietly revealed, "I fill my mind up with other things to keep busy and that negates my having to deal with any feelings." Although he clearly cared for his daughter, he could not disclose the intimate side of his feelings — not even to himself.

wives unaware While some wives indicated during interviews that their husbands verbalized about missing the children, more stated that, "He doesn't talk much about it." Rather, husbands preferred to stick to safe and basically unrevealing comments like, "Boy, it sure is quiet around here." Speaking directly of an emotional wound was too uncomfortable.

Perhaps Sue, a fifty-two-year-old mother of three whose children had been gone for a couple of years, reflected the most insight when she said, "I look around at the other fathers whose kids have left and I don't see feelings of loss. I think that it's natural for the mother, the nurturing one, to have them. Men are so geared to providing financially that I think that they're afraid to admit that a child leaving is a real loss...a personal one. Women are willing to say 'I really miss you.'

"My husband feels that you raise children and then they leave...you have good relationships with them and then things go on in a very sane way. He's more objective than I am. He's also very wrapped up in his job. I'm not implying that my husband doesn't have feelings about our children, because he does, but..." Sue's loss of words seemed to reflect her uncertainty about what those feelings were.

Another woman, so unaccustomed to knowing how her husband felt about anything, quite frankly admitted, "I don't know how much he has missed her. I should have asked, I guess, because

I'd like to know." Eight months had passed since their daughter left and yet they had never discussed it with each other.

children unaware Wives are not the only ones left in the dark. Because many children don't know their fathers very well, reading his emotions can be doubly difficult — as reflected by the student who commented, "My mother missed me a lot...I guess Dad did, too. The kids were a bigger part of her life. For my father I suppose the work was a bigger part...not necessarily more important, but..." As though they know that some feeling must be there, teens can be confused when trying to give a shape to it in words. How sad for some children and wives that the expression of a father's caring for his offspring becomes inexpressible, and a dangling "but..." leaves sentences fading away into nothing.

children who understand Luckily for certain fathers, however, children can be very cognizant of the emotions lurking beneath the surface and are not put off by a father's inability to express himself. Said one teen, "I know he cared but just didn't know what the hell to say." This awareness comes not only from the teenager barely a few months out of the nest but also from a mid-thirty-year-old man whose memories were keen and filled with emotion.

"I remember my father when I left. His eyes were real red and almost brimming and he could hardly talk but he wouldn't let himself cry. He couldn't. He couldn't even tell me that he loved me. All we did was shake hands. But I knew how he was feeling. Even though he couldn't express himself I knew that my leaving hurt him...I knew that the feelings were there. He just hadn't been raised to know how to express those feelings. Men weren't supposed to cry in his world. His feelings certainly weren't any less than a mother's...although it might have seemed that way."

THE SAME AND YET DIFFERENT

bad publicity for mothers Many reactions of fathers and mothers are similar. Both may mourn. Each may feel the lesser for the child's departure and the loss of the parent role. One or the other may try to manipulate the details of their children's lives, careers, and marriages. Either may try to keep the child at home for personal reasons that are not to the child's advantage. In spite of these potential parallels in parental behavior, though, mothers and their apron strings seem to get most of the attention and bad publicity.

a father's apron strings The apron strings of fathers are often overlooked. Twenty-year-old Carl, however, was aware of the pressure that his father had tried to exert. "My dad jumped around and said, 'Oh, you can't leave. Why don't you stay here and go to the university?' I'm sure that he would have liked to see me stick around. He had talked my brother into doing that for a year, but I didn't buy it. I was gone."

In another instance a father said, "I didn't want her to go that far away so I told her that she had to stay in the state for one year and then she could go to the school she really wanted. I felt like it was a good compromise: she was nearby for a while longer and then she could do what she wanted." The father's argument was compelling — he held the purse strings.

intense feelings Intense feelings by fathers also seem to get overlooked. Fathers do cry, but more likely in the privacy of their homes. "My wife had the same feelings as I did," said Robert, "but they were less intense. She was surprised at how intense my feelings were and even a little amused. I think that she thought that I hadn't been connected into what was happening for a long time...as though she was saying, ' I told you this was going to happen and I've been crying about it for years.'"

While the existence of emotions is not dependent upon their ability to be expressed, emotional responses are one way that feelings are effectively communicated between people. When fathers can eventually express these inner feelings, so much the better. "I was surprised at how much my husband missed Taylor...much more than I expected," said one wife. "He's hardly ever that emotional. It was nice to see."

When mothers view separation as a natural evolvement, they can provide emotional support and insight to fathers who feel cut off from understanding the child's growth process. Said a wife matter-of-factly about her husband: "He has a harder time letting go. For me, it's all part of the process. I tell him that."

anger versus depression Although either may react negatively to the empty nest phenomenon, men and women often exhibit a different outward appearance. Women are more apt to turn their anger at the children's leaving inwardly and become depressed; men may become depressed, but they are just as likely to lash out and manifest that anger externally. Inspecting this difference in his book, *The 40- to 60-Year Old Male*, Michael McGill finds two reasons for these reactions: first, that men are primarily responding not to the loss of the father role but to the loss of the breadwinner role; and second, that men focus their aggressive or hostile behaviors at the perceived source of the anger — their children or their working wives who are no longer home to take care of the nest.[1] In certain instances, they may displace the anger at other targets such as employees in the workplace.

Fathers may vent their rage simply because they are not comfortable dealing with the loss and sadness brought on by the youth's departure. This animosity exposes the family to a potential risk: repairing the damage done by a father's anger can be quite arduous.

William, a man of thirty, spoke about the disaster that occurred in his family because of his father's hostility. "I'm afraid that my father's inability to let me go in a positive way has had lasting repercussions on my emotional development. At the time, all I felt was hatred and emotional and mental abuse. He was a great man outside the house, but in the areas where he couldn't deal, and this was certainly one, he became nasty. I felt so hurt and rejected that I didn't go home for a whole year.

"Now that I'm older and have some perspective and maturity, I understand that there were intense emotional issues going on in his life. For one thing, he took the separation of each kid as a personal rejection. In retrospect, I realize that he treated all of the kids the same way when they left; but at the time, I took it quite personally."

no concensus Of course, there is no consensus about a parent's thoughts and feelings. They vary as much as the people themselves. There are no uniform patterns. Either mothers or fathers may camouflage inner emotional response; either may react outwardly. As a father may act, so also may a mother. Yet, even though many of their reactions are the same, on the whole, the reactions of fathers and mothers do seem different.

stepparents Stepparents, even though they share a residence with their stepchildren, are simply more removed when the kids leave. How much that response is influenced by the fact of being a stepparent and how much by the fact that most of these stepparents are stepfathers is difficult to determine. However, stepparents are not as emotionally bonded nor do they experience the depth of feeling that natural parents do when the nest empties. "It's not possible to bond as much to stepkids," articulated one stepfather, "biologically or philosophically. I'm here because their mother and I care for one another. I care for them not only because they're good people but because they're her children."

Because the duration of a relationship significantly influences emotional feelings, the reaction of a stepparent is highly contingent upon when he or she joined the family and took on a child-rearing role. Unless stepchild and stepparent have lived together for a long time (say, ten years or more) the stepparent is less likely to have a sense of emotional loss. Contrast the comments of Jake, a stepfather of two-year duration, and Von, a stepfather for twelve years when his stepdaughter left home. "I felt no loss," said Jake, "although I'm very glad to see her when she comes back. She called me up from school and said, 'Just wanted to tell you it's snowing.' My kids would never do that. I appreciate that kind of feeling. But miss her? No, I don't miss her."

"A real parent might feel more emotional stake in the separation. I'm more subjective," said Von. "But the stepparent also has an enormous role: by the time the kids go to college you hope that you've given them some stability through your caring, some basis to form moral and ethical judgments...so you have a lot at stake in seeing them succeed." Although Von shows more involvement, he's still aware of an emotional distance.

In fact, a stepparent may be quite glad that the child is gone: there may have been an unwanted financial responsibility associated with the child; there may be relief that the child-rearing obligation has ended; the stepparent may be longing for privacy; or the departure may signal the first time that the couple will be living alone. "I liked it," said one stepmother. "We had never had time to ourselves. I missed the kids but I didn't feel as guilty about what I was supposed to be doing and whether I was doing it right."

LEAVING THE EMOTIONAL STRAITJACKET

escape or change Fortunately, there are fathers who escape the emotional straitjacket during youth and others who actively change at some later point in their lives. These men are more comfortable nurturing and they experience separation much the same as mothers do. Although their ranks are growing, these men are still decidedly in the minority. Not unexpectedly, a large percentage of them are single-parent fathers, says Dr. Colley, because "most male single parents are more nurturing to begin with (by virtue of having accepted the single-parent role) so they are willing to show parental loss. They are intimately involved in their children's emotional needs."

emotional firsts Sometimes fathers spontaneously ignite a change by openly displaying emotions untapped for years — perhaps for a lifetime: the first hug since the child was little, the first "I love you" that the child remembers, or the only tears of the father's adult life.

The intense feelings which have been submerged for so long seem to explode, often surprising both the father and child, as well as other members of the family. Once the dam has been opened and the flood of emotions felt, a father may be able to continue letting go with more tears, stronger hugs, and continued expressions of love and caring.

This emotional opening up was aptly described by David as he talked of his father and family — a family composed of five children spanning a number of years. As each succeeding child left home, his father became more expressive. "Dad is more emotional about expressing things now. I know it's equal between the two...my mom and him...but he sort of breaks down and lets it show. That may be something that's a little more recent...as the second generation of kids leaves, it's coming out more. He didn't used to let his feelings show nearly as much."

"My relationship with my father changed a whole lot when I went off to school," said David's sister, Regina. She was the last child to leave. "We weren't close at all. We were fighting a lot. But before I went we started running and doing a few things together. When my folks took me to school, I said goodbye and I started crying...and he started crying. He said 'You know, you're just not like I thought you were at all. You're just like me: on the outside you seem so tough and on the inside you're mush.' My mom said he cried all the way to the airport.

"Then he wrote me a couple of letters and I talked to him on the phone. He had gone to prep school. His mom had shipped him off and he was really homesick, too. So we got a lot closer because now there was something for us to identify with together. He knew how I felt. He said in his letters that now we had 'a common bond. It's too bad that it took something as bad as that to bring us together but at least it happened.' So we changed a whole lot."

letters from dad Fathers may begin to open up by writing to their children after they leave home. While letters may not necessarily be intimate in content, as those from Regina's father were, they still may represent a form of one-on-one contact which has not previously existed in the father-child relationship. Most children are surprised to get a letter — an outward display of caring from dad. Some fathers, however, feel safer committing emotions to paper than saying them face-to-face.

Other fathers resist the idea of putting feelings in writing unless encouraged by someone else. One father discussed a letter he was writing to his freshman daughter, the first one that he had ever written her. "No," he responded, "I hadn't really thought of telling her that I missed her...but I do. I guess I should tell her." Her response was warm and loving; he was glad that he had taken a first step to bridge their emotional distance.

Sometimes fathers use letters (or phone conversations) to show indirect caring, a role with which they feel more comfortable. Speaking for someone other than themselves, they may write, "Your mother needs to hear from you." What they are often expressing is their need for a relationship with the child. They are saying that they care without saying it directly.

Letter writing also serves another function: that of repairing a parent-child relationship full of upheaval. Aware of the sometimes turbulent relationship of her husband and daughter, a mother said, "They've never had a very satisfactory relationship. He's always been hard on her, probably because they're a lot alike. He's written her a couple of letters and she was really touched. I know she was a little surprised to get them."

the nurturing void and guilt One thing that may awaken fathers from their emotional straitjacket is an awareness that they have not participated fully in the rearing and development of their own children. They may feel guilty. They may feel empty. They may feel as though they have failed as a parent, letting their children down. The lack of influence and intimacy with their children may suddenly seem unacceptable. From seeming obliviousness, they may begin to envy the emotional closeness that their wives have with the children. When these feelings act as a catalyst to change, the father may be more likely to move toward emotional openness. Unfortunately, many fathers are unable to take this step.

modern-day trend Indicative of the trend of fathers becoming more aware of their feelings and less reticent to admit to them, editorials addressing the difficulties and nostalgia of letting go of children have been written — by fathers — for some major newspapers. A decade or two ago this would have been fairly unheard of; mourning the passage of childhood in public was strictly the prerogative of mothers.

Even if a father has not been the primary nurturer for a child, a very special bond may have developed between them. Often this close relationship revolves around some physical activity which they share or participate in together, such as karate, fishing, golf, or other sports; for that reason the bond is more likely to develop with a son.

A factor that might contribute to a father identifying with his daughter is the fact that females can now attend those Ivy League schools, military institutions, or other universities which for so long reinforced only father-son camaraderie. Fathers take pride in daughters who attend their alma maters and often find a new and special closeness developing because of what they share together.

Actually, the trend towards androgynous fathers who actively participate in the nurturing of their offspring is not really a trend, but rather a slow movement toward change. Throughout society, being a nurturant father is the *in* thing for only a small number of fathers. Few children benefiting from this shift have reached their college years.

How these modern fathers will react to the separation process is as yet unknown. Perhaps they will feel much the same as mothers; for separation feelings are neither male nor female, as many single-parent fathers have discovered. Hopefully, other fathers, as well, will learn to face the difficulty of expressing both joy and pain in the same breath.

PROFILE

Robert Tyler, quoted earlier in this chapter, was a good example of a father caught unawares by the depth of his emotional attachment to his children, in spite of the close relationships that had developed during the teen years. Both his daughter and son left home within a week of each other and Robert's subsequent outpouring of feelings alarmed even his wife, Peg. By the time of the interview, he felt quite comfortable discussing his innermost thoughts and had clearly passed to a new stage of emotional awareness.

"I was surprised at the void. I was more affected than I thought I was going to be. I was shocked at how much more it hit me than my wife. She had probably played it out for a good bit of her life so she was prepared for it. I wasn't prepared at all...probably because I didn't think it was going to be that big a void. The feeling was as though they'd disappeared forever. We'd gotten very close for the summer...as if both sides could sense this was an end of an era.

"My feelings of loss moved into manageable levels over the next two weeks. Following that were some strong feelings of freedom and release. Peg and I had some enormous freedom...time freedom and attention freedom. The attention for each other, which we'd sort of forecasted, was really positive. It was not threatening...though it could have been if we weren't prepared. We'd paid attention to all the problems coming, but not the loss aspect. We became much more concentrated as a couple than we were before. There was a great exhilaration in our relationship...real significant feelings for sixty to ninety days. We did a lot together, spent time together by ourselves, focused more on each other than we ever have.

"Having two kids leave at once was powerful...like a tomb. We took the first to her room at school and got her nest built. I wanted to avoid an outward display of emotion and affection. I'm not emotionally demonstrative at all. But she could sense in me, and I could in her, the real feelings.

"Driving home I really had some sad feelings. I was laying in the back seat kind of dozing off and I rememember having...not exactly a cry but very, very melancholy, very lonely kinds of feelings about her being at school. It was not really emptiness...just a sad kind of a thing.

"Number two left about a week later. He was driving himself. We helped him pack, etc., so he could get off by five in the morning. It was sad. He kind of broke down and I broke down, and we hugged one another, which is fairly unusual for us. Peg was emotional but she's always pretty emotional, so that wasn't very unusual.

"I went back upstairs, walked into his room and looked around, and was really sad. I sat down and cried. I went back in his room several times during the next two or three weeks and I had the same response. It was a very pleasant response for me, but very different. The number of times I've cried in my adult life I can put on one hand. I hadn't cried in years. I registered surprise at the depth of my response. Peg was a little alarmed. I was not prepared for that sense of loss.

"My tears were from pride. The kids were ready...ready to handle what they were going to be up against. In some ways I was celebrating the end of parenting. I was celebrating...in not necessarily a positive way...and also realizing that it was over. This was the end of that dependency relationship. It was gone...and it was precipitous. It was clear to me that I was mourning its passage even though I'm much more responsive to an adult relationship than I am to a child relationship. I can't relate to young children very well.

"I spent very little time child rearing. Ninety-five percent of my energy until age thirty-three was spent in conquering the world. At thirty-four I decided that intimacy was also a requirement for my life and I altered those balances considerably. By age thirty-six my family occupied about forty-five percent of my time. So from about age thirteen to age eighteen of the kids' lives we had a pretty steady relationship. I spent a lot of energy on them. I feel moderately guilty about the time not spent until age thirteen, and real good about the time spent after that. So, in balance, I feel pretty good about being a parent.

"I'd been preparing them for years...a lot of freedom and a strong sense of the responsibility that goes with that freedom. Peg and I rarely say where they can go or can't go. And they've taken the consequences when that freedom is abused...mostly their own conseqences.

"I thought that they were very independent, unrepressed, and free before they went to school. They still bloomed and blossomed, and needed to do some testing and proving when they came home Thanksgiving...more so than I would have guessed. In retrospect, I should have known. But my feelings of missing and loss were so strong that they could have done just about anything they wanted!

"This summer there will be limits on their demands because they're less considerate, less responsive to chores, etc. They're less respectful of our space...which we've become more jealous of. They don't realize that they're living with somebody else who is not their servant for the moment.

"Our son announced that he would be living next year with three women. I know he wanted to see what Dad would do. I heard the test, I saw it coming...I perform very well when I see the test coming! I approved of whatever he wanted to do and helped him come to the realization of some problems that he hadn't seen. Then I just let it go. There's a lot of trust...a lot of maturity. He knows how to make the best of a situation if it gets difficult and gee! that's an experience...he's going to get married some day. This is going to give him a perspective he didn't have before. He's got a real good notion of how to handle the sex and emotional problems that the situation might have. (I'm glad that I have not given him my confusion over sex.) It's going to be an incredible experience. I'm not exactly personally for it, but I won't say that he can't do it. Things that on their face might look crazy...they don't get a *no*.

"Peg is very protective. The bulk of our fights have been about this. My protecting is more out-of-sight. The kids need to have a sense of their own freedom. I put my protecting far enough away so that they can mess up enough to get the lesson...but not all the way to have things come over on top of them.

"I felt very protective about the one child because of his minor physical disability. Yet he breezed on through. He exceeded my wildest expectations of how quickly he could become independent...leaving could have been the fix he needed. The other child I was less concerned about but she put herself under a tremendous load. So the situations were reversed in the sense that she needed the protection and life was tough.

"In the end, the kids leaving was the passage to a new stage for all of us...like your fortieth birthday, getting married, having kids... a part of life."

1. New York: Simon and Schuster, 1984, p. 144.

CHAPTER 6

ADDITIONAL STRESS FOR THE SINGLE PARENT

> *I have this little joke that I tell my friends about when the last one goes to college...how I'll find somebody and be married within three months. And the joke is: I hope he's nice.*

ALL ALONE

intense feelings and anxieties Of course, Joan laughed while she was speaking, as if in jest; then she added, "I'll just want to get someone else in this house, I know I will." These comments were in direct contrast to her later ones: "Isn't it amazing? I really like being a single parent. Sometimes I think...I don't really want to grow old by myself but...I'm perfectly happy living my life. I don't miss much and I have friends, men friends and women friends. I've never really felt single, alone." But Joan has always had her children around, except for brief visits with their dad. She wasn't sure how she would feel when her nest was really empty.

She had a right to wonder. The fear and anxiety leading up to the separation of the last child were very real for Thelma, a mother of two. "I began having trouble with anxiety attacks. Suddenly I went to pieces. There was a lot of tension. I think I was very nervous about taking care of myself. It was the end of college for me and I would have to get out and make my own way...my own living. I would also be alone.

"I was worried about not having a man in the picture. I wanted a love interest. Getting married was a goal for me from the time I got my divorce. It was always important for me. I was never comfortable with the idea of being alone or managing alone...although I've done it for six years. I wanted somebody in that house." Thelma echoed Joan's feelings.

"I moved out of my house partly for financial reasons. The house would be too big so I bought a small condo. Actually, the house was not that big, but it felt big. It felt empty...even though my daughter was still at home.

"So when she graduated in June, I got married two weeks later. In a sense, it just worked out that way...but the getting married was no surprise. (Well, it was a surprise that I did because you never really think that you will again...but that's what I had always wanted to do.)" Thelma had resolved her worries and anxieties about being alone.

Single parents often feel the separation more because they face it alone. Being alone seems to intensify all of the normal separation feelings and anxieties. Single parents are very aware that when the last one leaves, there's no one left. No one. The starkness of that reality is rarely experienced by married parents who at least have the familiar noises and patterns of each other. Even if the marriage is not in the best of shape, there is still another body — a physical presence — around.

Not so for the single parent. The emptiness of being all alone can initially be terrifying. Said one father, "I just seem to rattle around. At first I felt unfairly abandoned and very empty...like I was adrift." Perhaps anticipating this reality for herself, Joan had added one more comment about her youngest child, "She'll probably go to the university here and I'll probably let her because I'll want the company. I'm hoping I won't but I see how that could happen."

In an empty house or apartment a single parent may feel a real loss of identity. Such a loss often breeds resentment and anger, as reflected by thoughts such as these: "I shouldn't have to go through this by myself. It wasn't supposed to be this way." "Someone else was supposed to be here to share these feelings and this empty space. Someone should be helping me get through this." But no one is. Single parents must make the transition alone.

Many single parents have kept, maintained, and improved the nest without the help of a partner, perhaps for years. When the children fly the coop a mother or father may suddenly ask: "Who cares any more?" "Why bother?" "Will I ever have a mate again?" "Will the other side of my bed always be empty?" "What happens next?" "How can I face being alone the rest of my life?" "I did so many things for the kids and now there's no one around to appreciate what I do. Do I want to keep doing it just for myself?" Sometimes the answer is simply no.

As a single parent, Warren decided that his house was too big and he sold it when his son graduated from high school. Yet, he described his current apartment as "...temporary. It's a lonely situation and I'm not happy with it. No matter how you slice it, I'm still coming home to an empty house...there's no one waiting for me at the end of a business trip. I know it's something that I have to accept but there's an emptiness. I seem to be surviving day to day rather than enjoying the life I lead. Also, my mother died last year and that was a real load. It complicated things.

"I don't know any men in my circumstance," Warren confided. "All the single men just run around. I have a few buddies but I'm missing good companionship. Three years ago I could have gone to Europe to work but my son didn't want to go. Now I would go because I need something different to do but I can't find employment there. And, wouldn't you know, he's the one in Europe; he got stationed there. It would be a help if I got more rewards from my job...but I don't.

"The bad feelings don't carry through for long periods of time. I feel them half-a-day here, two hours there. I have to put my energies elsewhere. What I really need is a permanent solution...changing my surroundings, the apartment, my job, my career, settling with a mate. I'm not tied to a geographic location. I didn't really prepare myself for this...everything feels temporary." In spite of the fact that Warren's younger son lived with his mother and still came for visits, Warren essentially felt that his parenting days were over. Unfortunately, life was on hold.

predominately women Overwhelmingly, the single parents facing these situations are women. For this reason the chapter emphasizes the experiences of mothers who have been single parents for a number of years, although single-parent fathers will experience many of the same feelings. While the numbers of male single parents are increasing, by and large social customs have traditionally placed children in the custody of their mothers and, because statistics show that divorced men remarry more quickly than women, fathers with custody may not actually be single when a child leaves home. With divorce rates continuing at high levels, the single-parent category has been growing at an astounding rate.

The dilemma of single parents can be partially understood by looking at two typical situations. A traditional family consists of four people: mother, father, and two children. When one child leaves, the family dynamics change twenty-five percent. The same single-parent family consists of only three people: parent and two children. When a child leaves the energy force within the family shifts by thirty-three percent; when the last child leaves there is a fifty percent change in the makeup of the family. These larger percentages reflect, at least symbolically, the greater impact that the single parent is feeling. In addition, because the children *are* the family for the single parent, when they leave the family unit seems to break up or disappear, perhaps to be resurrected only during holidays or summer vacations.

holidays and special occasions Worse felt are the holidays and other occasions of family sharing when the children can't make it home. Facing an empty house at Christmas for the first time, one mother clearly knew that her coping skills were being put to the test. "I don't want to talk about it. I'm trying to ignore Christmas and pretend it isn't even happening." Suddenly tears welled up in her eyes and she walked away. The fact that she would be flying to see her daughter on the twenty-eighth did little to ease the pain of being without her children on Christmas Day.

Being alone can be especially trying during events such as a high school graduation, going off to college, or parents' weekend. At those times, a parent may have to deal once again with the other parent — that person who symbolizes failure or incompleteness. Not only may that person represent the inability to have a successful marriage, but the parents may not like each other. One may resent the fact that the other is still around intruding — even though the parent has a right and need to be involved in the child's life.

Deeper feelings aroused by special events may also be sentimental in nature. Graduations are often a time of nostalgia for mother and father as reflected by the comments of a noncustodial father about his daughter, Ann: "Her mother and I felt so proud. We'd all experienced a lot together even though there were things that I'd missed out on because of the divorce. Somehow Ron (Ann's stepfather) just didn't belong...he wasn't really a part of her life. Funny thing is, I think Ann's mother felt the same way and would have been happier if he hadn't been there."

Parents' weekends are also a sensitive time. Commented one mother, "I think that my only regret about being divorced comes during parents' weekend. We can't really go together as a family so either I go or their dad goes and then one member of the family unit seems to be missing." Continued expectation of the traditional family unit is unrealistic and yet difficult to avoid sometimes.

STRESS AND THE SINGLE PARENT

total responsibility The culmination of stress arising from a child's leaving, though, seems to be inherent in the single-parent role, itself. Throughout the period of being a single parent, there is a feeling of total responsibility which rarely lets up. Single parents may get a weekend off or a few weeks vacation but the unrelenting enormity of the responsibility usually persists month after month, year after year. Illustrating this point, one mother whose oldest boy no longer lived at home remarked, "When the other two kids were gone for spring break this year, it was the first time in nineteen years that I was alone for more than a weekend! Can you imagine that? The first time in nineteen years...that's a long time." Indeed.

trying harder yet feeling guilty The burden of being a single parent often means trying harder, as if to make up for not being a normal family. Situations continually arise which make a single parent feel guilty. "Raising kids takes four hands," said a single-parent father. "I only had two."

The overwhelming effort and energy that go into meeting so many, if not all, of the child's emotional, financial, and physical needs are exhausting. Wanting what's best for the child and not always having it can be demoralizing and undermine a single parent's self-esteem. Material items denied the child and other deprivations, real or imagined, contribute to the stress. Taking personal time or building a career continually gets in the way of spending time with the children.

Finding the middle ground where neither too much is given, nor too much taken, by the parent is difficult. Being *super mom* or *super pop* is clearly impossible and yet single parents try — generating feelings tinged with guilt or failure. As if to strike a crowning blow, the children occupy such a commanding and important place in the single parent's life that the adjustment to a life without them can be more difficult and lengthy than the transition faced by other parents.

loss of emotional support When children leave, they can no longer meet the single parent's emotional needs. Because there is rarely another adult in the home to give emotional support, the mutual sharing that single parent and children have established is understandable and expected. This interdependency is intensified if just one child exists; parent and child have only each other to give primary support. That person is — in a sense — irreplaceable.

If the parent has relied too heavily on a child, if the parent has invested spouse-like qualities in a child of the opposite sex, or if the parent has gradually become taken care of or parented by a child through a process of reversed roles, then that single parent will feel more alone and perhaps dysfunctional without the child as support.

This overdependence is not healthy for either the child or the parent. In fact, it can be a huge burden on a child.

Understanding this, one college student described the situation with his freshman roommate: "His mother had been divorced for years, and she was real protective and strict with him and tried to keep tabs on him when he went off to college so he had a terrible experience. She called him a lot and he was always gone and I'd have to pamper her. You know...I'd have to talk to her and tell her something about what he was doing...and say that he'd call when I knew he probably wouldn't. She was a single parent and felt dependent on him. She ended up pretty insecure because he was gone. He had been the man of the house and she missed that. He was homesick but he was so glad to have the freedom of college that he really did go overboard...so far, in fact, that he ended up flunking out." As a result, he had to move back home — thus reinforcing that emotionally dependent link.

avoiding mutual dependency Cautiously avoiding overpossessive or clinging ways, single parents are often aware of the need to sever the apron strings. They carefully analyze whether they have tied the child too closely — simply because they are alone in the child-rearing process. To counterbalance this temptation, some single parents take precautions, such as sending kids away to school or away for the summer, to insure that neither the child nor parent develops a dependency on the other. Financially, however, this is often not possible.

separation from noncustodial parent Ironically, the very distance that may separate children and noncustodial parents — a separation often reflected by different mannerisms, dispositions, or life views — may allow for an easier transition into an adult relationship. The child, quite literally, does not have to break away in the manner that must occur with the custodial parent.

Aware of this difference between his parents, one son commented, "Dad liked retreating to college life when he came to visit me. I think he's taking more of an interest in my doings because he liked college. He sees me two, three times a year so he can notice changes, successive steps. My mom sees me constantly so it's harder for the realization of my being an adult to come through. My dad and I can go to a bar and have a couple of beers and I feel like an equal. I can't do that with Mom. I don't know if it makes her feel bad, but probably it does." The mother has continued to parent, perhaps without letting go; the father has let go, perhaps without continuing his parental role long enough.

There are, of course, noncustodial or joint-custodial parents who have an active, close, and ongoing relationship with their children. That parent may live close by, frequently seeing the children and participating in their lives. Naturally, these parents will feel the loss of their children more — but perhaps still not as much as the parent with whom the children have spent a larger percentage of their time.

In an interesting twist, a noncustodial father spoke of the apron strings which he had pulled in getting his son to go to the local college. "I had just moved back to town and I wanted to hold on to what we didn't have...so we could build from there. I needed that chance to get to know him again. I encouraged him to stay so that the relationship would improve."

feelings of loss and rejection Although the departure of a child may be the most traumatic loss many parents have experienced, this is often not the case for single parents. The first loss may well have been the loss of the marriage through divorce and the child-loss reactivates the same feelings of despair and failure that were caused by the marriage-loss. Not only does the role of parent seem to be evaporating, but there is no role of spouse to fall back on. The child-loss may be compounded by feelings of inadequacy and abandonment originally tied to the divorce.

The child's leaving thus becomes viewed as a rejection, particularly if that child is of the opposite sex. This child may, at times, have acted as a *date* or served to bolster the single parent's sagging ego. Consciously or unconsciously the parent may have compared potential mates to this child. One particularly honest mother was a little embarrassed by her admission. "A while back," she said, "I had to honestly admit to myself that I really wanted someone like my son. He's intelligent and I enjoy the stimulating conversations. He has a witty sense of humor, is good looking, and, most importantly, knows how to handle me...most of the time. Our temperaments are much the same so we can fly off the handle and then it's over...no bad feelings. We both enjoy being alone so we know when to stay out of the other's way. There's a mutual respect without being confining. And, of course, he really cares about me.

"Somehow men I go out with don't seem as smart, or are too shallow, or can't deal with their emotions...or something. There's always something. Sometimes I wish I could clone him...and yet, heaven knows, he's not perfect. I can't bring myself to settle for someone that's not at least his equal, someone that he can respect and look up to...even though he's grown. Facing the prospect of never having someone romantically in my life as neat as he is...is downright depressing. I know he's not really mine...and he and his girlfriend have a relationship that I envy.

"I can see why some single parents feel alone or rejected when their kids leave. But you can't hold them back, can you? That would be much too selfish. Besides, things like that always backfire."

worry about relationship role models Because they have not been able to provide a role model for a healthy, happy relationship between spouses, single parents often worry about how their children will cope with and handle romantic relationships. The issue may be compounded if hostile feelings for an ex-spouse are projected onto a child. A mother may project negative feelings toward men onto a son, or a father may do the same to a daughter by bad-mouthing females.

Perhaps because single parents know pain and being alone, they wish to protect their children from similar experiences. As if to hush the harshness of what she was saying, one mother spoke in quiet tones of her fears: "I worry that Angie will have trouble with men...that she'll think she doesn't deserve much. Her brother was mean and her dad doesn't know what to do with her. She certainly hasn't been able to learn what to do from me."

Single parents resort to hoping that cautiousness on the part of their children, healthy relationships between child and single parent, and knowledge of what *not* to do will bring wisdom to children when they seek a mate for marriage. There is little consolation in the knowledge that children of divorce often have many scars. Despite the fact that the home environment is no longer marred by a bad marriage, experts indicate that single-parent children can still be quite needy and vulnerable. They frequently have problems and frustrations centering around relationships in general. A single parent may regretfully understand and wish it weren't so.

COMPENSATIONS

parent no longer indispensible In spite of being alone and dealing with stress related to the single-parent role, fortunately, there are often some compensations for the single parent facing an empty nest. While these may not be the exclusive property of single parents — they can certainly apply to married parents, as well — they are often foremost in the mind of a single parent.

Perhaps the most significant is that single parents often realize that, should anything happen to them (for example, should they die), the children are basically equipped to take care of themselves. This is especially important if the other parent has not been active or present in the child-rearing role. The fear of not being able to finish the job of parenting recedes, as does the huge responsibility that the job entailed — with exhilarating relief. The parent is no longer indispensable; the children can manage on their own.

delicious freedom Without the weight of daily childrearing obligations and the stress of constantly being a parent, the emptiness of the home becomes delicious, delicious freedom. "Being all alone in my home is wonderful!" exclaimed a single-parent mother. There is no longer a need to check in with someone; there is no one monitoring a single parent's whereabouts. For some parents who married young, this may be the first time in their lives that they do not have to be accountable to someone. They can come and go as they please.

Energy previously poured into children can now be channeled elsewhere. Not even a spouse is present to require attention or place demands. Single parents have even more space than married parents to make life changes. Single parents are free to pursue what they've always wanted — whatever that might be.

independent children One factor that helps to offset some of the stress experienced by single parents is the knowledge that their children have a keen sense of independence and the ability to cope with life's frustrations and vicissitudes. (This can, of course, also be said of many other children.) Part of this has been forced upon the children; part comes from the role model of a mother who has taken responsibility for her own life. Psychologist Wendy Fidao articulates this independence as follows:

> By and large, single-parent children are apt to have more coping skills and are less sheltered. They have had to grow up faster and learn earlier how to do things for themselves — something as simple as doing the laundry. They have more of a sense of self-sufficiency. When single parents have learned to cope, they become a favorable role model: the way that they cope with stress and adapt to the changes in their lives is an example for the children when they come up against the same situation...whether they consciously remember or not.

During their interviews, single-parent children, particularly, talked about their sense of independence: they saw themselves as more independent than many of their peers from traditional family settings. Teens from the traditional, dual-parent family mentioned independence far less frequently.

Sam, whose two older brothers had already left home, was keenly aware of the positive aspects of his situation. "We've been pretty independent. Mom gives us a certain freedom and it's been that way for a long time. When we were younger she had to go to school so we had to cook our own meals and that...so she's grown used to it. She likes it. She doesn't have to worry about us as much and we can take on all the responsibilities and usually she gets off free and she doesn't do anything around the house anymore. We do all the cleanup, dishes, this, that, and we have certain privileges. We don't have to come in at twelve o'clock or anything like that. So it's real nice. It's like being an adult at your own home. We don't have to play child and mother; it's just friends."

When asked how his mom will feel when he leaves, Sam gave a small laugh. "Ah ha...she's dreading the moment because we've gotten real close together and she's going to be real...I don't want to say it, but...lonely. I'll feel a bit guilty. It's going to be a little rough on my mom to get used to having no one here and I'm the last one. I don't want to leave...and in a way I really want to leave and be out...gone off to college. I'm just hoping she bears it well. She may get a little more fond of the dogs!" He laughed at the idea.

"Mom says that she's getting in her hugs now before I leave." Sam chuckled again. "She's getting her affection now...storing up." Interestingly, Sam wouldn't be departing for one and a half years and yet the act of leaving and its consequences upon his mother were already heavy on his mind.

toughened fiber Paradoxically, the lack of material affluence that negatively affects so many single-parent families may sometimes contribute to a toughened fiber that allows those children to have a better chance of making it on their own. They know what it means to struggle. They've had to assume responsibility earlier in life.

That some economic deprivation has a positive impact on values was articulated by one mother as follows: "The kids are much more independent because I work. Some of our friends (both kids and adults) are very smug with that confidence or security that you get when you've never had to deal with not having money or things. I'm not bitter or unhappy, but there are times when my friends who don't work drive me crazy. Don't talk to me about how tired you are from carpooling, or that your maid didn't show up, or that the carpenter who's putting the new room on the house can't work because it's raining. I don't want to hear it, thank you very much. You can talk to me about a lot of other things but not the problems of being a housewife.

"Too much affluence can give kids a warped perspective. I felt security growing up because I could have something if I really wanted it...but what kind of security is that, really? There's a fine line between how much you give your kids because their father is gone and they've already suffered and how much spoils them from striving for things. Where is that fine line? That's one of the hardest things. But I do know that not having things has helped my values. Out of economic necessity I have to ask my kids how badly do they want something. 'You want a pair of shoes for fifty dollars and here's one for twenty-five. Is it worth it to you to come up with the other twenty-five dollars for those extra stripes on the side?' If their commitment isn't there, it certainly isn't there for me.

"I have a friend who takes her kids breakfast in bed and then she wonders why they don't appreciate her. Can you imagine what she's doing to them? To their future husbands and wives?

"There are so many things to do...the dishes, the grass, etc...it's hard to find time to have fun. Kids know this...they don't expect things of single parents as much. Maybe single parents do a better job because we know that it's up to us. Did you know that more accidents happen to kids when both parents are home than any other time? Maybe one parent feels that the other parent is talking to them. It's easy to shift the responsibility. Single parents can't do that."

a survival shared By having survived, both the child and the single parent may share a special closeness. They have struggled and made it. They feel successful in having gone the distance alone...together. There is a feeling of unity. They definitely feel an unspoken sense of pride.

charting new ground Children leaving home in the 1980s constitute the first big wave of single-parent children reaching maturity, a wave that will continue to surge during the 1990s. In spite of this, single-parent mothers appear to show no greater concern over the departure of their children than do married mothers.[1]

These single-parent children are also charting new ground in other ways. Daughters understand that a husband cannot necessarily be counted on for lifelong financial support. Their mother's strong sense of self may lead to a more positive role model than might otherwise be the case with a non-single-parent mother. Sons no longer expect mothers to wait on them and minister to their every desire. Sons are more likely to develop emotional sensitivities and attention to domestic chores without giving these items a *feminine* label. "My son's a great cook!" one single parent mentioned proudly. "He probably does more cooking than I do."

But more than that, these single parents are producing a new brand of future husbands and fathers who may show heart and balance in their family life — something men have not always sought to achieve. Said one mother, "I can't believe what a neat husband he's going to make someday."

special bond While almost all parents advocate for their children, these children may overwhelmingly advocate and protect the single parent, perhaps because there is no spouse to fill that role. One mother touchingly described a scene which she remembered: "It was holiday time and the stress of preparing Thanksgiving dinner for all the family finally got to me and, after I had thrown everyone out of the kitchen, I was crying and trying to regroup...and who were there to comfort me and rally round the wagons? My children, of course. They had to take over the job that a spouse would do. I don't think that it bothered them to assume that role, but I was keenly aware of their support. We have a very special bond."

Said another, "There's something special between Janie and me, and I think that it has to do with having to go through a really tough time and being able to talk about it. I think that the bad stuff makes really good stuff. You can't have the good until you've known the bad in relationships." The unique bond between the two helped to compensate for the difficult times. Even though this special bond is, in many ways, never quite the same when a child leaves, its strength and fiber is sustaining to the single parent — and often continues, even should the parent eventually remarry.

Thoughts of the last child leaving can be particularly frightening at times. Nancy, a single parent in her early fifties spoke of these fears while acknowledging the importance of the parent-child bond. "Because the kids often represent the most important and only other significant person in a single parent's life, it's so much nicer when their leaving is okay. It's nice if your kids can leave in a good way and things are okay between the two of you. The happier you are with a person the easier the parting is if it's supposed to happen. If you're insecure or guilty about a person, you can go through a lot of grief about a departure because it's so uncertain. It's good to clear the decks. Then you don't have to deal with all that baggage later on. It's not always easy though. There are a lot of fences between parents and kids. It scares me to think of the last one leaving, but I think I'll fall into it and like it pretty much...and the spaces will fill up."

Because single-parent children are generally in tune with their parents, insight and understanding are often reflected by their comments. Said one son four months after his departure for college,

"My mom felt empty, strange...a loss of sorts. It seemed pretty normal to me. Here she was, a single parent with two children...basically, it was no surprise. I could understand it." In contrast, young adults leaving the traditional two-parent family setting often seemed unaware, during interviews, of their parents' feelings beyond the most superficial of observations.

parent as person Yet another compensation arises from the single-parent dilemma. Along the way, the parent usually realizes that she (or he) can't be both the mother and the father. There are limits to what one person can do — limitations that many single parents willingly admit to their children. (Again, this is not exclusive to single parents; married parents may also develop this openness or the special bonds alluded to earlier.) They confess when they're tired, or frustrated, or angry. They don't have enough energy not to. So the child matures seeing the single parent as a real person, one with strengths and weaknesses. In this environment, children eventually become more comfortable with their own limitations.

Over the years, this honesty gradually leads to acceptance of each other on equal terms and helps to facilitate the transition to an adult-adult relationship. The strength of the friendship between parent and child seemed more apparent during interviews (with either parent or child) involving single-parent families than those involving families where the parents were married. This should not be surprising: without a spouse for a friend, one of the most available choices is the child.

Not all single parents, however, develop this relationship with their children. Some single parents are insensitive; some have serial marriages or lead disruptive lives; some pawn the kids off on the other parent or a family relative. The strength of any relationship, obviously, is dependent on much more than marital status.

no "debt" for the kids Where single parents have accepted full responsibility for divorce choices, the sense of failure or guilt arising from the divorce itself is muted. These parents do not feel that their children owe them for the sacrifice — either the sacrifice of staying in a bad marriage or the selflessness reflected in the single-parent role.

"One of my decisions," said one mother, "in leaving their dad when the youngest was two was that I thought...if I stick around for their sake, there will come a time when they're gone and I'll feel like they owe me a *lot*! And they won't. They're not asking me to stay and I don't want to feel resentful that I gave up or stayed with their father all those years for them, because it's not fair to them."

Consequently, her children were leaving home without obligation; they were not in debt to their mother nor responsible for her mental health.

vindication Judy told another story. Tucked away in one corner of her mind was a feeling of vindication and a relief from guilt. "It's as if I could finally say to my family and my parents...'See, I made the right decision years ago. In spite of two failed marriages I have raised this successful kid who is off to the Ivy League. She is my badge of success. She is the ultimate proof that I could make a family that works. She vindicates all the hard times, the problems, the feelings of failure...she has justified everything.'

"Fortunately, I've grown wiser since then and have let her off the hook. She can do what she wants without having to prove anything...to me or for me. I've lifted that pressure from both of us.

"But those feelings of pride and success are still there. By virtue of the fact that I'm a *single parent*...that term alone makes me different...I think that I've always felt that I had something to prove. But no more. Perhaps part of it is that I don't have to feel guilty anymore." As an afterthought Judy added, "Finally, I can get back to worrying about who I am and not how I've done."

UNLIMITED OPTIONS

perhaps too many The possibilities are endless — too many, in fact. When single parents are honest with themselves, by far the most stressful part of an empty nest can be some of the unlimited choices which are available: move, sell the house, change jobs, go abroad, get married. While these same options may be available to married couples, the single parent makes her or his decisions alone without having to consider or report to anyone else. It's like starting at ground zero and having no one else to blame if the right decisions aren't made.

In spite of an aura of potential excitement that starting anew can evoke, subtle terror may lurk as previously neat boundaries that guided the parent's life seemingly disappear — boundaries predicated on the children's needs. Selling a house or changing a job — all alone — can be frightening. Dropping out or taking a sabbatical for a year presents a real risk when there is no backup person for support. Yet single parents face these choices, whether they are willing to admit it or not.

freedom to find a mate The option to remarry or live with a mate, of course, is not a new one for single parents; but an empty nest may represent the first real opportunity to consider it seriously. Although hesitant to admit to being glad that the children are gone, parents may intuitively understand why the departure brings relief: they would have felt guilty giving energy to two sources, the children and a new mate. Single parents may tacitly acknowledge that the children would not have wanted the competition or another authority figure in their lives.

"After John and I broke up, I decided that my life would be a lot simpler if I didn't live with anybody until my son left," related a mother as she spoke of the man that she had lived with for a year. "I knew that I could if I really wanted to, but my son, Tim, had been surly with John and sometimes showed downright contempt. He didn't want to have another adult around telling him what to do, although John didn't try to play parent or boss him very often. Tim was aware that he could manipulate me much better without any interference. I also think that there was some jealousy involved... there had to be.

"All I know is that life was easier when there was only one male in my life, and that had to be my son...at least until he grew up and matured." Whether this mother should have put her life on hold for so long is perhaps questionable, but with her son's leaving the burden was lifted.

Sometimes there appears to be a hurried rush to fill an empty house. Just as, in the beginning of the chapter, Joan feared the emptiness and Thelma got married to avoid it, so, too, did Tina use her anticipated freedom to find a roommate.

"About two years ago," related Tina, "I read an article in *Reader's Digest* by a father whose child was leaving. It was poignantly written about how many more breakfasts they'd have together and those kinds of things. I saved it. It was real touching and it really upset me. I began to emotionally prepare myself for Drew's leaving. I almost felt that it was a countdown. It would always come to my mind that he wouldn't be with me that much longer...I ought to do this, I ought to do that...I ought to appreciate him.

"I became aware that I didn't want to live alone...that I was scared of being alone. For a while I encouraged Drew to stay at home and go to college. Then my fantasy was that I might get my sister to move in. I thought about who I knew that might be a good roomie for me because I wanted somebody to come home to, have meals with, talk to, share things with. Living with someone was also a financial necessity; I might have had to move.

"I met Kevin in April. Right away we were practically living together. We talked about it and laughed about it...I recognized that I was avoiding being alone. Drew felt protective of me. He was worried about my being alone so he was real happy when he heard that Kevin was going to move in...then he didn't have to feel guilty about leaving. As soon as Drew left for school, Kevin moved in."

Not only do single parents in search of a mate feel a freedom from children. There is also the freedom of dating patterns no longer confined to the familiar older-male, younger-female format. On the contrary, women dating younger men has become quite common. A few parents may explore their sexual orientation; others may now be more open about their homosexuality.

There is, unfortunately, an obstacle to traditional matehood. The media is full of studies and surveys (and cartoons) which detail the unavailability of men for women of all ages — particularly the older women get. The single-parent mother who worries about finding a mate with whom to share an emotional, intellectual, and physical intimacy has a legitimate concern.

sowing wild oats For those not seriously in the mating or marriage market, the opportunity may exist to bust loose and act like a kid again — maybe even sow a few wild oats. Spontaneity need not be tempered with thoughts of the children. At the first real sign of freedom, getting settled again may be the farthest thing from the single parent's mind. Children no longer ride secret herd on the parent's comings and goings, acting as a kind of *morals-review committee*. Replacing children as inhibitors, today's sexual encounters must now be tempered with thoughts of the numerous sexually-transmitted diseases, particularly AIDS. To some, a cruel joke.

nonsexual relationships For many single parents, however, easy sex is not the answer. Years of isolation from sexual companionship may leave a parent unsure of his or her attractiveness or sexual appeal and lacking confidence in romance skills. Grateful for more time to spend with others, intimacy comes rather from earnest friendships with men or women which outside interests may gradually broaden and expand.

PROFILE: The Single-parent Mother

Pat Kelly had been a single parent since her only son, Matt, was almost three years old. Financially, life had not been easy. Matt's breaking away from home was complicated by the death of her father and the fact that Matt lived at home for a year because he decided not to go to college. Self-confident in many ways, including her management of a nonprofit craft store for Appalachian art, Pat still spoke with a certain degree of hesitancy about her future.

"Matt first left home for an extended trip to Europe. My father was dying at the time so I felt very insecure and I wanted Matt here but I knew he needed to go. The hardest part was the lead up...knowing that it was going to happen. I was a miserable, horrible person for a long time...not for a week, but for a whole year. If there were any way that I could have frozen him in place I would have done it. I did not want my life to change, even though some part of me did. My next door neighbor was like a cheerleader saying, 'Great, let go.' But it was painful for me.

"That summer at Yoga camp I met a woman working with physical therapy. I felt, although I couldn't really put my finger on it, that I had this heaviness. She did some work with the muscles under my arm and ribcage and, all of a sudden, it was release time and I just cried and cried...and what came out was that everybody that I depended on was leaving me. It's interesting how things in your life group and those two events were a double whammy.

"Finally Matt moved out. I didn't really want to live alone but it didn't hit until later because I was busy. I thought...oh, I'm doing great...no problem. But one night I found myself wandering around the kitchen and I was angry that there was a stack of dishes in the sink and I thought...when is he coming home and why isn't he washing these dishes?" Pat paused to laugh. "Then I realized that it was just totally irrational. My subsconscious came gurgling up all of a sudden and I realized he's not coming home. I don't have to keep my ear cocked in the evening anymore.

"That's when I understood that there were more dimensions to this than I had first realized. I'm glad he's out living his own life but it's like a mourning. I've had this little sidekick all my adult life, and he's not there. There were things that I would do and places that I would go as long as he was sitting in the front seat of the car next to me...things that I would never do on my own.

"I'm a fairly possessive person and some of my close friends have teased me about my phantom apron string. You know how if people have a limb removed there's this phantom feeling about it, so they're teasing me about my apron string just sort of flapping out here in the breeze!" She again laughed at herself. "For a while when Matt didn't go to college and he was hanging around longer than some kids, I would think...oh gosh, have I tied him too close to me? I wanted a way to make him more eager to get out and earn a living. Maybe as a rationalization, I thought...well, some people are ready at different times and it's really okay to live at home.

"Just the other day I said to my neighbor whose five kids are all gone, 'I think Matt should come back and help me keep this place up. He should help me cut the grass. I can't do all this myself.' She said, 'Look, when they go, they go. You just have to cut them loose. He shouldn't have to come back and take care of you.'

"I feel the emptiness, especially in the evening. I feel restless. I want someone else to be in the house...it's a big space. I'm not happy being totally alone, but I also don't want a roommate so I'm just going to have to see how it evolves.

"I've noticed changes in my personal life. I don't take the care in cooking for myself that I did when there was another person. Matt loves to cook. He's a very good mix of feminine and masculine qualities which...I think in a lot of ways he's a kind of new breed. More and more men are...it's really nice to see. I'm really looking forward to being a grandmother.

"I neglected Matt a fair piece and I think that's why he's turned out fairly well." Pat stifled her laughter. "I know I've had a powerful influence on him but, on the other hand, he had to be independent. I used to spend a lot of weekends out in the country and at a certain point he let me know that he didn't want to go. So I said, 'Look, here's how to change the fuses and here's how to reach me and you may not have parties or people in,' and he stayed home. It was better than having a moping adolescent around.

"Do you remember teaching your child how to ride a bike and how you hold on to the back and you go along with them and, when they don't even know it, you let go? Letting go of kids is kind of like that I think. If you haven't given them the big things throughout their whole lives, it's real hard to make up for it...like the feeling of love and respect. Those things you don't do overnight; they come over a long period of time. But kids need practical information, tools to survive. They need to know how to run a house and how to buy groceries and how to have a checking account and how to deal with people. I don't think I've done all of them successfully but I don't know if you can or if you're supposed to. By and large, I think that I've done a pretty good job as a parent.

"Sometimes I'm sorry that Matt didn't have the experience of having his mother and father together throughout his whole life. I just think it's a really beautiful thing if it works that way. I wonder how it's going to go for him. Will he look for one person, or be real loose?

"I've watched a lot of things come back on myself. I keep growing and changing, and Matt's coming along and even though he's an independent person also directing his own ship, I see all this garbage that I put there coming out," she started laughing, "and I think...oh brother! My biggest regret is that hole in his middle years when I was so self-absorbed and totally drawn into self-awareness things. But it's okay for a kid to be a little weedy for a while. I did all the things a parent is supposed to do...it's not so bad that I snatched time for myself. There's no point in feeling too guilty. Besides, those feelings are offset by the good relationship we have now.

"You know, the other night I had a dream that I had a baby. I just love the way they feel. Apparently, I'm not ready to say that I'm not going to have a family any more, that I'm going to be this single, independent, professional, career person. It's just all a big jumble in my mind.

"I was driving to work the other day and I suddenly wondered...if I just took all my resources that I could gather and set myself totally free...how many years could I live without ever having to work? What would taxes be if I sold my house and didn't buy another one? What if I started a business? I'm sick of the United States; I could live in Greece. I'm sick of who I've been and I just want to try something real different.

"That's fantasy. I don't know if I could do it. Am I scared at the unlimited choices? If I think of it seriously...but I stick pretty close to the grind stone. I also feel that when it's time to do something else, not hell or high water can keep me from doing it."

PROFILE: The Single-parent Father

Nick Walsh had been divorced for years but not until his son, Zak, was fifteen did single parenthood begin. Immediately after the divorce, Nick had lived out of town for a few years, finally deciding to return so he could be closer to his son. Because his career opportunities in the creative arts might suffer by the move, it was a major decision — but one he did not regret.

"I'm an empty nester and it's a drag. I feel like I'm living my life around someone who isn't even here. I have to sit here and guard this nest while, when he's home for a visit, he's free to come and go and leave me home on a Saturday night.

"When he left I was decimated. It was worse than breaking up with my wife. I didn't see any reason to do anything. It was empty...but it was necessary. I was proud of him.

"At first I thought that it was going to be kind of fun. I could go out and party. There would be no interruptions. But I missed the dinners, the visits, the talks...the texture that the relationship provided. It was anything but shallow. Going out, having dates...in the end that just amounted to how many shallow experiences could I stuff into a hole trying to make up for something valuable that was missing. It didn't work.

"The most important thing in my life is my son, and when he

decided to move in with me, it was an answer to my prayers. I had moved back to be with him. It is not an accident how kids turn out. That's why they need to be the highest priority in life. I don't regret having done it. It's been a blessing for me. Raising Zak has been the major thing for me.

"I do have some feelings of resentment. I can't just take off and go. I can't say, 'Look what I've done for you.' My friends and family are excited about me doing for myself now. But it's not so much to cut him loose as I have to cut myself loose. The dilemma is to not let him become an excuse for my not achieving personal goals. Anything's possible...it's up to me. People seem to expect a lot of me. They're always saying, 'You're different than we are,' as if there were a *we*. Sometimes it's a little scary."

1. Joan Z. Cohen, Karen L. Coburn and Joan C. Pearlman, *Hitting Our Stride* (New York: Delacorte Press, 1980) p. 129.

CHAPTER 7

WHAT THE WOMEN'S MOVEMENT DIDN'T TELL US

A BIT OF HISTORY

hidden messages The women's movement had a lot of messages in its early days. Many were straightforward and easy to understand — like the message *equal pay for equal work*. Others were much more subtle. Some were so subtle, in fact, that no one immediately grasped the potential underlying meaning.

This chapter deals with one such subtlety which even self-proclaimed feminists may not readily identify as a factor influencing the empty nest phase of their lives — but a few will. The women's movement brought not only changes to mother's lives, in general, but also changes in the way some women viewed the separation issue: they thought they would be immune from feeling a loss when the kids left home. In order to understand how and why this happened, one must understand the impact feminism has had on many mothers' lives. (The scenario outlined below is not meant to negate the many beneficial effects of the modern-day women's movement; but rather it examines one possible outcome in a movement that contained anything but cookie-cutter results.)

the movement The momentum for the women's movement began with Betty Friedan's 1963 book, *The Feminine Mystique;* the founding of the National Organization for Women in 1966 served as a catalyst for enlisting thousands upon thousands of women (and some men) in the cause. The fight for equal rights and the subsequent impact on people's lives resulted in one of the most dramatic social revolutions to occur in so short a period of history. In spite of the fact that the Equal Rights Amendment has not been ratified on a national basis, the changes which occurred during the first ten to fifteen years of the movement were truly monumental. Almost without exception, those long-overdue changes were good and positive for both men and women.

a nonhomemaker role For some, becoming a feminist implied a clearcut message: nothing should stand in the way of a woman's right and ability to be a wage earner and have a career — not husbands, lovers, children, housework, uncooperative employers, or anyone or anything else in society. No longer would a woman live her life through husband and children. She would have other interests, intimate friends, and a career — in essence, her own independent life. Feeling that men were a stumbling block to aggressively pursuing a career, many women lost their mates or remained single. Only rarely did mothers abandon or lose their children but many put off having them, decided against it altogether, or psychologically neglected them.

Women who were raised in one era began experiencing adulthood under another. Openly eschewing the traditional female role of homemaker or working for economic reasons, women flocked to the business world in the early 1970s, dressing for success in the long struggle to the top. Those time-honored values of family, caring for others, and love sometimes hovered on the precipice of being judged a sign of weakness. Slowly, women learned when not to cry, when to mimic the male hierarchy of values, and when to avoid anything that might remotely be thought of as feminine. In fact, femininity was frequently a dirty word.

a price to be paid The road was not easy, and it was often lonely. Placing a value on things and achievements above people exacted a price. Men had been paying that price for years; to women it was a new experience. The price was often steeper than expected: unwittingly, many career women gave up a husband and family permanently. The media has frequent coverage of the plight of successful business and professional women who are single and still *looking*.

Having coveted the man's world for so long, some women gradually discovered that success was not everything it was purported to be. Not to say that there weren't benefits and rewards to financial aspirations, but frequently these were achieved at the expense of other human needs.

Perhaps women had given up too much or, at the very least, some of the wrong things. In the effort to be more *like men*, women had assumed that whatever the men had and did was, by definition, good. Because men seemed to be in control, women easily overlooked the fact that the male value system might have profound weaknesses. After all, men had the money, money meant power, and power obviously went a long way. The absence of a balanced, encompassing system of values, which had not been readily apparent to women by virtue of their seemingly second-rate position in the eyes of society, was now noticeable.

As they began to achieve the financial rewards of business success, some women gradually began to have time to sit back and think, to analyze exactly what they did have and what it was really worth. What had they lost along the way? What was the price they were paying? Should they now consider giving some of it up? They couldn't have given it up earlier because, in the final analysis, one can only give up what one has, not what one doesn't have.

a second look By the end of the 1970s, the tone of what was being written about women had begun to change. Although not revolutionary like her earlier book, Friedan's *The Second Stage*, published in 1980, argued that the family had been ignored by the women's movement and, unless now addressed, forward progress for women would come to a grinding halt. The well-known voice articulated in print what many women were feeling about the dilemma of balancing career and family, of putting a value on these two important aspects of life. In 1984 Megan Marshall's book, *The Cost of Loving*, examined women's fear of intimacy and how the "myth of independence" often resulted in an empty life — one without nourishing love relationships.

Another aspect of a balanced life which was overlooked was the spiritual quest which Jung identified as the purpose of midlife and old age. "I think that the biggest thing that the women's movement forgot was the importance of the spiritual in our lives," articulated one person during an interview. "The inside is much more important than the outside."

Nor was any mention made by feminists of the pain women might experience, in spite of having careers and independent lives, when children left home. "I think that it's been said the the women's movement forgot its heart," said another interviewee. She was talking about her own *separation gap*.

THE SEPARATION GAP

expectations vs. reality This so-called separation gap represents the difference in feelings between what a mother expects to feel when a child leaves home and what she actually feels. If expectations and reality match, there is no gap. But if, as in the case of the author, the reality is more painful than expected, then a gap does exist — perhaps the more painful because it is unexpected. And if that gap exists because of a subtle message conveyed by the women's movement (a *nonmessage* might be more appropriate terminology), then there is an additional surprise.

This element of surprise was echoed in a piece called "Apron Strings" by columnist Ellen Goodman when she described driving her daughter to college. She talked of her "approval, pride, pleasure, confidence" and "giving away her...(daughter's)...hand in independence." She talked of her sense of loss. She also echoed many women's thoughts when she said:

> A long time ago, I thought mothers who also had work that engaged their time and energy might avoid the cliche of an empty-nest (sic) syndrome. A child's departure once meant a mother's forced retirement from her only job. Many of us assumed work would help protect us from that void. Now I doubt it.
>
> Those of us who have worked two shifts, lived two roles, have no less investment in our identity as parents, no less connection to our children. No less love. And no less sense of loss.

Later she asked:

> What do you do with all the antennae of motherhood when they become obsolete?...What use is there for the expertise of motherhood that took so long to acquire?[1]

Surprise makes the separation gap appear to be a sign of weakness in the mother and contrary to the precepts of the women's movement. The message seems to be: because women don't need offspring to feel complete, when their children do grow up and leave home the parting should be easy and without trauma. Strong mothers don't mourn.

a mother's heart   To her amazement, Sarah did mourn — just as other mothers. Mother of two, she was totally surprised at her reaction after son, Jeff, left home: "I've been enormously successful in the business world, especially for a mother raising kids all by herself. But, I'll tell you what, in spite of all the headaches, all the energy I've had to give and all the mistakes I've made, and in spite of the fact that society often just pays lip service to the value of mothers, I wouldn't trade it for the world. Raising those two has given me a sense of purpose that outweighs all the negative feelings that society has about the role of women. It's given me more meaning to life than any of my career successes.

"I didn't realize it until my son left home and wow! was I feeling neat about him as a person...someone who could function and cope. Not that he doesn't have his ups and downs or that sometimes he flounders around...you can't expect a nineteen-year-old to have all the answers. But he's going to do just fine; they both are. It seems that women devalue what they do and the approach that they have in life (because they're not paid for raising children) until men give it a value. But oftentimes I think that it's men who have the misplaced sense of value. Well, shoot! I know...and being the best law partner in the world at age sixty-five is not going to give my life an inner spiritual meaning or be more important than molding my kids' lives. Of course, I wouldn't have wanted to be a full-time mother for all those years; I think I'd have gone mad! And one does have to eat, right?

"When he left, I couldn't believe how bad I felt. It was awful for a few weeks. Not that I went around crying all the time or anything like that; there was just this inner loss of major proportion. I guess you could say I moped around...like I was crying on the inside. Somehow I thought that I would escape those sorrowful feelings...I'm not sure why, but I just did. Maybe it's because my life was always so full and I thought that I was above it. Maybe I felt too feminist to be so caught up...so connected to Jeff. Boy, was I wrong about that! I missed him a lot...he was really a part of me."

Somehow, the movement forgot to tell women that anytime they invest eighteen years in another person, no matter how independent the lives they lead and no matter who that other person is, a separation is going to be a jolt. Children's leaving hurts, and mourning is not a sign of weakness but rather one of caring, love, and shared experiences. Missing someone is okay. The women's movement may have lost its heart, but mothers have not.

DOING IT OVER AGAIN

pipe dreams How often has an adult said, "Oh, how I wish that I could be a child again...wouldn't it be wonderful"? The illusory "it," of course, is not the image of youth involved in wiping away the years but rather the image of freedom and being totally carefree. Such pipe dreams don't come true because one can't understand freedom from responsibility without having experienced full responsibility; that doesn't, however, prevent the daydream from popping up every now and then.

A similar paradox arises for working mothers. Enmeshed in the hustle and bustle of running a household, being a good mother, satisfying the needs of a mate, balancing a career, and finding personal time, a woman can easily forget to enjoy her children. While the chore of raising children so often seems endless, it is finite: the older they become, the less care they demand until, finally, they require very little.

In hindsight, career women often discover that they did not value homelife and children enough. Women may make this discovery at almost any time: some will make it immediately after children depart; others may not acknowledge it until later, even as much as ten years later.

Either way, the phenomenon is one which has arisen mostly over the past decade. Enough time has elapsed that career women have been in the work force for a number of years and they have also been a partially-absent parent during the childrearing process. A mother may say to herself, "I should have enjoyed them more while I had them. Why was I always so busy and preoccupied?" Some women may even feel that they neglected their children and desire to begin over, saying, "How I wish that I could raise them again now that I'm mature enough to appreciate doing it." Fantasies of another child are largely counterbalanced by the reality of all the work involved or by thoughts of being the ever-patient grandparent.

no role model Feeling guilty after the fact occurs often. By then the role of parent is over and a career can more easily be devalued because it has no competition. Yet, when the parent is in the middle of balancing both, making such a determination is not simple and each mother attempts to find the best equation she can. Feminist career women have been charting new territory, and being a pioneer is never easy.

1. *The Courier-Journal*, September 16, 1986, p. A7.

CHAPTER 8

LETTING GO: LAYING THE FOUNDATION

Your children are not your children.
They are the sons and daughters of Life's longing for itself.
They come through you but not from you,
And though they are with you yet they belong not to you.

You may give them your love but not your thoughts,
For they have their own thoughts.
You may house their bodies but not their souls,
For their souls dwell in the house of tomorrow, which you cannot
visit, not even in your dreams.
You may strive to be like them, but seek not to make them like you.
For life goes not backward nor tarries with yesterday.
You are the bows from which your children as living arrows are
sent forth.
The archer sees the mark upon the path of the infinite, and He
bends you with His might that His arrows may go swift and
far.
Let your bending in the archer's hand be for gladness;
For even as He loves the arrow that flies, so He loves also the bow
that is stable.

THE PROCESS

children not possessions of parents These beautiful words by Kahlil Gibran from his book, *The Prophet*,[1] give one clear message: children do not belong to their parents. Understanding this is the key to letting go. Parents are but the apparatus launching their children into life, just as the bow propels the arrow into the air. The ability and willingness of parents to act positively during the weaning process will, to a large extent, determine the type of relationship that is established with the child maturing into adulthood. Just as freedom and love are given to all of *God's children* as they can find their own way in life, so too must parents do the same for their offspring.

letting go from birth Separation between parents and child begins early, from the day the child leaves the mother's womb. A little at a time the small steps of breaking away emerge as the child learns to feed itself, dress itself, think for itself. Change that initially predominates in the outward physical sphere gives way to change that manifests itself in the internal, emotional world of the child. Separation is an ongoing process, not a one-time event.

When the separation is largely accomplished during the teen years, when both the child and the parent are prepared for the transition, the child is more able to function as a mentally healthy adult; when emotional separation is delayed until the adult years, the child (as adult) usually suffers and may have psychological scars lasting a lifetime. If the parent doesn't give independence to the child, then the child must take it. But most importantly, by preparing a child to function on its own, parents prepare themselves to let go.

a difficult task How does a parent let go? Is it too late to start? For most parents, whether they consciously admit it or not, letting go requires concentrated effort over a prolonged period of time. Because parenting techniques are often passed from one generation to the next, parents who have difficulty letting go are probably repeating the pattern of *their* parents.

Maggie, a mother of two, suspected that she illustrated this behavior. "I was a very overbearing, overprotective mother," Maggie reflected. "I didn't let go. I may have said it but then I churned on the inside and didn't let go mentally.

"Kids need to be allowed to fall on their faces and not be picked up. I always found it difficult to find that right line between disciplining and a few basic ground rules...and then let them go from there. Parenting didn't seem easy to me. Perhaps I wasn't parented well." As an afterthought she added, "I'm much more tolerant, now, of other people and their problems raising children."

Some parents think that they are letting go when they are not. Many times during the interview process parents stated that they found letting go of their children easy to do and indicated that their children were independent individuals. These parents then proceeded to talk about how they gave unsolicited advice to their offspring and freely offered opinions whenever the occasion seemed appropriate. This is *not* letting go.

A further aspect complicating the letting go process arises from the many unconscious and nonverbal messages that occur within intimate relationships. Oftentimes these messages contradict and sabotage the conscious, verbal messages that kids get from parents.

The difficulty of developing autonomous children who continue to relate well to their family after leaving home was evident in a study of the teenage transition from high school to college. A highly selective group of students was chosen based on competence, academic success, good peer relationships, and effective participation in social groups. In spite of this selectivity, at the end of freshman year only fifty percent were "self-reliant and effective in college yet enjoying increasing intimacy with parents during vacations." The other students fell into two groups: in the first group students were low in autonomy and experiencing difficulty being on their own; in the other group students were high in autonomy but breaking away from home by going their own way — primarily because the "parents were found to assign a role to their offspring that was more in keeping with their (the parents') interests than the interests of the son or daughter concerned."[2]

historical perspective   Society has come a long way from the condescending view and abusive treatment of children described by Charles Dickens in the mid-1800s. Worrying about children's psyches is a modern-day occurrence. The evaluation of parenting skills is a phenomenon arising only during the past few decades.

There is no one correct way for parents to let go; trial-and-error is usually required. If parents can accept and openly embrace the process of letting go, then they will be mentally ready to prepare each child for the launch. They will be able to project themselves into a new role after the children have left home.

ACCEPTANCE

overview   There are basically three facets to parental acceptance. First, the parent must understand the transformation of the son or daughter during the letting go process. Next, there must be an understanding of the parents' role during this period. Finally, there must be acceptance of the inevitability of the parent-child separation.

understanding the individuation process   The word *individuate* is a clinical term which has been used by psychologists and psychiatrists for years but, more recently, has appeared in popular self-help books. A child individuates as the individual self evolves its own identity and becomes a person distinct from and independent of its parents.

In the process of finding and establishing this separate identity, much of what has been overlaid on the child by the parents must be rejected. Parental authority is replaced by peer standards. Parents are challenged on a continuing basis. When contemplating a particular course of action, children may use parents as sounding boards to see what the reaction will be, to see if anger or disapproval will result. Because children may or may not follow through on these actions, parents may never know if the child is just *testing the water*, is actually swayed by parental opinion, or automatically discounts the advice given because her or his mind is already made up.

role of conflict and hostility The period of adolescent testing is not only very confusing to parents, but it creates hostility between parent and child. Parents are continually wondering how much to give, how much to pull back. A trying time for both, the atmosphere of conflict is, unfortunately, inherent to the individuation process and cannot be avoided, although the magnitude may vary significantly from child to child. As mentioned before, such confrontation often sets the stage for easier detachment.

child in need of own agenda One of the reasons that acceptance of the individuation process is so difficult is that, no matter how open-minded they think they are, most parents develop a *hidden agenda* for their child. While parents may not think in terms of having this agenda, they can usually admit to having hopes, desires, or goals for the child. In all likelihood, many of these expectations are communicated unconsciously — both verbally and nonverbally — to the child. This agenda may reflect what parents didn't do in their youth, but wish they had. Parents may thrill at the idea of bragging about the accomplishments of their child as a form of self-validation, or they may see themselves in the child and be vicariously reliving a part of their lives.

When the young person is merely enacting the parents' goals, the motivation to continue on this course may, at some point, evaporate. Often this is the case when kids drop out of school to *find themselves*. (Later still, it may occur during a midlife crisis.) The difficulty for parents is to let go of their expectations and, at the same time, leave their child alone to develop his or her own agenda.

Not surprisingly, this progression is rarely accomplished in an easy or efficient way; upheaval and uncertainty seem handmaidens to individual growth. Sadly, some children never do create their own road maps.

child in need of independence Children need to be independent if they are going to learn to cope in life. Overprotective parents send subtle messages that children can't make it on their own. Young adults who seek too much advice from their parents, who too often return home for financial and emotional security, may not be maturing and may find it difficult, if not impossible, to develop a singular wholeness. Not only may they have trouble adjusting to adulthood, but there is the likelihood that they will have problems with intimate relationships. When the ability to be independent is impaired, for whatever reason, the parent-child relationship stagnates and remains *status quo*; the parent is not accepting the emergence of a young adult in a new role.

A feeling of ambivalence does surround the act of becoming independent. Like an actor straddling the world of pretense and the world of reality, the child has one foot moving forward to adulthood as the other drags behind in the security of the familiar. One minute kids can act autonomous and grown up, while the next minute they want the parent to tell them what to do — even though they subsequently lash out and criticize the parent for butting in. One time an independent adult emerges; next time, the dependent child. In spite of the difficulty of living with this yo-yo effect on a daily basis, parents should realize that this is a natural, normal reaction to growing up and that children do not really want their parents to intervene or rescue them — it only looks that way.

parents letting go of control The second challenge of acceptance is for parents to examine their own role. There's an old saying about letting something go free — to see if it will return to be loved of its own free will. Parents must not only let go of the physical presence of the child, but the child's thoughts and mind, as well; then they have to sit back and see what happens.

Enlightened parents contribute to a healthy and loving parting when they are able to say, "Go with God and take care of yourself," without making the child feel guilty for leaving. They realize that they can no longer presume to know what is best for their children. These parents do not *own* their children, but act as a vehicle for their growth and separation — just as the bow launches the arrow. Giving up control means giving up protecting children from unpleasantness and difficulties.

When parents cannot give up authority over their children, the parents' lives (as well as the children's) skip a critical phase of emotional growth. This may occur particularly for parents who never made an effective break from *their* parents. Some parents may even "avoid the pain of the young generation's separation by separating from *them* beforehand."[3]

parents who polarize Parents who resist letting go can polarize their teens into action instead of loving them into adulthood. This is what happened to Tom, a very determined young adult. "I needed my independence," he stated flatly. "I needed to show my parents that I could make it on my own without their help. They were threatening me and holding this hammer above my head and saying, 'Well, you're not going to make it, you should do what we tell you to do.' They don't like me making my own decisions, doing what I want to do. When I come home they really wish that they had more control over my life...whereas they don't." He was unsure that they would ever accept him as an adult and this saddened him. He felt helpless to change the deteriorating relationship.

Because his parents were fighting so hard to keep him at home, they threatened to withdraw all monetary support should he carry out his plans to attend college out-of-state. They followed through on their threat but failed in their objective: Tom still left home. Unfortunately, use of such drastic financial measures is not uncommon by parents who can't give up control. If the threat succeeds, departure is only delayed, not avoided, and the home environment can become saturated with frustration and resentful feelings.

Tom's case was an interesting one. After he had been gone for a semester, his father became ill and, out of a sense of obligation, Tom moved home to finish his freshman year at a nearby college. He felt that his mother had manipulated the situation by exaggerating the severity of the illness and her needy dependence upon the oldest son. This time she won. Had he not responded, Tom's sense of guilt would have been overpowering and his love for his family would have been questioned and possibly compromised. After the crisis passed and Tom made plans to leave home and return to school for sophomore year, his mother begged and pleaded for him to stay. She "made a big stink" and resorted to cajolery with such statements as, "What will I do without you?" and "Your father needs you." Tension and acrimony permeated the household. But Tom's resolve held firm and, once again, he left.

parents letting go of expectations Throughout the childrearing, individuating, and separating process, parents who seem to be the most accepting of their children are those whose expectations have been kept to a minimum. Ray Shafer's ideas from his earlier Profile are worth repeating here: "There's a one-way thing from parents to kids...there's no justification for me to expect anything...because if I do, I'm going to be disappointed." There is perhaps no better indicator of how well-adjusted parents are than the level of their expectations for their offspring.

Not only can expectations lead to disappointment but they also place undue pressures on children. Still struggling with this pressure, a twenty-eight-year-old child said, "It's a hard thing living up to parental expectations." One wonders when the pressure stops. Kids may feel that a parent is looking over their shoulders, being critical, inhibiting their ability to ask for guidance or advice with the threat of being judged.

When parents are content with their children, a supportive message is sent. "Maybe one of the reasons that I'm so happy at school is because of what I have here at home," related a bright young woman. "My parents don't put pressure on me as lots of other parents do for getting As, selecting the right major, and expecting too much. They're happy that I'm happy." This support does not begin when children leave home; it begins early in a child's life and provides the foundation and environment for successful individual growth.

parents no longer molding child Ironically, during the senior year of high school there is a tendency on the part of parents to make last-ditch attempts to influence or change their children. More often than not, parents are evaluating an academic, behavioral, or social pattern that has consistently been a part of their child for years. The situation is not new, but the parents' reaction is. Parents begin putting pressure on kids to *get their act together* and may contact the school for professional advice. The focus of this effort is to get the child to change before leaving home. Parents seek to *repair* the trait that they don't like, a trait that they think may cause the child problems down the road. The trait may even mirror a characteristic found in one of the parents.

Not only are these last minute efforts futile, but they can sour the parent-child relationship. Parents have to accept that it's too late to force major alterations in young people whose values were internalized years earlier. At this point only the children, themselves, can initiate and assimiliate change into their lives.

Parenting during the teen years doesn't basically alter children. Parents have to accept their children as they are. But what parents can do with late parenting, as astutely expressed by Robert Tyler who was profiled earlier, is "preserve their life relationship with their children. Beginning with the teenage years, about all you do is decide whether you're going to have a relationship with your kids for the rest of your life. You don't alter their life choices, personalities, or values very much, but boy! do you powerfully alter the relationship that they're going to have with you."

parents accepting pain Although discussed before, it bears restating that most parents must accept the fact that when children leave, the pain cannot be avoided. (There are parents, however, who claim not to experience any pain.) Even an intellectual acceptance cannot override the emotional reality: letting go hurts. Some parents become so sad when their child leaves that they literally cannot enter the child's room and shut the bedroom door until the child returns home.

Pain can't be avoided, but it will pass — sometimes quite quickly. When a parent cannot let go while the child still lives at home, pain may become disguised as anger. Intense anger can provoke a parent into threatening to kick the teenager out of the house; a few parents carry out this threat, sometimes well before the child is ready to cope. Ironically, parting angrily is often easier than coming face to face with the sadness.

inevitability of parent-child separation Ultimately, parents must accept the inevitability that children are going to break away; they are going to be different and have distinctive lifestyles; and they are going to be uniquely on their own.

The parents' challenge is to help in this process as much as possible and, finally, to work themselves out of a job. Children who are leaving home are ready to start making what *they* want with their lives. "I was no longer growing for my parents or growing for my friends, I was growing for me," related a college freshman about his first thoughts of true independence, "and I was going to grow into something that I liked. If I didn't like it then I told myself that's not the way I'm going to go. That's how I did things...my way."

To children whose parents have been accepting, the separation is a natural process. Parents who are not supportive miss out on this exciting stage of their child's maturation. One son sadly described the gulf that now existed with his parents: "They just don't see what I'm doing. They don't really know what I'm like, what I want, my goals." This child saw leaving home as moving ahead; in resisting his departure, his parents chose to see only a finality, an ending. They couldn't accept that they were not losing a child, but gaining a unique, thoughtful adult.

This theme not only echoes in real life, but literature as well. One of the best illustrations is a revealing line of dialogue in Marsha Norman's Pulitzer-winning play, *'night, Mother,* when the daughter angrily lashes out at her mother, "I am what became of your child." The breaking away is inevitable. Parents must let go.

When parents feel that this letting go process is off track for any reason, seeking professional advice may be the best course.

PREPARATION

love and self-discipline In laying the foundation for a child's independence the most important ingredient is love, for with love children develop a sense of value. In his book, *The Road Less Traveled,* M. Scott Peck thoroughly develops the essentiality of love in preparing children to cope with life. Because life is made up of a series of problems, he says, parents must equip children for making the decisions and personal choices that are required in the everyday world. In order to develop this skill, children must see their parents as role models of self-discipline, willing to take responsibility for their own actions.

Parental power over children exists, Peck continues, because of the offspring's dependency on their parents for well-being. When parents abuse this power, children are powerless to change the situation — their choices are limited. But, in adulthood, choices become unlimited and conscientious parents will prepare children for this responsibility by acting on a commitment to let go gradually throughout the adolescent period. Children then develop their own self-discipline; they learn to love and parent themselves.

Failure to let go under the guise of *protecting* children actually deprives them of needed information for processing decisions, reinforces parental control, and allows parents to escape being challenged on an adult level — a level which might call for change in their lives. The message to the children actually is, Peck concludes, "Look, kids, you go on being children with childish concerns and leave the adult concerns up to us."[4] This is not a communication of love: the growth of the child is being ignored.

a child's self-worth When parents value their child, that child grows to like and value himself or herself. Before modern conveniences freed people from many household chores, children were needed to bring in the hay, stoke the fire, sew the clothes, raise the vegetables for canning, and contribute to the survival of the family. Children could get their sense of value from these contributions. Because the tasks assigned nowadays to children (e.g., mowing the grass or doing the dishes) are rarely essential to survival, developing a feeling of worth must come from a different source if children are not to feel like a liability to the family. Says Dr. Tom Colley:

> Children must be valued for who they are, not what they produce, what they contribute, or what they accomplish. A parent must be able to say to the child, "Your contribution is in just being yourself — someone who is fun to be with, someone who makes me proud, someone who doesn't cause me problems. You are special, not because of your achievements, but because of other things — you have good friendships with other kids, you're well liked, other kids can come and cry on your shoulder. You are developing a uniqueness that pleases me — even if it's not what I expected, it's different than I am, and it seems brand new. I appreciate and value you the way you are."
>
> By doing this, parents prepare children so that they have a good system of enhancing their own self-worth based on their uniqueness and orientations — not those of their parents. This allows children to make their own way in life. When parents look only to the child's accomplishments, trophies, grades, or other signs of success, children may not feel valued for who they are inside. The end result is that children feel pressure — social pressure, academic pressure, athletic pressure, career pressure. When they no longer feel content with who they are, their self-worth declines.

Parents have the responsibility to make available different resources and experiences from which their children can develop their uniqueness, define their goals, and, hence, mold an agenda. Children need to be encouraged to explore what is different and new. To be well equipped, they need raw material from which to draw conclusions and make judgments: different jobs, summers away (such as camp, visits to relatives, athletic programs, or survival training), language study, student internships, music lessons, YMCA/YWCA/4-H activities, Little League, scouting programs, swimming lessons, summer dramatics, special hobbies, exposure to other adults and lifestyles, after-school experiences. Some of these ideas involve a financial commitment but others do not. What *is* important is parental support.

As children spend time away from home and have other interests, parents will have an easier time letting go. They will have taken steps to prepare both themselves and their child for separation.

values Children need to grow up with a clearly defined set of values. Such values show love, reinforce self-discipline, and provide an environment within which a child's self-worth can flourish. These values may be within a religious or spiritual framework; they may not. By knowing what their parents stand for and what the family standards are, children feel secure. Wise parents will not stifle differing opinions or prohibit debate about these values or other important issues, for this dialogue helps children define themselves.

giving time "Give your kids everything: give them your time," says psychiatrist Dr. Keith Auerbach, emphasizing the importance of this factor in the parent-child relationship. By giving time to children, including time to discipline them, parents show caring and love. Only with time do relationships develop. Time provides parents the space to find pleasure in their children, doing things with them and for them because of wanting to, not because of having to.

All too often as children get older, parents are too busy. Bemoaned one mother: "Who has time to play a game anymore?" With this question comes the realization that parents frequently don't take the time to enjoy their children.

listening Giving time also means having time to listen and Peck has valuable thoughts about this process. Because listening requires tremendous effort and total concentration on the child and on each word, he says, listening becomes a labor of love and the rewards to the parent who listens are many:

> First, your willingness to do so is the best possible concrete evidence of your esteem you can give your child.... Second, the more children feel valuable, the more they will begin to say things of value....Third, the more you listen to your child, the more you will realize that...your child does indeed have valuable things to say...and you will come to realize that he or she is quite an extraordinary individual.... Fourth, the more you know about your child, the more you will be able to teach. Know little about your children, and usually you will be teaching things that either they are not ready to learn or they already know and perhaps understand better than you. Finally, the more appropriate your teaching, based on your knowledge of them, the more eager your children will be to learn from you.[5]

Peck is well aware that the listening process begins early in a child's life. But even those parents who have not paid much attention to their child's conversations can begin to listen. A forty-eight-year-old mother of two grown sons, Ruth regretted all the years that she had not really listened, years when her boys had discipline problems culminating in the need for a drug treatment program. Only after seeking group therapy counseling had she been able to understand her role in her sons' problems.

"Kids are real...really people. I was dominating, dictatorial. Kids have feelings. Parents need to listen to kids. Things that they're concerned with are genuine to them, even if they don't mean anything to me." The process of mending her relationship with each son was slow and painful, but it was progressing.

Leo Buscaglia in his book, *Loving Each Other*, discusses the results of a survey that he conducted to determine what people think are the qualities in a relationship that most enhance continued growth. While, not surprisingly, communication is at the top of the list, the ability of parents to implement effective communication is often lacking:

> One of the greatest complaints among the young today is that though they are given so much in terms of objects, money, and physical comforts, they feel deprived of close communication. They miss the type of talk which helps them to hear their own voices, discover their own resources, make their own mistakes and seek their own solutions in a supporting environment. They often feel that true communication between themselves and those they love is, if offered at all, of limited value.[6]

The difficulty, of course, is that while good communication is dependent upon certain identifiable characteristics, such as the abilities of both parties to listen to each other and to be open about themselves, communication between parent and child cannot always be programmed in advance. A parent cannot say to a child, "After school today I want to have effective communication with you." Or, "Let's get together and really communicate on Saturday for one hour." It doesn't work that way, which can be frustrating to parents. (Although this approach may become more effective as teens make the transition into adulthood.)

Parents have to be available, receptive, and patient, as the thoughts of this mother reveal. "My husband and I decided early on that the most important thing was to keep the kids talking to us no matter what they said...even if they were cursing us. What that implies is that you can't say things to turn them off. You have to make them comfortable enough that they are able to tell you the things they are thinking." If not, teenagers won't discuss the important things that are happening to them — real situations like being pregnant or being gay. These situations may evoke panic in a parent, but the alternative is a child who becomes a stranger.

praise and a positive attitude Because so much of a parent's outlook on life is communicated directly (although perhaps unconsciously) to a child, the importance of parents having a positive attitude cannot be emphasized strongly enough. If parents accentuate the positive, rather than the negative, then children tend to do the same with their lives. Parents need to consciously praise and reinforce children for who they *are*, not dwell on who they are not or what they do wrong. A predisposition toward negativeness can become a way of life, one that rarely allows children to get out of the quagmire and test their wings with confidence.

Reminiscing on all the lost opportunities for positive support and praise, Ruth concluded, "I regret all the years that I didn't do that." Said another mother, "The greatest gift you can give a child is to make them feel that they're most special. Then they feel attractive to others because they feel a mother's security and love. It's hard to do sometimes." Her thoughts were confirmed by one study which showed that when mothers are loving and share a close relationship with their children, the children demonstrate more self-esteem. These mothers show respect, firmness and care when exercising parental control; they rely on praise rather than punishment.[7]

trust and support Peppered throughout these pages is the importance of parents trusting their children — trusting their judgment and their decisions. When children are trusted, positive messages are sent: love, respect and support. Trusting parents don't closely supervise children as they mature. Trusting parents communicate honestly, knowing that their children can handle information in an adultlike manner. Trusting parents are more able to let go.

Jennie's father was finally able to trust and let go on one of her visits home from college. "Dad was trying to impose curfews on me. Finally I explained to him that at school I may not come in until the sun comes up so he was being pretty hypocritical to watch the clock now. If he could trust me at school, he could trust me at home. He agreed. The curfews disappeared." In her father's eyes, Jennie had finally grown up.

physical contact "Have you hugged your kid today?" is a bumper sticker that has more meaning than first meets the eye. It is actually an indictment of parents and the quality of physical and mental health that they often provide their children. Parents who don't hug their children? Sad, but true. Scores of fathers have not hugged their sons since early youth, excusing this pattern with a statement to the effect, "I'm not a very touchy, feely person," or "I don't get into that." This attitude may be okay for the father, but what about the feelings of the son who gets a hug only when he leaves home?

Because there is a positive correlation between the physical closeness children experience and their physical and mental health,[8] parents should make a commitment to hug their kids frequently, even during the teenage years. Said one mother, "I remember when my son was in junior high. Those were troubled years for him; he really withdrew and didn't have many friends. I knew that if I didn't hug him he might not get touched all day, except to be bumped in the halls at school. So two or three times a week when he left for school I would make a point to say, 'I'm your mother, so hug me.' and then I would tell him that I loved him. He wasn't wild about the whole idea but he accepted it. I knew he needed it — even if he didn't think he did." The love that a hug shows speaks to people of all ages.

space and privacy Just as children need the closeness of touch, so also they need the distance of privacy. Another part of letting go is giving children space and respecting their right to that space — usually their bedroom. This should be a place of privacy for them, a space that parents do not casually invade. Inability to give privacy shows a lack of trust and respect on the parents' part. In this place of escape, children are becoming young adults, individuating themselves from their sometimes stifling parents.

humor When parents are able to acquaint their children with the value of humor in dealing with life's problems, kids have one more tool which prepares them for the task of coping with life. The ability to laugh at oneself and not take one's problems so seriously, if learned in youth, lasts a lifetime. Sharon, mother of a nineteen-year-old, firmly believed in the importance of humor and shared her thoughts about the first Mother's Day card that she received after her son left home.

"I was really surprised that he remembered to send me a card at all. I hadn't reminded him and so I had no expectations. You can imagine my surprise when it arrived in the mail, and on time, to boot! I felt touched...really good inside. Mother's Day followed a period at school during which he hated his job, the car he bought broke down, school work seemed oppressive and As impossible, there was no time for physical exercise, and the rooming situation for sophomore year looked dismal. On the outside the card said something about teaching him to laugh at life's little problems.

"But the inside was the best." She chuckled, remembering the card. "I remember it said, 'I'm in hysterics,' and he had added a note about how he was going to get me one of those mushy cards saying what a great mother I was, but none of them could do me justice and besides, this message seemed pretty appropriate. I know his problems didn't disappear, but at least he had a perspective that worked in his favor instead of making him feel totally overwhelmed. I was glad that he could laugh at himself. When you can laugh at yourself, things usually get better."

friendship Parents who feel good about letting go are those who gradually develop a friendship with their children. They enjoy each other's company in a friendly, congenial way, especially after the child has left home. They have fun together. They look forward to spending time together.

When people are friends, there are certain *things* that they don't do to each other and people who disregard or violate the basic precepts of friendship do not remain friends. But for some reason family members often feel immune to such rules of behavior and can be thoughtless and insensitive when dealing with each other. Parents who want young adults to enjoy coming back home to visit can't be interfering in their children's lives. Said one parent: "It's very difficult to button your lip and think before you speak. They have to be treated as friends. You don't treat your friends like that so...if you want your kids to come around...and I want my kids to enjoy coming around. That's very special to me. I always want them to want to come home, not come because they have to."

Contrast this to the statement of a college student about his feelings of home after having spent two years away: "My mother still worries about things like when the roads are slick. I point out to her that I've been away and she hasn't been there to point these things out and I'm fine." In the end he looks forward to returning to school. "These Christmas breaks are about a week too long." How sad that this mother henpecks her son literally out of the house.

openness The foundation of any friendship is that people know each other in the sense of sharing who they really are. This applies to parents as well as children. By opening themselves up, by not being hypercritical, and by exposing themselves as vulnerable human beings, parents have much to gain. Of course, they have to be willing to give up domination and superiority over their children's lives.

"The most important things that parents give a child," said one young adult, "are love and respect and honesty. They're all equal. We need them all in relationships. Parents are dishonest when they expect a child to tell them everything that goes on in the child's life and yet they try to hide things that happen in theirs. There is a point when a child is old enough that the parent can level with the child and explain things. It's not fair for parents to expect it of the child and not give it equally."

Said a father along similar lines: "It's best for parents to expose themselves to kids and let the kids draw their own conclusions."

When children see their parents as vital people with real problems, people who admit when they are wrong or make a mistake, then children are learning valuable lessons about how to cope with life. When they see parents acknowledge weaknesses, as well as strengths, then children are better able to assess themselves realistically, not overembellish their strong points or ignore their weak ones. When they see parents as distinct individuals who wrestle with life's problems, who are open to change, and who actively seek growth, then children are better prepared to accept the challenges of life rather than shrink from them. When children see their parents' emotions unshielded and exposed, then children learn how to deal with their own feelings. When they see parents as open and receptive, children can come and share the truth, even when unpleasant.

In spite of all the barriers of protection parents may raise, ultimately, children evaluate and draw their own conclusions about their parents. The impact of parents is as role models, not in what they preach. As children begin to understand these lessons and to know and value their parents, children can also begin to appreciate their need for other people in their lives and recognize that this need is not necessarily a sign of dependence.

understanding change Change is a catalyst for personal growth. As mentioned earlier, children often leave home feeling that because of a new environment they have been given a *clean slate* and change will be easy. They are unprepared for the hard work that change demands. Children who have an understanding of the effort, personal introspection, and diligence required to effect change will be better prepared to seek their own personal growth. Having a parental role model plus loving acceptance from parents creates a climate in which children can risk change without feeling less whole. Ultimately they experience the freedom of being who they are in a dynamic and evolving sense.

removing guilt Parents are not letting go when they make children feel responsible for the parents' well-being or make children feel guilty for wanting to lead their own lives. This is a form of manipulation that yields children unable to know themselves or to make decisions without always feeling the impact of those decisions on their parents' lives as an overriding factor. It also occurs when parents closely *program* their children's lives and make them feel guilty for attempting to write their own agendas.

Such manipulation by the parents verges on, or may actually be, mental child abuse. These parents invariably lack self-value and self-esteem. That they believe they can only keep their children's love by holding on is best illustrated in another statement from Buscaglia's book: "And how little we value ourselves when we manipulate someone in order to keep them, when they would rather be elsewhere."[9]

Mothers can be particularly guilty of this if they are so wrapped up in their children's lives that the children are seen merely as extensions of the mother and not as separate individuals. A mother perpetuating this pattern must stop seeing herself at the center of her child's world. While interviewing Helen, a mother of five, about her own feelings and children, a story apropos to this situation emerged. She began speaking of her forty-six-year-old husband and the relationship with his mother.

"His mother has never let go but I'm getting him to realize that he has to. If he calls our children on one particular day of the week as they grow older and then they don't call us on that day they'll feel guilty, like he feels guilty if he doesn't see his mother every Saturday or call her two, three times a week.

"I have been intimidated for years by his mother. We don't have her over every week like we used to. We owe ourselves things. She even expected our oldest daughter to write all the time from college. That's when it hit me. She made me feel guilty for years and she was not going to do that to my girls. They owe her nothing. I've gotten very resentful. I'm doing exactly what I want to do now, on my own terms. My kids have their own lives and they don't owe me anything and they don't owe her anything. We have been her entertainment and her life for twenty years."

As she spoke, Helen's built-up resentment of this manipulation made her angrier and angrier. "She called me everyday for twenty years and I finally squared her away on that! If the kids were sick, she called two, three times a day! I never felt I owed my parents. The only thing our kids owe us is to be happy, responsible citizens who contribute something to this world. And if they are happy doing something they like, that's all we expect." In the final analysis, it was Helen's mother-in-law who had set herself up for disappointment and rejection. Helen was determined not to let that happen with her children.

PROJECTION

parents in a new role   For parents to be ready to let go, they need to be able to project themselves into the future, to see themselves in the new role of parenting less. When parents anticipate the changes associated with a child's separation and begin to shift gears ahead of time, then the potentially negative aspects surrounding the leave-taking can be minimized or capitalized upon and used to the parents' advantage. By being willing to change as part of the natural growth process, parents stand to benefit from their children's individuation and maturity as much as the offspring. Change is healthy. By rising to the challenge, modifying attitudes, and responding to children, Peck encourages parents to "become the parents our children need us to be."[10]

new goals   By the time children leave home, parents have channeled vast quantities of energy into child rearing. Although difficult, this energy must now be redirected into their own lives. In his book, *The Children of the Dream*, Bruno Bettelheim addresses this issue with the following: "The dreams parents dream for their children never come true — though neither are they wholly in vain. One cannot dream up a life for the other, one can only fashion a life of one's own."[11]

Parents must decide what direction the next decades will take, what goals will be achieved, what changes will be made — in *their* lives. Some parents are quite young (in their early forties) when all their children have left the nest; others may be much older. On average, however, parents have at least twenty to forty years left ahead of them, much of it healthy, productive time. When there are still children left at home, this period of introspection and reevaluation can be deferred for a while. But overall, parents will have an easier time of letting go of their children's lives when they have planned in advance.

leaving as a process   As they experience the beginning of a new phase in their lives, young adults adjust fairly quickly; only a very few get homesick. Parents, on the other hand, are experiencing the end of a phase. For this reason, the act of children leaving seems very final. Feelings of emptiness contribute to the air of finality. But because of the upheavals and ambiguities that beset children during their difficult transformation into adulthood, the *end* is not nearly as final as it at first seems. There is no real closure to what is, after all, a process.

kids as a long-term investment If parents can come to view the time, energy and money spent raising a child as an investment, then once the child has left home the parents must relax and wait for the investment to mature and yield its return. There are no immediate results and parents do a disservice to their child if they are prematurely evaluating what they see.

The parents' need to have instantaneous answers is somewhat understandable: because they are no longer in control, they want to know the final outcome. But indicators, such as successful or unsuccessful, mature or immature, are inappropriate and may only serve to trap a young adult under a harmful label. Children do look to their parents for evaluation and approval of their life choices. Children do need to feel that their parents are being supportive, regardless of whether things work out right away in the new environment.

parents letting go of mistakes At the same time that parents wait for the returns, they also need to let go of the mistakes, real or imagined, that they made in rearing their children. There is no such thing as a *perfect parent*. When reflecting on parenthood, there is often a tendency to forget the good and dwell on the things that were *screwed up*. Parents need to resist overpsychologizing what they did. Regretting the past is pointless.

children in a new role Projecting the child into the future is every bit as important as projecting the parent there. During their first year away from home, young adults change dramatically as their independent status becomes more defined.

The problem is, as mentioned earlier, that parents are not privy to much of this change and their image of their offspring tends to remain static. One freshman summed the dilemma up in this fashion: "I come back home and they take up where we left off. For me, I've been through a lot of changes but I still see that parental authority not letting go. They're not treating me as a full adult. Parents have to reevaluate kids and treat them as their behavior merits. They can't assume that behavior hasn't changed. The difference between senior year in high school and the first Christmas break in college is tremendous."

Said another, "My mom was still telling me what to do, eat my carrots or whatever, and it's a shock to come home to that. I'm used to school where no one tells me to do anything. I do what I want. To go home and have my mother remind me to eat carrots, is just way off base. I became resentful. I do just fine in school by myself, so don't bother me. I know what I'm doing."

Because both parents and children can easily fall back into the old habits and patterns which put the child in a dependency position, parents must work very hard to catch themselves when they are not letting go. This new course will avoid feelings of resentment and aid in furthering the emerging adult-adult relationship.

1. New York: Alfred A. Knopf, 1955, pp. 17-18.
2. John Bowlby, *Attachment and Loss, Vol II: Separation* (New York: Basic Books, Inc., Publishers, 1973) pp. 348-50.
3. Scarf, p. 298.
4. New York: Simon and Schuster, 1978, p. 60.
5. Peck, pp.125-126.
6. Thorofare, New Jersey: SLACK Incorporated, 1984, p. 56.
7. Bowlby, p. 342.
8. Buscaglia, p. 133. Author also states that there is a "positive relationship between adolescents who use drugs and those who come from homes in which there is little or no touching," based on studies conducted by Jack Pankaepp of Bowling Green State University in Ohio, as described in *The Gift of Touch* by Helen Colton.
9. p. 128.
10. p. 149.
11. Toronto: The Macmillan Company, 1969, p. 320.

CHAPTER 9

LETTING GO: PRACTICAL APPLICATION

It's hard to be a parent. It's hard to lose. It's hard to give your children everything and walk away. It's hard to be in this unrequited love affair that is parenthood.[1]

NUTS 'N BOLTS PREPARATION

parents' duty to prepare Two decades ago the doctrine *in loco parentis* prevailed on campuses around the country. This doctrine stated that the administration of a university acted *in the place of the parents* while children were in attendance. The university accepted this responsibility by enforcing rules, regulations, and dormitory restrictions. As times changed, the universities gradually conceded more responsibilities to students in the context of daily decision making.

Today, while the university may still be legally accountable, children have actually been delegated the responsibility for their lives. Parents have the duty to prepare children for this responsibility. Even though college is somewhat protected from the outside world, it does require many more coping skills than the sheltered environment of home.

checklist of a teen's responsibilities If children have been given a broad range of responsibilities, then they have the tools to deal with the real world. Responsibility provides children an outlet for the incredible amount of energy they have and allows them to exercise power over their lives. Because teenagers often think that they have all the answers, being able to implement them — whether successfully or not — in some fashion takes the monkey off the parents' backs. Responsibility usually requires kids to do more than just *go with the flow.*

Because responsibilities should be specific, not general in nature, a checklist may prove helpful. (As with any list, there are undoubtably items which have been overlooked.) While it may appear long, the importance of each item cannot be ignored. Before they leave home, teens need to:

* hold a job
* get themselves up in the morning
* have a checking account, savings account, and/or possibly a credit card
* acquire money sense, developed through managing a clothes budget and earning all or part of their spending money (teens should not be given an allowance during the summer when they can work)
* do their own laundry
* go grocery shopping a number of times
* cook at least some of the meals — their own or for the family
* contribute to household functioning, e.g., cleaning, mowing, weeding, shopping
* develop good work habits
* take care of any car that they drive regularly
* adjust to demands made on them
* take care of themselves in most ways
* make most of their own decisions
* understand the decision-making (problem-solving) process of thinking something through rationally, evaluating alternatives, and examining the long-range implications of their conclusions (they need to think beyond the moment and not just look for the quick fix)
* spend part of a summer (or several summers) away, preferably for longer than a week
* meet a variety of different types of people
* pick the college they want to go to and, perhaps, have an idea of what they want to do with their lives
* go away to college, if possible
* deal with the consequences of their actions and mistakes
* set their own curfews (with parental consent) by their senior year
* understand the etiquette of thank you notes, respond to invitations, and fulfill their own obligations as required
* know how to request information and make inquiries or com-

plaints in person or on the phone
* know how to stand up for themselves if being misinformed or taken advantage of by sales clerk, mechanic, school official, or someone else
* take primary responsibility for packing and getting ready for college

privileges and freedom Responsibility means privileges. Privileges and a sense of control over one's life brings freedom. Students who have not had this sense of freedom at home can go overboard when they're finally on their own, ranging from excesses of sex and drinking, to staying out all night, skipping classes, and leaving school for days at a time. Carried to the extreme, students can flunk out or physically harm themselves.

Students able to handle the freedom have a much better sense of themselves. Said one student: "A lot of people when they leave their parents have a new thrill...the thrill of freedom, doing what they want without...the busting loose part of cutting free. But for me it was no big thing."

Another student, Bill, was a confident, college sophomore in a five-year engineering program. He had spent one summer in Israel in a work/study endeavor and another as a camp counselor. Each year he came back and spoke to high school seniors about college life: what they needed to know and how it differed from high school. Because of his time away from home, he had felt well prepared when he went off to college, "...so for me it was not nearly a shock. I knew how to do my laundry and generally knew what I was doing. Most kids aren't that way. When I got there, my roommate, after letting his laundry pile up for a couple of weeks, pulled out the box of Tide that his mother had bought him and said, 'Now, how do I do this?'"

The roommate was eighteen, attending a college costing thousands each year, and yet he had never had responsibility for doing a single load of wash. His mother (and father), by being overprotective, had left him unprepared for the simplest of tasks.

As each child matures through adolescence, parents must analyze when to let go, when to stop waiting on that child in a servantlike manner. Even though younger children may still require attention, at some point such behavior is inappropriate for older brothers or sisters. Children who are used to being waited on ultimately suffer a loss of freedom.

guidelines and rules Setting out good, clear guidelines for children is important. Children must have some authority to identify with when they are growing up. Because idle threats, demands, or punishments that are not backed up are a waste of time and teach a disregard for authority and for parents, mother and father need to agree on certain non-negotiable rules which carry consequences if not followed.

If there are but a few firm rules, then children have a wide latitude in which they may function in the decision-making role. Teens will usually not break these rules, at least not directly in front of a parent. Yet they have something to fight *against*, out in the open — a crucial element in helping children define their separateness from their parents. Such rules might be: no smoking in the house, babysitting on a particular night for a younger brother or sister, no drinking and driving, calling if unable to meet curfew time, and so forth.

Rules should not be arbitrary and should have some justification. If not used too often, sufficient justification may be as simple as saying, "I'm not comfortable with that and if you live in this house, on this one issue, my being uncomfortable is enough." The child may rant and rave, but usually begrudgingly accepts the outcome. Rules that impinge on the child's lifestyle, such as dress, neatness of bedroom, amount of makeup, or length of hair, are much more difficult to enforce and are, perhaps, unfair or unwise. Rules that affect the child's health and safety or impact the parents' lives have more justification. When children provide input, negotiated rules work best of all.

When conflicts arise, parents need to depersonalize them, especially when bickering about relatively unimportant things. Children are not necessarily *against* their parents and don't necessarily dislike them. What the child does, or doesn't do, does not relate directly to whether the parents are bad parents. But what does impact heavily and can lead to problem children are parents who say *no* to everything or those who are inconsistent to the point that children cannot predict whether their parents will think something is right or wrong or whether punishment will be given or not. Wise parents will realize that if children break the rules and suffer the consequences, then parents must be willing to *drop it*. They must let go of the situation and trust that children have learned from it.

role of consequences One more word about consequences. Everyone has consequences in life. When people rob banks, they go to jail. When people are consistently late for work, they lose their jobs. When people drink and drive, they run the risk of having an accident, perhaps injuring or killing themselves or others. Being independent means being able to deal with consequences outside of the home. Learning how to do that begins *in* the home.

Some parents make that a very clear message to their children. "I tell them..." said one mother, "you make the decision, you live with the consequences. If they get bad grades and can't get a job later on, it's their lives, not mine, that are affected. My life is in enough uproar without worrying about everything in their lives also. Not that I won't help them, and they know that, but they're old enough to take their own responsibility."

Certainly parents can help their children if they need it, but parents should not *rescue* children so they escape dealing with deserved consequences. All too often parents stand up for their children when the time has come to let the children stand up for themselves. Protecting children from unpleasantness and consequences ceases to be in their best interests. Sometimes children have to suffer and learn the hard way.

parents' fear as a hindrance to preparation Parents today seem afraid — afraid of asserting parental rights, afraid of standing up to children, and afraid of fighting with them. Parents are afraid of not being loved or needed; they are afraid of saying *no*. Some parents see only the risk of rejection when conflict arises, or else they do not have the energy to stick to their decisions. Saying *yes* becomes the easiest, fastest, and safest way out. Even though children may have succeeded at that game they know so well — manipulation — the result is poor parenting. The kids get shortchanged.

Interestingly enough, most parents seem to know when they are being manipulated, they just feel helpless to do anything about it. Said one observant college student reflecting back: "It's really nice to be able to lay your troubles off on your parents if they're willing to take them. At college it's all on your own shoulders." Children seem particularly adept at finagling extra money for clothes or cars and getting parents to repair or replace items broken because of the child's neglect. Parents end up feeling *sorry* for children; oftentimes such sympathy is inappropriate and simply allows escape from responsibility.

affluence as a hindrance Certainly money, in and of itself, is not bad. But when money is used as a crutch for a child's weak self-esteem or as a substitute for love and spending time together, the effects are bad. When children are given too much by affluent parents and grandparents, money can become debilitating and stifle growth and identity development within the child. To be a seventeen-year-old driving a seventeen-thousand-dollar car may be a thrill, but it does little to shape character.

A child's relationship to money is molded by parents and is perhaps a greater responsibility than many parents acknowledge. So important is its effect that world-recognized child psychologist, Bruno Bettelheim, lists society's affluence as one of three factors leading to adolescent revolt.[2] For parents to overlook this sensitive issue is a mistake. They may incapacitate their children for certain aspects of adulthood.

differences for sons and daughters If any differences exist in the growing-up and breaking-away process which are unique to the sex of the offspring, they might be oversimplified by the following comments. In a nutshell, boys need to be encouraged to express their emotions and to nurture their development of intimate relationships. Waiting until a midlife crisis strikes to achieve this end is a long wait. Girls need to be encouraged to develop a career path, even if interrupted by child-rearing responsibilities. Statistics clearly indicate that at some time in her life a female will most likely have to be self-sufficient economically or contribute financially within a relationship.

experience as the great teacher As much as parents try to prepare their children for a life away from home, there is only so much that children can absorb without first-hand experience. Talking about greater responsibility or a new and different life can never approximate the actual experience of coping in an unfamiliar situation. Nor can children be taught to appreciate home by being warned that they may miss home more than expected. All of these discoveries will come. How they are handled depends on how well the children are prepared.

DISTANCING

a vote of confidence Preparing children to be on their own means watching them pull away slowly, as described by one mother: "There's a certain distancing in the senior year. They were allowed more independence. We built it up gradually during the high school years. The rules began to fall away a little bit at a time. Kids tend to be more physically absent and that sort of goes along with an emotional pulling apart." By letting children gain this freedom, parents are giving a vote of confidence in the child and, even more importantly, showing the parents' own comfort level in trusting the child — which is sometimes not easy to do. Parents often do have difficulty in seeing their eighteen-year-old as capable of functioning alone.

The irony of this underestimation of children's ability suddenly showed up during an interview with Kit who, herself, left home to get married at that early age. She was speaking of her son's money sense and certain financial obligations that he had to assume because he had not gone off to college, but rather had chosen to attend a local school and live at home: "I'm hoping that he's learning something out of this that he can apply to budgeting expenses when he gets out on his own. It would be really hard if he never had to pay for anything and all of a sudden he moved out of the house and had to face rent and utilities, insurance, and all that. How in the world would anybody...how did we do it?" A quizzical look appeared on her face and then she burst into laughter throwing her hands into the air, laughing at herself and her husband and the realization that she could not imagine her son now doing what they had done at the same age. "How did we do that?" She paused. "I don't remember. I honestly don't remember!"

acceptance of friends Parents can also let go and show a vote of confidence by accepting their children's friends without judgment and by making them welcome in the family home. Manipulating the selection of friends or acting jealous of time spent with them gives children the message that parents want to be in control. Jan loved her father but after one year away from home was able to reflect: "I don't think he wanted me to grow up. Whenever I brought somebody home (after I started going out with boys), I was real insecure. The same was true with all my brothers and sisters. Nobody liked to bring anybody home because we always got the feeling that he was not being friendly to them.

"I guess in a way that's why I think he didn't want me to grow up...or at least that had something to do with it. It made him even madder when I was out with my friends. Before I was staying home a lot and going to movies with my parents or watching TV with them. I started to do my own thing, I guess, and he didn't like that...and then, when I sort of totally blocked him out by not talking to him about what was going on, that made it worse." Parents who drive a wedge between themselves and their children only harm the relationship; letting go gracefully enriches it.

letting the kids decide An important part of distancing dictates that parents begin to limit their involvement in decision making or problem solving about their children's lives. As kids grow up, parents should gradually get in the habit of offering advice when situations come up, and then letting children make the final decision. Later parents can slip into the pattern of only giving advice when asked. In other words, they encourage a child's autonomy. At times, parents must force children to make a decision; the children may try to take the easy way out by automatically letting parents decide for them.

Advice is a two-way street and one daughter offered these words to parents: "First, give children lots of encouragement. That helps them. When parents say, 'That's okay, these things happen,' it also makes the parents realize that things will be okay. You can't push. It helps parents cope with everything when they think...the kids are going to be okay. The kids will be responsible.

"Second, parents should guard their tongues and not give too much advice when it isn't asked for. It builds resentment and makes kids mad. Parents need to realize that while kids are living at home they are growing more responsible every day and parents need to treat them that way, too. It lessens the tension and resentment. Lots of kids are just so eager to get out that they jump into things without thinking."

When parents too readily offer their opinions, children may do whatever is recommended without going through the decision-making process of evaluating alternatives, identifying consequences, and making a selection. When parents do not let their children persevere with difficult problems to arrive at effective solutions on their own, then children do not learn to break problems down into manageable-sized pieces. The parents become a crutch, instead of a valuable resource.

Obviously, wise parents do not thrust undue responsibilities or decisions on their children before they are ready; this, too, can be detrimental to maturing children. Parents still have the obligation of cautioning children whenever there are irreversible consequences to a path they might be considering. Many decisions that are made can be easily reversed but some cannot. For example, if a child is contemplating relinquishing a scholarship to a particular school, the likelihood is that the scholarship will not be reoffered once declined. Parents can encourage their sons or daughters to ask, "What's the worst that could happen if I do/say such and such?" This is an extremely useful tool in the development of decision-making skills.

Confidence building for children includes: letting them have their own opinion during arguments or discussions; letting them experience the mutuality of parents who sometimes *give in* or admit that they are wrong; or letting them be the first to solve a problem. When parents take it upon their shoulders to have all the answers, all the time, for any issue that arises, they are usurping their child's prerogative *to be a winner*, sapping the child's struggle toward self-will and self-knowledge. How arrogant are parents who presume to know the *truth* for their child's life.

showing flexibility   A good example of distancing was related by Barbara, a woman in her early forties. The conversation with her son began one night after she came home from work just before the beginning of his senior year's winter break. "When my son said, 'Gee Mom, it's too bad that you're not going on vacation next week,' I knew it had nothing to do with his concern for my welfare! He couldn't afford to go anywhere and if he had to stay home he didn't want me around. He wanted to feel on his own. I wondered if I could find a solution for what otherwise might seem like a dismal week to my son and probably me, as well.

"Eventually I came up with an idea which I thought I could live with, even though I knew it would be difficult. I told him that he could pretend that I wasn't at home for that week...he could come and go as he pleased. I would appreciate any information that he cared to give me, but he didn't have to disclose his whereabouts. He thought it was a great idea! The first night he was out until 4:30 A.M.; I heard him come in. But then he was probably home before midnight the rest of the week. It was a little nerve-racking but I survived.

"It did a lot for his self-image and feeling of independence and that feeling persisted throughout the rest of the school year. In making the decision, I was very aware that once he was at college he could leave campus whenever he wanted for as long as he wanted and I might never know that he had gone to California or Florida or wherever. Going from total control to no control seemed too drastic...like a transition was needed. I don't think parents think about that enough. This seemed like a good way and it worked for us."

open discussion   The final act of preparation, and one recommended by professionals, is for parents and child to sit down and talk openly of their feelings before the actual separation occurs — their feelings of missing each other and yet looking forward to the break. More effective than a single conversation is an ongoing dialogue started during the student's senior year in high school. Regular conversations encourage both parent and child to become comfortable with the process of separating. When done with an air of understanding, there is much less chance that parents will feel hurt or angry, less chance that the child will feel guilty or overprotected.

Because feelings may be conflicting and at opposite poles of the spectrum, there is often a hesitation to speak on this topic. But children can deal better with their parents' pain when it is realisticly counterbalanced by the positive feelings parents are also having. And parents can give support when children feel apprehensive or scared. Both have an obligation to listen and learn how the other feels about this natural parting of ways.

catch-22 As hard as parents try to let go, it may be even harder to feel that children are *gone* when they come home in the summer. Many kids have a tendency to drift back into a childlike role. They may resume patterns of behavior that parents have not had to put up with for months. Said one mother of her son, "When he comes home, it's like having another adult come to live with you when your routine is altogether different. It's disruptive."

The independent-dependent, push-pull struggle can intensify, causing anxiety and confrontations unpleasant in nature. The parents' patience can be severely tested, causing them to lament, "Why should I have to put up with that in my own house when I haven't had to for the past nine months?"

Why indeed? And yet children are hard-pressed to realize that their absence goes hand in hand with a diminished sense of ownership. Slowly their home with its implied prerogatives and privileges is becoming less *theirs* and more *their parents'*. When parents and children don't understand the nature of this transition, the letting go process is prolonged.

SELF-ASSESSMENT FOR PARENTS

why parents don't let go Professional therapists are not the only ones who have insights into the letting go process. A mother of two who admitted to having trouble making the break gave this account of why it is difficult for parents to let go: "I think it's a dependency on the parents' part. Probably they don't feel good about themselves unless they have someone dependent on them, so they want to hang on to that child for their own self-esteem. That's what makes them feel like somebody. The need to be needed is probably very instilled, especially in mothers.

"It's hard to let go little by little, gradually. My husband helped me when he said: 'You can't hang onto them forever. We have raised them as best we could and we raised them so that they'd become responsible human beings and, in order for them to leave home, you have to let go.' It turned the lights on for me. Sometimes it was hard to remember what he said...those words would come back to haunt me from time to time."

Perhaps an example of *not* letting go would also be helpful. The interview with Pam, a mother whose daughter was attending her alma mater, one of the best schools on the West Coast, revealed that her daughter's life had been tightly controlled. The mother confused age, living at home, and the asking of advice with the ability to be independent. Financial dependence, which was the daughter's situation, did not automatically dictate abdication of autonomous ways and independent thought. Pam, by her own admission in an earlier part of the interview, described her daughter as "dependent" and felt that many parents raise dependent children to "reinforce their own self-image." Yet, midsentence, while defending her right to persuade and influence her daughter, she suddenly realized that this might not be in the daughter's best interest, that maybe the daughter was not making up her own mind but merely acting out her parents' expectations.

"At nineteen she's not an adult, not independent. I think that she still likes to have my opinion on subjects. I don't think that she would make any major decision without being sure how both of us felt and, in the end, she usually takes our advice. She usually comes around to the way we think about things..." and here Pam stopped, eyes wide with surprise, "...which is terrible in a way, I guess, but it isn't. It makes...I don't know...I feel like I'm falling in a trap...saying something I didn't mean to say...that is not quite true. Just suddenly going away to school does not make an adult out of somebody. She is transforming into an adult. It's something you earn.

"I think we are giving her the tools by helping her. We may be molding her too much. I still believe that at age nineteen, and eight months into college, she is not an independent person. She gradually will be over the next three years. I think that she still needs...wants help from us. I wouldn't feel good about not offering that help or not giving my opinion. It would be unlike me not to tell her how I feel. I think she...I just want her to know clearly about it. And then if she gathers the information and decides something else then that's fine. I don't think it's manipulative of me to express my opinion. She makes the decision, but she needs the strong opinions that I hold whatever the subject is."

Is the daughter getting the tools to transform into a self-functioning adult? Perhaps not.

Resistance to letting go may be more evident with the *last* child. Parents may throw up innumerable roadblocks to deter separation — such as manipulation of financial support, as already mentioned. Postdeparture, they may maneuver to bring a child home by requiring, for example, unreasonably high grades. While some of these *techniques* may work, clearly, letting go is thwarted.

questions parents should ask themselves Is there a litmus test to give parents a quick indicator of how they are doing in the process of letting go? Of whether they are being supportive and empathetic, without being critical — even when they don't really understand where the child is coming from or what is going on in the child's mind? Of whether they are adequately preparing their child for life after high school? While the list below may not predict success, it may act as a barometer of how well a parent is doing. While some items are aimed at the older teen, many can be phased in during the early teen years.

Note: A *yes* answer signals a caution flag, an area for reflection and reconsideration or an area for discussion with daughter or son.

Areas of self-reliance
* do you cook dinner every night?
* do you always do the grocery shopping?
* do you tell your teenager what to eat?
* do you still wake your teenager up in the morning? make sure she or he gets to school on time? to work on time?
* do you pick up your teenager's room? make the bed?
* do you remind your teenager to do homework? get involved in doing it?
* do you always go clothes shopping with your teenager?
* do you always wash and take care of your teenager's clothes? do her or his ironing?
* do you do your teenager's mending? sew on missing buttons?
* do you tell your teenager what to wear?
* do you tell your teenager when to get a haircut?
* do you pay the insurance on a car your teenager drives all the time?
* if your teenager has a fender-bender, do you take the car for the estimates? to get it fixed?
* if your teenager bounces a check, do you cover it?
* if your teenager runs out of money, do you consistently give more?
* do you often tell your teenager what to do?
* do you always make dentist/doctor appointments for your teenager?
* have you been making college visitation appointments for your teenager?
* have you been more involved in the college selection process than your teenager?

Areas of respect
* do you ever put your teenager down? act rudely? make accusations?
* do you expect your teenager to do something exactly when you want? the way you want — all the time?
* do you tune out when your teenager is talking, especially if the topic seems a little boring? do you interrupt? if busy, do you say so but forget to get back with your teenager later?
* do you trivialize things that seem important to your teenager?
* do you devalue events in your teenager's life by saying, "It's just a phase"?
* do you forget to keep your promises?

Areas of independence
(or, more commonly, "Mind your own business!")
* do you nag at your teenager?
* do you give advice before being asked?
* do you jump in to solve your teenager's problems?
* do you feel that you should always tell your teenager whether you agree with what he or she is doing?
* do you meddle in your teenager's business?
* if someone calls your teenager, do you usually ask who called?
* do you usually ask your teenager how his or her money is spent?
* do you ever open your teenager's mail?
* do you try and monitor what your teenager reads?
* if your teenager's bedroom door is shut, do you walk in without knocking?
* if you are cleaning your teenager's room (and, by the way, why are you?), do you snoop, look into notebooks, read folded pieces of paper, take access to whatever might be out? do you snoop at other times — especially when your teenager isn't home?
* do you always ask your teenager where she or he is going — even during the daytime?
* do you always ask a lot of questions about your teenager's activities, such as who was at the party, what there was to eat, what everybody did?
* do you always make your teenager attend family get-togethers, no matter what? always go with the family on vacation?

more questions   There are other questions which can be asked which demonstrate whether the parent is showing love and mutuality for the child (or getting it from the child) and whether the parent has the ability to reverse roles with the child and be the recipient of nurturing and wisdom. A *yes* answer shows that the relationship is becoming one of interdependency and sharing; a *no* answer means that the parent really wants to keep control over the child and is probably impacting the relationship in a negative way.

Of course, because no parent can expect to be *perfect*, a few negative answers must be expected — at least in certain situations. They should be regarded as areas for future improvement or for discussion with son or daughter. Parents must also keep in mind that when their unconscious wishes and desires are at cross purposes with the verbal statements being given to a child, the resulting message is negative — a *no* answer. Words and behavior go hand-in-hand and must be mutually reinforcing.

Note: A *no* answer signals a caution flag, an area for reflection and reconsideration.

* do you let your teenager see your weak side? admit that you're not perfect?
* do you ever ask your teenager for advice?
* do you learn from your teenager?
* do you let your teenager know when you're upset and may need some TLC (tender loving care) when the reason has nothing to do with the teenager?
* do you let your teenager love you?
* if your teenager disagrees with you about something, can you listen to the reasons and sometimes change your mind?
* do you accept it gracefully if your teenager *wins* an argument?
* do you feel proud of your teenager for standing up to you about something she or he believes in — because you can appreciate the streak of independence being developed, appreciate that this person is a separate person from you?
* if something needs to be decided, do you ever say, "Let's toss a coin"?
* do you sometimes say to your teenager, "I think that's your decision to make"? "Do what you want to do"? "You decide"? "Trust your own judgment"?
* do you sometimes say, "It doesn't matter what I think or feel, what do you think"? "What do you feel"?
* do you ask open-ended questions?
* do you usually show the same respect to your teenager that you would to a friend? talk the same way? act this way?
* do you take what your teenager says seriously?
* if your teenager is not treating you with mutual respect, do

you point it out? stand up for your own rights?
* if your teenager evades an issue under discussion by digressing or changing the subject, do you point that out?
* do you support your teenager — even if she or he does something that you don't understand or wouldn't do personally? even if it seems *a little crazy*?
* if your teenager wants to be alone, do you respect that desire?
* do you show respect for your teenager's wishes, even if you don't gratify them?
* do you show support for your teenager's career goals or other life dreams?
* do you regularly tell (or show) your teenager, "I love you"? "You are a neat person"? "You are special to me"? "I like you"? "I have confidence in you"?
* do you hug your teenager?
* when you think of the future, can you envision your teenager on his or her own? making decisions? operating just fine without you?

IMPEDIMENTS

the economy Aside from inherent human weaknesses in the letting go process, there are also roadblocks thrown up by society. Chief among these are the economy, the lack of support for high-quality education, the rate of change in society today, and the television. Aspects of the economy are almost dichotomous: affluence has raised many of the expectations of young adults to a point that cannot be satisfied upon graduation from college. For these are the *children of entitlement*, children raised to believe that they are entitled to certain things: jobs that give quick advancement, salaries that allow a better-than-average standard of living, and living quarters that measure up to those left at home.

But the prosperity of the 1950s and 1960s when corporations anxiously sought college graduates in an expansionist economy have not returned. Over the last two decades, the economy has been racked with recessions, foreign competition, inflation, and government spending to the point that salaries have not kept pace with the cost of living. Affluence has prevented many youth from knowing the real struggle of want and from desiring independence badly enough to be willing to struggle financially. It is simply easier for young adults to move back home when things aren't as expected. For parents who haven't let go, saying *no* is often impossible.

lack of high-quality education These thoughts, as well as the importance that education plays in preparing children for life, are best captured by the words of psychologist Dr. Lee Epstein:

> My main interest is youngsters' ability to adapt and find appropriate careers for themselves. They have a problem in being able to enter the system through understanding and picking careers. Of the twenty- to twenty-five-year age group, many are lost. Parents and schools haven't shown them what people do in the world, how one starts thinking about that early, or how to prepare for those options. Kids used to do what their dads did. Now there's a high degree of competitiveness (the baby boom has grown up) and it's hard to enter the area you want. The jobs are not there.
>
> Parents should give their child the best education possible and really promote it, maintain it, and discipline it. Children who are prepared educationally have the best chance of separating. If they have a poor education and poor functional skills, they can't succeed in separation. Going back home is a problem. Oh, my God, it's unbelievable!
>
> Kids can't establish themselves in a job and have not learned to tolerate great difficulties to earn money. Kids haven't seen struggle. Parents make it too easy and kids can't deal with doing it themselves. The kids who are doing best are from lower-economic (but not poor) homes—as can happen in single-parent homes.

accelerated rate of change This book is about change, about the transition of parents and children into adult relationships. But human institutions do not prepare people for change, they seek to maintain the status quo. The legal system, government, schools, churches, marriage, and even family and child-rearing practices are meant to insure a sameness based on the assumption that all relationships are permanent.[3] These institutions do little to help individuals adapt to the changes that people can bring to their lives or that can happen to them. Nor do human emotional needs change as rapidly as the outside world.

In some ways young adults are caught in the midst of a society where change is the norm, where values seem in disarray and flux, and where parents try to cope, doing the best they can when the job of being a parent keeps changing. Parents aren't sure what's right or wrong oftentimes.

In a rather short space in history, there has been a decline in religious practice, an increase of sexual activity and contraceptive use, some social acceptance of the use of drugs, an increase in abuse of drugs and alcohol, heightened awareness of child abuse and incest, a dramatic rise in divorce rates, an increase in mobility, a decline in the neighborhood sense of stability and community responsibility, threat of nuclear holocaust, an increase of violent crime, a breakdown of respect for other people, and a recognition that in many ways we have become a narcissistic culture. When parents divorce, remarry, blend families, switch jobs, or change residences, constant adaptation is required.

As a result, parents have to raise children in an unfamiliar environment, one that they did not grow up in themselves. Most people do not plan to be single parents and yet many must adapt to that pressure, as must their children. None of these circumstances make it easy to be a parent.

television Finally, a word about the television. This instrument of escapism has done much to create unrealistic levels of expectation in young people today. Not only are material goods deemed necessary in order to be *in* or *with it*, but most of life's major problems are solved in less than sixty minutes. In the commercials, headaches disappear in less than sixty seconds, cars make a person sexy, and charge cards buy possessions or trips with no worry of later payment. In most of the sitcoms, children have all the answers and parents are made to look stupid. Violence gets high ratings. Real life looks boring. Life has to be sped up and jazzed up to look exciting. But that's not real life. In the midst of all this, parents must raise children who can cope. A tall order.

PROFILE

Susan Lynch had one son, Steve. Although her marriage was a bad one for many years, she did not get divorced until he was in high school. Steve, who left home three years ago, was nationally ranked in football and had his pick of numerous scholarships before deciding on a college six hours from home. Since his departure, Susan had become the top real estate producer in her office and had married a man eight years her junior. They lived overlooking a lake in a home that they had recently built. Susan was clearly a happy woman.

"I felt terrible when Steve left!" She laughed just thinking about it. "At first I thought...what am I going to do without him?...because we became such close friends after we went through the mother-son stage, the teenage stage of fighting each other, and then finally the stage where we learned how to work with each other. We were the best of friends and he was protective of me. Steve's like me. He's a toucher and a hugger. He's emotional and he cries. For that first year he was homesick and I missed him. I didn't sit around and pine away over him but just cried my heart out everytime he came home and had to leave. Or, if he called, I would cry.

"Then one day after about five months...I have no idea why...the transition was made. It was after work and some people were going out and I thought, gosh, I don't have to go home because Steve's not there. I can go home at four in the morning or do whatever I want to do. After that it was kind of neat!" She laughed again. "It marked the first time that I made the transition from being a parent to being a single person. I probably had guilt feelings about how good I did feel because the responsibility was lifted from my shoulders.

"One place where we developed our relationship was that I could look him in the eye and say, 'I was wrong. I got mad about this and I hollered when I shouldn't have.' We went through bad stages. We fought with each other, at first about what he could and couldn't do. You can treat kids like adults to a point...but you can't just forbid things. You can't make threats or punishments that you can't back up. In other words, you don't say, 'You're grounded for a month.' Who wants a moping teenager around for a month? Nothing's worse than that...so you have to be sure that whatever you do or say you stick by it regardless. So if you're going to ground him just do it for two days!

"Was it hard to let go? Yeah. In high school you still think of them as your little boy (or little girl) but they have to have room to make their own mistakes. What's hard as far as being a parent goes is that because you're older and more experienced you know that there are some mistakes that they can make that are irreversible and you want to try and guide them in the right direction so they won't make them.

"One night I was out late because I was showing my horse at a show. I was on my way home and going to bring pizza so I called. Every phone in the house answered! The kids were having this tremendous party. My first reaction was to be mad, but I said, 'Sounds like you're having a good time.' 'Just a few people here,' he said. Well, hell, few people my foot. 'I'm going to get a pizza and be there in twenty minutes.'

"There wasn't a beer can, there wasn't a thing! It looked like my cleaning lady had been there. It looked fantastic. I thought about it on the way home. I was still mad, but I realized that I would rather have him at the house than out driving around on the streets. So thank goodness I had the ability to think it through. A lot of people would have just screamed and hollared and grounded him for a month and that wouldn't have solved a single, solitary problem.

"So what we were able to do, because I was able to keep my cool, was allow him to come to me in the future and say, 'Can we do this? Can we do that?' rather than sneak around behind my back. I told him that I couldn't guarantee him that I would never get mad or disagree but if I found out that he was lying to me it would be twice as bad. It didn't work out all the time but eighty/twenty is not a bad deal." Susan's eyes twinkled and she chuckled. "It worked out better in the long run.

"We had certain guidelines and rules. For example, nobody was allowed in the house if I wasn't there. I did not let him spend the night out. I would buy beer and make kids call their parents when they were going to spend the night. He had a car and he could drive if certain chores were done but he couldn't drink and drive.

"One night he came home tipsy, all puffed up like big toad. In our former relationship I would have been...God...just furious. But I had learned that if I screamed like a shrew it was just not going to work, so I said: 'I thought we had a deal.' He said: 'Fuck you and your deals.'" Just thinking of Steve saying this made Susan laugh. "And I said, 'Oh, well maybe we just better talk about it in the morning. Why don't you just go to bed?' All the time I'm thinking I could just kill the brat, just kill him. He said: 'I'm going over to Joe's and spend the night there.' 'No you're not.' 'You can't stop me.' (Now, he's so big that he's probably right!) 'Well I probably could stop you if I wanted to.' 'Well how you going to do it?' And I thought, Jesus, Mary, and Joseph, what am I going to do?

"So I walked out into the garage, and I got this broom. He said, 'What you going to do with the broom?' And I said, 'You said you wanted to leave. So go ahead, but this broom is going to go with you, sweetheart, and I think it's going to be somewhere where I don't think you want it.' My heart's going like this." She made a fast-beating sign on her chest with her hand. "'Humpf! Well, I'll just wait till you go to sleep.' 'Bet I can stay awake longer than you do.' And there we stood staring at each other, and I thought what am I going to do? This is the most ridiculous thing. I think I'm going to cry. I'm going to lose it in about two seconds. Finally, he just turned around and tucked tail and closed his bedroom door and that was it. The next day he sent me some roses with a note and from then on he called me the broom lady. He told everybody about it. I guess it was just our test. Of course, I just cried and bawled and it was terrible. But what else could I do? Let him go? I don't think so. It worked, whatever it was.

"Before he left there was more closeness. We spent more time together. There was more consideration, with Steve not wanting to run around with friends all that much. He came to appreciate more some of the things he had taken for granted, knowing that he was going to leave. We went out dancing. Some people even thought I was his girlfriend. I think he knew he was going to miss the friendship and the home that we had created.

"I miss the companionship. I miss having his friends around. But you can take anything in your life and say, 'Woe is me,' and drown in your sorrows. You make it what it is. You have to look at things on the positive side. I got to go watch his games...and then it was only a few hours to Florida and the beach!

"After he left I had more time for my career. It became more important. I could work more nights and weekends...all those extra hours! I became the best performer that year.

"There was a transition to doing things for myself. I had married at eighteen and now, all of sudden, I was number one for the first time ever. I exercised. Took dancing lessons. Did my makeup and hair and nails. Made a lot of money. My son was just as proud of me as he could possibly be. So it was fun. It was fantastic! One night after my dancing lesson, I stopped to check on my horse and that's how I met my husband.

"I do have a fear of getting old. I don't feel old but I can look in the mirror and see lines and stuff. Recently Steve said to me, 'You get your hair frosted?' 'No,' I said, 'it's just getting gray!'

"It has to be a big change for a kid when you've been as close as we have, to have someone else come into your house. Then my husband and I built this house. I don't think Steve feels that he belongs anymore. But then, he's got his own life to look forward to."

And so does she.

1. Writer Marsha Norman, as quoted in "Marsha Norman hopes to stay on top of Wheel of Fortune with her first novel" by Ira Simmons, *The Courier-Journal*, May 3, 1987, p. 19.
2. In *Children of the Dream* (p. 207), Bettelheim discusses adolescent revolt. In addition to (1) affluence allowing society to refrain from child labor, thereby perpetuating the economic dependence of youth, there must be (2) customs that parents expect to have perpetuated by their children, but which are actually breaking down, and (3) a cultural expectation that children will be sexually inactive after sexual maturity has already been reached.
3. Gail Sheehy, *Pathfinders* (New York: William Morrow and Company, Inc., 1981) p. 96.

CHAPTER 10

MYTHS OF MIDLIFE

> *I was talking to my son about his sister leaving for school and all of a sudden he laughed and said that he'd have to get me a rocking chair or something. He saw my life as almost over.*
> *I see it as just beginning.*

MISCONCEPTIONS

perception of distress About the time children start leaving home, most mothers and fathers have entered the midlife phase — generally defined as that period between age forty and age sixty. While thoughts of self-examination may not necessarily be a direct result of a child's actual or impending departure, there can be little doubt that the two are often closely linked in the parent's mind. The letting go that occurs during the teen years sets the stage.

For some parents, the midlife transition is relatively smooth; for others, a dramatic upheaval. To deal with this period in people's lives, words or phrases have evolved which immediately call to mind an individual in distress, an individual victimized, an individual out of control: empty nest syndrome, male menopause, menopause, midlife crisis, male climacteric.

reality as alternative While perceptions in people's minds are one thing, reality may be quite a bit different:

* "I'm still waiting for the empty nest syndrome to happen. It hasn't happened yet so I'm beginning to wonder what's wrong with me."
* "Their mother was in med school so she didn't have time to

miss them. There was no empty nest for her because she was never in it!"
* "I don't want to wake up when I'm fifty and decide hey! I should have done this when I was thirty or forty. I've got things to do and places to go. A year is just no amount of time."
* "All of a sudden being chairman of the board or president isn't nearly as attractive as I thought it was at age twenty-five. I make a certain amount of money...for what? Four weeks of vacation are nicer than two; six nicer than four."
* "My new Porsche...that's my midlife crisis! And according to Mary it's better than my getting a new wife!"

Do these sound like statements of distressed individuals? People depressed and overcome with dysfunction? Mothers and fathers unable to continue with life? Of course not.

Could these be statements of people looking at and evaluating their lives? Individuals making changes in their lives? Fathers and mothers embarking on a new phase without the responsibilities of children? Definitely.

labeling A number of factors seem to contribute to misconceptions about the midlife years. One is the automatic inclination of our society to put a label on people, things, or happenings that can be grouped together. While this practice makes identification easier, it also increases the tendency to categorize something or someone when not appropriate. The label may take on the air of being all-inclusive or infallible, even when future studies indicate that most people do not fall under the label or that there is a trend in another direction.

midlife relatively new stage Another factor leading to misconceptions about middle age is that a complete understanding of this period, as representing a distinct stage of adult development, is still evolving. Few people worried about midlife at the turn of the century: life expectancies were such that midlife did not really exist. Life expectancy at birth for the average American was age forty-seven; many died during childhood. (Once past childhood, of course, an individual's life expectancy rose.) In addition, women in the 1900s had their last child at an older age than most women currently do — primarily because women today have smaller families — and were often in their mid-fifties when the last child left home.[1]

Thus, as life spans lengthened and the dropping birth rate expanded parents' *child-free* years, the period of middle age took on an identity of its own. In contrast to the almost nonexistent empty nest life at the turn of the century when couples often had only a year or two together before the husband died (frequently he had already died before the last child left), couples in 1970 could expect to spend thirteen empty nest years together before one of them died.[2]

Although often closely linked to the departure of children from home, the term *midlife* typically relates to an individual's age (i.e., age forty to age sixty) and not to the status of her or his children; a middle-aged individual during the 1990s can be parent of a two-year-old or grandparent — or both.

Most major books on midlife have been published during the past two decades. While Gail Sheehy's best seller, *Passages*, investigated both men and women, other midlife books have predominately covered the lives of men who were married. Best known among them is Daniel Levinson's *The Seasons of a Man's Life*.

Understandably, the indepth look at men made sense: as breadwinners and financial supporters of the family unit, husbands in a state of midlife crisis had the potential to be a threatening disruption to the time-honored expectations of society. One suspects that the midlife passage of women was not worth investigating because of its relatively small economic impact. Only more recently have books addressing the midlife concerns of women reached the bookshelves.

changing demographics   As existing midlife books age and new ones are written, research data and subsequent conclusions may have a difficult time keeping up with and reflecting current reality because the demographics of society are shifting so rapidly: the traditional two-parent family supported by the husband is slowly disappearing, women now work in increasing numbers, more and more women have careers of long standing, some couples delay having children, single-parent families continue to increase, more fathers gain custody of children, many people remain unmarried, single women (and men) decide to raise children, and blended families proliferate. All of these changes mean that there is no clearcut role model for women. In particular, the image of a midlife mother covers a wide spectrum: she may have young children, have children leaving home, or already be a grandmother; she may not work at all, work part-time, or have a consuming career; she may be married, divorced, or never-married. There is no norm.

Not only is the middle-aged population extremely fluid, but it will remain in a state of continual change for years to come. Perhaps this fluidity and the newness of the middle-aged group are the reasons that researchers have difficulty identifying predictors of midlife crises, although education and economic security do seem to provide a safe framework for introspection. Ultimately, a midlife transition may have not only a cost in terms of real dollars, but also in terms of security forfeited — as might be the case for a parent who leaves a high-paying corporate job to become a farmer or storekeeper.

Generalizations about people often persist because they have a certain validity. But at what point does that validity disappear and no longer apply to a whole group of people? The uncertainty of what to make of middle age combined with the penchant for labeling people, it seems, are precisely the reasons that misconceptions or *myths* of middle age have arisen — so-called facts which do not hold up under close scrutiny.

WHAT ARE THESE MYTHS?

myth: most midlife symptoms are hormonal and unpleasant The symptoms of midlife can be numerous: depressed feelings, physical limitations, confusion, fear of the future, anger, turmoil, self-doubt, emotional instability, introspection. Popular belief could lead one to conclude that these symptoms are most unpleasant and stem simply from changes in the body's hormonal system, as reflected in the steady use of the terms *menopause, male menopause,* and *climacteric*. Particularly this belief is prevalent about women: midlife fluctuations are regularly attributed to *the change of life*.

Fortunately, midlife is more than just hormones. It encompasses a breadth and magnitude of experiences and feelings that cannot be conveyed easily by one or two words. Instead of reflecting the positive side of midlife and the possibilities for growth, comments often dwell on the negative aspects.

In the end, a person must understand that these symptoms are not abnormal or unnatural. *This* is what midlife actually is. Each individual passing through middle age is helping to create a revised image of midlife in America's society. Yet for the sake of using popular jargon in the media, the labels stick, making midlife not a time of healthy change, but a time to be dreaded.

myth: some fathers suffer from male menopause Menopause means a cessation of the menses. By definition, then, male menopause does not exist. What the term has come to mean, however, is those eccentric conditions which manifest themselves in men when for years people wanted to believe that only women could be the victims. The symptoms are more correctly ascribed to the male climacteric (a lessening of sexual competence and activity) or to the midlife transition, itself.

myth: most mothers suffer from empty nest syndrome Empty nest syndrome is a clinical term used to describe a state of depression in women brought on by the departure of children from the home. A complete description of the syndrome, though, goes beyond just missing one's children; its symptoms include profound despair, loss of self-esteem, inactivity, difficulty in thinking and concentration, sleeplessness, loss of appetite and sexual desire, inability to deal with daily affairs, and the inability to relate to anything in life in a positive manner.

Original study of the empty nest syndrome was conducted on hospitalized women already in a state of crisis, without reference to an unbiased sample group including nonhospitalized women. The implication was that most women would suffer from empty nest syndrome in spite of the fact that, says psychologist Ann Block, "By the time we found a label, things began to change." Once again the label stuck in people's minds and the empty nest condition had been anticipated in the lives of countless mothers.

Psychologist Lillian Rubin in her book, *Women of a Certain Age*, describes the perpetuation of the empty nest myth in some detail by examining studies of postparenthood women in the late 1960s and 1970s. When early studies reported acceptance and feelings of relief after the departure of children, the findings were basically disregarded because they contradicted the notion of the empty nest syndrome. Experts concluded that the women surveyed had repressed their true feelings. By the mid-1970s, surveyed women were revealing increased marital satisfaction. Studies in the late 1970s which showed not only greater marital contentment, but an increased sense of well-being, received little attention because they did not conform to the supposed stereotype of the grieving and depressed mother. This led Rubin to conclude that the "myth of motherhood" is so strong and pervasive in our society that women have been encouraged not to express their feelings and are made to feel guilty or unnatural as mothers if they are not sufficiently upset over the departure of their children. This dictum of how *perfect* mothers must act perpetuates the notion that womanhood is synonymous with motherhood.[3]

While some women may experience such symptoms, evidence that most do not is mounting. Today's women in their forties and fifties are much more mentally healthy than their counterparts of twenty years ago.[4] Thanks in large part to the women's movement, options pertaining to *what to do with my life* and *what to be after the children leave* are primarily limited by a woman's imagination, energy, and drive. More and more women plan ahead to prepare themselves for their children's departure; they are not caught unawares by an empty nest cliché.

When asked about their feelings during interviews for this book, "Wonderful!" was a common response by both mothers and fathers who no longer had any children residing at home. Yet Rubin's theory on the myth of motherhood was frequently borne out by the embarrassed laughter of mothers which followed this reply, often with a quick glance to see if anyone else might have heard this ever-so-honest admission.

myth: most fathers have a midlife crisis In spite of all the research conducted about midlife men, statistics and conclusions are somewhat contradictive and inconclusive. Certainly, many men do have midlife crises but there appear to be too many variables to draw any firm conclusions — variables like exactly how the term *midlife crisis* is defined, what role normal anxiety plays, and which precise age group is affected most. For example, one researcher said that eighty percent of the small sample of surveyed men were affected; the maximum age of the group was age forty-five. A larger survey said midlife symptoms were most evident in the forty-five- to forty-nine-year-old group when compared to younger men. As researchers continue to examine adult development stages, statistics are often not used and one is forced to speculate if perhaps the change which occurs during each development stage is not more the norm and less a state of crisis.

In his book, *The 40- to 60-Year Old Male*, McGill defines the midlife crisis as a time when there is "a rapid and substantial change in personality and behavior" which is "not necessarily negative or disruptive to the individual's development" and which affects close to one third of the men in this age group.[5] So, although a sizeable number of men do experience a midlife crisis, according to this researcher, the majority do not. For those who do, the transition is not necessarily as debilitating as the word *crisis* denotes and, for this reason, the phrase *midlife passage* has gained popular appeal. Also, as men have become more open in discussing their personal feelings, the perception may have arisen that a great many men are in crisis when, in fact, they are not.

myth: no empty nest syndrome for fathers/no midlife crisis for mothers "Men have a midlife crisis, right? Women either react against it or they're the victim of it. Empty nest syndrome, that's what women have."

While this comment by a well-educated mother echoes the perceptions held by many people, such narrow sexually-stereotyped conclusions about individual lives are coming under attack in current literature. As women are trying to free themselves of the empty nest label, some psychologists are using it to describe fathers. Because empty nest depression in midlife women has often been associated with menopause, depression in men over the loss of children has not been viewed as a potentially significant factor in the male midlife crisis.[6] In other words, if being depressed over the loss of the mother role could happen to women, it didn't necessarily follow that men could mourn the loss of the father role. Yet, fathers can be very wrapped up in their children's lives and activities; some fathers can and do play a nurturing role within the family. Others may live and achieve vicariously through their children, especially their sons.

Conversely, because many professional women have been in the work force for a number of years, their pattern of self-evaluation may more closely parallel the man's middle-aged passage and involve a critical career or marital analysis, not simply a readjustment to life without children or a menopausal transition. Women, then, are candidates for full-fledged identity crises. The empty nest and menopause can cease being the general catch-all for every symptom and problem which occur during a woman's midlife passage.

myth: anxiety about retirement from motherhood is pathological
If women view children leaving the nest as an end to their *jobs* as mothers, the situation is no different than men who retire from their jobs at age sixty-five. Many men do have an extremely difficult time adjusting to retirement, including periods of depression. And yet, only women are seen as having a *pathological attachment* if distressed when they retire from motherhood. Both situations, though, are similiar: each involves a retirement from an attachment which has provided a sense of purpose and identity.[7]

myth: midlife parents have all the answers   As people get older, there is a tendency to assume that they have discovered all the answers, that they won't be changing much, and that their lives are fairly set for the future. But that's rarely the case. They don't have all the answers. In fact, sometimes they feel like they don't have any answers. Change is still an important component of their identities. Their lives are not set. Separation from one's children is one more step in the developmental sequence of adulthood and, just as one may initally feel unprepared for parenthood, nothing can totally prepare parents for the second phase of their lives — that of living without children once again.

myth: "with-it" mothers don't feel intense loss when a child leaves
While most women do not sink into depression at the departure of children, there can often be a brief, but intense, period of emptiness and loss. The issue is oversimplified by asking the question, "Do mothers get depressed or do they feel relief?" A middle ground exists where the sadness and mourning for the departed child can be expressed and cried about — a middle ground where parents deal with an empty heart, not an empty nest.

Both parents need to understand that it's okay to feel sad, to feel lonely, and to grieve for a few days, a few weeks, or even a few months. Such grieving rarely leads to long-term devastation. Parents do not have to deny that they are going to miss their children by making comments which only express their feelings of relief. Perhaps the aspect that is most indicative of whether the *missing* is healthy or not comes from an honest acknowledgement of exactly what is being missed. Missing the child-as-person is healthy. Missing the relationship and times shared together is healthy. But resenting the loss of the active role of mother or father is not healthy; this is clinging to the past when life is moving on.

1. Judith Treas and Vern L. Bengtson, "The Demography of Mid- and Late-Life Transitions," *The Annals of The American Academy of Political and Social Science*, Vol. 464 ed. Felix M. Berardo (Beverly Hills: Sage Publications, 1982) pp. 13 and 15.
2. John Kotre and Elizabeth Hall, *Seasons of Life* (Boston: Little, Brown and Company, 1990) p. 281.
3. New York: Harper & Row, 1979, pp. 24-27 and 228-229.
4. Cohen, et al., p. 9.
5. p. 43.
6. McGill, p. 138.
7. Linda T. Sanford and Mary Ellen Donovan, *Women and Self-Esteem* (Garden City, New York: Anchor Press/Doubleday, 1984) pp. 222-223.

CHAPTER 11

PARENTS FORCED INTO SELF-EXAMINATION

> *When I was a boy of fourteen, my father was so ignorant I could hardly stand to have the old man around. But when I got to be twenty-one, I was astonished at how much he had learned in seven years.*

ISSUES OF MIDLIFE

principle issues Parents find this gem of wisdom by Mark Twain humorous because it is, obviously, the child who has grown up and matured. But not only can the child discover the *new person* within, the parent also may evolve and change in a process of self-discovery. Studies show that several issues exist for adults during middle age:

* launching of children and letting go
* realizing that their bodies are looking older and running down
* coming to grips with their own mortality (usually due to the death of a parent)
* evaluating and measuring a career on the success barometer
* readjusting personal relationships
* taking stock of personal well-being and general quality of life
* setting of new directions

change Exactly what these issues mean to men or women may vary. Whether or not each mother and father chooses to confront any or all issues, and when, also varies greatly. By their very evaluation, however, change is a common byproduct — for introspection or self-criticism without follow-up is pointless. Because the nature of human beings is to resist change and cling to what is familiar, individuals who avoid this process resign themselves to protecting the status quo and may even deny the actual truth of what is happening in their lives. Yet the family unit and parental roles are not permanent; previous patterns of relating do become outdated and ineffectual. Change becomes a challenge, yet *what to change* and *how much* are not easy decisions.

Uncomfortable as change is, the act of facing the unknown, of making a decision, and of going forward serves to bolster self-confidence and create a pattern of growth. As much as people would like, growth does not come without a price — as expressed in the oft-used phrase, "No pain, no gain." In order to move forward, something must be given up or put at risk, and a person often endures a preliminary period of discomfort. This is the reason people sometimes talk about doing a *cost accounting* to determine the costs of making a change, to balance these costs against the rewards, to weigh the positive against the negative.

When the rewards are obvious and outweigh the costs, then change may be easy. When the costs of not making the change jump out (for example, "If I don't do thus and so, I can't pay my bills"), change may become inevitable. When disgust or anger or fright of current behavior is great enough, then an individual may finally be motivated to change. When an event happens *to* a person, change is almost certain. The more dramatic the event, the more certain and, perhaps, dramatic the change.

When a child leaves home, an event has occurred in the parents' lives that may or may not seem dramatic. If the event has been actively anticipated, change may already be in process. If preparation has not been made in advance, change will still result but be forced and unwelcome. Ultimately, this difference is reflected by whether individuals feel that they are taking action or being acted upon.

"I've always welcomed change," said one parent. "Change excites me. That's what life is. That's the process and I love it." Parents benefit when they view change as having a positive effect on their lives. Change is complicated and not always external and visable to friends and family; it may be internal and intensely personal. Change takes energy and time. And because the rewards and pleasures of change are not always immediate, keeping a long-term perspective can be extremely important.

phases of transition Gail Sheehy's book, *Pathfinders*, outlines the four phases that occur during a passage or transition in a person's life. First is the anticipation stage where an individual achieves a receptivity or openness of mind in preparation for what lies ahead. Next is the separation and incubation phase during which time the old rules and restrictions are put aside in order to make room for new ideas and a revised self-image. At this point a person must grapple with the issues and acknowledge that there will be consequences, personally and for others, arising from the changes made.

The third stage is that of expansion: a person makes a firm commitment to change patterns of response and the people support systems that they interact with on a regular basis — as though rewriting life's script. And, finally, in the last stage a person reaches the incorporation phase when survival seems easier and there is breathing room to absorb what has occurred, to relax, and to reflect in a feeling of well-being.[1]

children's leaving as catalyst The departure of children can act as a catalyst for introspection, motivating or forcing parents to recognize that they are in a midlife passage. Identity issues that may have been shelved while the kids were still at home can now be addressed.

By their very act of leaving, children free enormous amounts of their parents' time, energy, and, if not immediately then eventually, money. Parents are generally not aware of how extensive the inhibiting nature of children is while they still live at home, but once they are gone parents have the space to address issues more clearly, however painful. Parents can begin to question what they want to do with this excess time and energy now that their role as parent has diminished or viritually disappeared. What they really ask is: "Who am I? What do I want to do with the rest of my life?"

For the first time in a long while, parents have space to think, to be themselves, to do for themselves, to look inside themselves. No longer do they have to give constant consideration to the effect something might have on their children's lives. No longer do they have to do something just to escape from their children's interruptions, demands, and presence.

growth at midlife What is this midlife process? Although there is a danger of oversimplifying in chart form something as complex as self-discovery, the following will provide a framework for discussion.

Growth at Midlife

Area of Self-evaluation	Self-discovery: Men	Self-discovery: Women
role as parent	*feelings of completion or regret at having missed out *end of provider role (and perhaps nurturer role)	*feelings of completion or failure *seeing children as validation *end of nurturer role (and perhaps provider role) *overcoming resentment or anger
aging and the body	*concern about sexual performance and climacteric *acceptance of age	*concern about sexual attractiveness and menopause *acceptance of age
mortality	*dealing with own mortality	*dealing with own mortality and shorter life span of husband *possibility of a life alone
job/career	*decreasing importance, changing careers, or making final push to top	*starting or returning to work, going back to school, or accepting homemaker status *enjoying financial independence *discovering thrill of power *career women: same evaluation as men
personal relationships	*effort to improve nurturing skills and develop friendships	*importance often decreases
	*marriage: acknowledgement that "we have to live with and for each other" may lead to marked improvement and sharing, but divorce or acceptance of status quo not uncommon	
life assessment and setting new directions	*looking beyond image derived from job and role as provider	*looking beyond image derived from relationships and roles as wife and mother

There are a number of excellent books on middle age based on interviews with men or women, some supplemented with a broad spectrum of questionnaire responses. The space of this chapter and the next cannot possibly condense the content of many books, except in summary form. But the impact that children leaving home contributes to this process can be examined. One of the first areas that parents look at is the kind of job that they have done as parents.

ROLE AS PARENT

positive feelings about parenthood Raising children usually gives parents a great sense of accomplishment. Wonderful feelings may arise when parents reflect positively on their role. Said one mother of raising her daughter, "I've done a very good job with her. I think that she is a super, super, neat person. I hope that I can pull it off with the second one."

A father echoed similar thoughts, "I'm proud of them. I like them. I think they've turned out pretty well...especially if you look at all the things that can go wrong nowadays. I don't know if we get all the credit, but I'll certainly take some of it. Being a good parent is not easy."

Parenthood may also create a healthy bonding within marriage. During one interview, a father touchingly reached over and placed a hand on his wife's arm. "A better mother they couldn't have had," he said. "All the boys have realized that." She was a little embarrassed but clearly enjoyed sharing this special moment with her husband.

"Some mothers feel relief," said Ann, a mother of four. "To a certain degree I do, too. Given all the circumstances I think that I've done a pretty good job and I think my kids reflect that. I know my kids love me. We've had our squabbles but they know I care. They know they can come to me for help. I do feel a sense of loss but I feel a sense of satisfaction." The tears were gently welling up in Ann's eyes. Then she added, as if bringing herself back to reality, "Of course, I also feel a sense of freedom to do what I want to do."

The enrichment and joy that children bring to parents' lives is often of a general nature — part of the big picture. As the nest empties, parents may specifically ask themselves, "What kind of job did I do?" In examining their roles, doubts can arise. Those areas which have caused difficulties may be foremost on parents' minds. So, instead of discussing the positive aspects of parenthood, parents' comments often reflect the complications that children bring.

children of choice Before further investigation of how midlife adults evaluate the job that they have done as parents, speculation about the underlying cause of the guilt that so many parents experience is tempting. Rollo May, in his 1969 book, *Love and Will*, speaks to the root of the problem — the "dilemma of personal responsibility" which arises from

> ...the freedom to choose to have a baby or not. It has been possible to plan babies for the last four decades, and though we have acted upon that power, we have never accepted the psychological and personal responsibility for it. Our blithe evasion of that issue comes out in the guilt we feel as a whole society toward our children. We do everything for them, we cater to their development and their whims, we count it a sign of our broadmindedness and virtue that we give in to them on every moral issue (and now on marijuana) so that the poor children have an impossible time trying to find something about these always-giving-in parents against which they can revolt. When they go away, we say, "Have a good time," and we get worried if they don't have a good time and worried if they have *too* good a time. And all the while we are secretly envious of them and their youth and resentful at how good they have it as compared with how hard we had it. Through all of this treating our young like little royalty, heirs apparent to heaven knows what, we are the maids-in-waiting, chauffeurs, cooks, nurses, bottomless money-bags, home teachers, camp leaders—until it is no wonder our children stand up and scream, "For heaven's sake, leave us *alone!*" And that is the biggest threat of all to us — for we are filled with some nameless, pervasive guilt about our children and can't let go. And the guilt we are expiating is not about some specific thing we did or didn't do in rearing them; it is about the basic fact of having children in the first place. For no longer does "God" decide we are to have children; we do. And who has even begun to comprehend the meaning of that tremendous fact?[2]

Of course, not all parents feel that their children were planned; often they were not.

negative feelings about parenthood Frequently, parents submerge negative feelings brought about by offspring. Such feelings may surface as the kids leave, confronting parents with the fact that:

* they never really wanted children

* they had too many
* the timing was bad
* they wanted a different sex
* in hindsight, they shouldn't have had one or all of the children
* they never really loved one or all of the children
* they are much better off now that the children are gone
* they were constantly reminded of an unwanted or unloved spouse or relative by one of the children and, consequently, projected bad feelings onto that child
* they didn't like one of the children for a particular reason(s) and are glad that the child is no longer around to make them feel uncomfortable on a daily basis
* they tried, but they were't made to be parents
* the investment in time, money, or effort wasn't worth it
* the relief that parenthood is over offsets any negative assessment about the quality of the job done

In fact, many parents admit that they wouldn't have children if they had it to do over again — not that they're necessarily sorry they did, but rather they're not sure that they would repeat the experience. Suppositions based on hindsight may not be terribly important but they do indicate some of the more honest thoughts parents may be having.

children as women's identity The evaluation of parenthood is of particular significance to homemakers (and often working mothers) for just as a career becomes the essence of many men so, too, the child becomes the reflection of countless women. The child has been the homemaker's career; evaluating the role as parent is synonymous with assessing the career of her lifetime.

Mothers who have dedicated their lives to rearing children feel a crucial validation resting with the results. When mothers (particularly those who have remained at home) have closely shaped their children's lives and religiously met the children's needs, offspring must not only prove themselves, they must vindicate their mothers — including the sacrifices she made, the effort she expended and the personal goals that she aborted along the way. Having dedicated so much (perhaps too much) of their lives to their children, mothers can end up feeling insignificant — even of no value when those children leave home. By having assigned special qualities to themselves and their nurturing skills in order to justify their *being*, women often convince themselves that staying home and taking care of the children is the ultimate purpose in life.

Consequently, when children leave and there is no longer a

family member to take care of, the value of these magical and special qualities doesn't hold up. There is little left but a psychological dependence. Some women can only conclude that the sacrifice wasn't worth it — they were sold a bill of goods. Mothers may ask themselves, "If my kids don't need me, who does? Who am I really?" Mothers with large families may particularly feel the impact when the last child leaves. Up until that time, the loss seems gradual. "When the last one left, the whole bottom dropped out," reflected the mother of six kids. "It was the whole impact that hit me rather than the one child that had just left. Suddenly, I didn't have anybody."

While some mothers worry that they gave too much, other mothers (particularly those who worked outside the home) fret that they didn't give enough. When there is another family member upon whom these special qualities can be displaced — say, an aging parent — then the crisis may be avoided.

Joyce was an example of a parent who judged herself a failure. Although she had not sacrificed her life to her children and had a meaningful career, there was an air of defeat when she talked about her son who had left for the Army after numerous high school failures. She had given as much as she could to this son but the effort never seemed adequate.

"It went real fast from the time he was born until he was gone. It's like all those things you think that you'll have as a tradition later...but you never got started. You think you've got these kids forever when you're changing diapers. You don't think it will end...and then it does and they're gone. I don't have a lot of regrets, it's just that...I always wanted to take a motor trip out West with all the kids...and it's gone...we never did it.

"It seems like there's a whole lot of stuff I didn't tell him yet. You know how people are always saying, 'My mother was so strong,' or 'My mother did this,' or 'I couldn't have done it without my mother,' or whatever? I can't look at him and think that I did that for him at any level...except maybe a seat belt. And you know, that's not a very big accomplishment for all those years. I don't like him a lot...some of the time. I am beginning to enjoy him when I don't live with him." Undoubtedly she gave him more than she stated here, but the pain of her feelings of failure was evident.

judging children Children who are judged *successful* mean that mother, and therefore the parents, have done a good job. Mom may have done most of the work raising the children but the *halo effect* applies and dad gets the credit, too. Anger can erupt when a woman gets in touch with her resentment at this seemingly unfair situation.

Ironically, the reverse does not always hold true: mothers often receive more blame when things go wrong. Nonetheless, if the accomplishments of the children outweigh the feelings of loss, then most parents reflect a sense of satisfaction.

Children not yet in control of their lives, those floundering or having troubled times, those parents disapprove of, or those who seem unsuccessful cause parents, particularly mothers, to evaluate themselves harshly and feel that they are to blame. Sensing that their role is unfinished or that they have failed can intensify feelings of grief at the child's departure.

Such premature evaluations of children, and thus their parents, are grossly unfair to everyone involved. To place a *final* evaluation on twenty-year-olds who have perhaps three-fourths of their lives ahead of them verges on the absurd. Yet parents all too often view a young adult as not measuring up — simply because the parents expect too much. In the end, both parents and child suffer negative side effects.

judging parents Direct or inadvertent criticism — particularly if that criticism comes from the spouse or the daughter or son — can trigger much self-doubt, anger, and dejection. A man can be challenged for his generation-linked work values — those which consistently paid the bills and yet are now put down by his children as morally unethical, lacking in social awareness, or causing an unbalanced life. Men who isolate the philosophical issues from direct criticism of themselves are better able to dilute their own hostility and resentment.

A woman can feel that a huge part of her life has been discounted or trivialized when her skills as a mother are questioned. Only when women redefine themselves as separate beings can the interweaving of their self-image with that of their children stop. Only then can women feel comfortable not needing their children now that the children no longer need them.

Working mothers may be even harsher in their self-evaluation because they know that their children did not always come first. Even though working mothers compare favorably to nonworking mothers in the amount of emphasis that they place on the importance of children and the value of motherhood,[3] they know that there were times when the socially-defined role of mother took a back seat to a pragmatic balancing of career and mothering, and they felt guilty deciding exactly where this balance lay. If fathers were not as often caught in this bind, mothers may have residual resentment toward the parenting duties that constantly impinged on their everyday life. If fathers were not a part of the family unit or the child's development, then the single-parent working mother may hold herself doubly responsible for the child's outcome and, if things went wrong, feel that there is no one to share the blame. Only when parents can free themselves of the *have to*s — those feelings of compelling responsibility — can they be more accepting of themselves as parents on their own terms.

When self-criticism does arise, it need not be flagellating but can be reflective in nature, as shown by the following comments:

* "My son has no strategies for making plans and following them through. I assume a lot of guilt for that because I can do that at the drop of a hat. I think I probably paralyzed him when he was younger...I always had forty ideas for his social studies project...or it could be just his nature. That's the situation mothers get into: you don't know whether to bear the guilt or not. And, of course, it doesn't do any good to feel guilty."
* "I regret letting her manipulate me too much. She doesn't have money sense...maybe she should have had a job. Maybe I should have been firmer. At least I know she manipulates me."
* "I don't think I did a fantastically wonderful job but I don't think that I did a terrible job either. I guess it's the kind of person I am...a mediocre, middle-class..." This mother paused to laugh. "I guess that's the category I fall in as a mother as well. I feel that we did give the children a Christian home and in doing that we did more for them than anything else we could have done. Even if they drift away from the church for a time, they will remember and get back to it."
* "I figure that I did a pretty not-okay job in her early years and misunderstood who she was and how she was put together and hoped that she would conform to what I thought was the way a girl would be. She was not very disciplined and I was afraid of her. I didn't want to have to handle it. Then I feel that I did a number of personal things that got my act together so I could accept what she wanted to do. It was her choice and her life by that time. She seemed to really appreciate that I had made that decision...we can even talk about it now."
* "There were things I did when my daughter was young that I regret intensely. I was much too immature and innocent and my husband and I were going through a period of great stress in our relationship and I had nowhere to turn. I reacted by getting angry at Kim for things that she hadn't done at all. I took out my own frustrations on her. Now, when something bothers her, we probe back to those years to see if they are the cause."

clinging to parenthood   Women who are not able to reconstruct themselves emotionally and who are feeling useless often find ways to cling to the mothering self-image through outlets that they seek or through active involvement in the upbringing of their grandchildren. One mother who felt that she had let her children down postulated that "...perhaps grandchildren let you complete what you didn't finish." Even when they know that it makes no practical sense, women may yearn for another child to fill the void or because they sense that they could do a better job. As shown in the Profile of Ray Shafer, fathers with younger second wives are tempted to act out this wish — and some do.

Other attempts to prolong the parenthood role are not uncommon. One young adult explained how her parents had begun adoption procedures for a hard-to-place child. Its failure to go through had been a real blow to her mother. "I think that it will be strange for her not to be a mother, not to be raising children. She's amazing at it and she wanted to keep doing it. In a way, it's the one thing that she feels that she's really done well in her life." Two years later her parents were divorced.

A touch of irony, perhaps, also plays a role in this clinging to parenthood. For, in many parents' minds, just as they have finally finished the nest — nice furniture, house fixed up, life in an orderly fashion, a settled marriage — the fledgings leave. Having worked hard and established the means for a secure family life, parents want to sit back and enjoy the nest — only to see it empty. To some, it seems a little unfair.

empty nest jolt for some fathers   When fathers have spent the largest part of their lives in pursuit of the breadwinner role, an empty nest can be a big jolt. The physical and psychological separation of children becomes symbolic of a father's loss of the role as patriarchal head and his loss of dominance over the family. Suddenly fathers may want to turn back the hands of time, knowing that they did not spend enough time with their children, realizing that they do not know their children very well, and fearing that it may be too late.

Fathers may feel resentful that they let their wives be the go-between with their children year after year. As mediators and interpreters between husband and child, mothers often cultivate, subconsciously or consciously, a power base within the home by manipulating and controlling these roles. Fathers who discover too late that they have not shared in their children's development now wish that the family had not so often played second fiddle to seemingly-important career involvement. When a father of four suggested that Harry Chapin's popular song, "Cat's in the Cradle," would express his thoughts and regrets with regard to his early parenting days, tears came to his eyes and his voice was choked. Clearly these critical words of the chorus held sad memories for him.

> When you coming home, Daddy?
> Don't know when,
> But we'll get together then.
> You know we'll have a good
> time then.[4]

timetable for departure Parents usually have a mental timetable for determining when and how their children will leave home. For some, the leaving occurs at the first point that the child is gone for more than a month or two; for others, the job as parent may not be over until the child has taken everything from his or her bedroom at home or is financially independent or married.

Although departure age is not fixed and leaving does not guarantee that a child acts as an independent person, when departure does not occur as anticipated, once again, parents may judge themselves harshly. If they feel confined to the parental role, they may actually put off dealing with certain midlife issues or approach them with less intensity. Yet, ironically, if children leave and are surviving beautifully without their parents, seeds of unexpected resentment may creep into a mother's or father's mind. Parents may forget to congratulate themselves for a job well done when children are taking care of themselves without parental help.

"perfect-parent" trap The measuring rod of whether parents have been successful is frequently gauged by outward appearances. Because being a parent is so hard and advice from professionals often points to parental shortcomings, perfection as a parent is truly a distant goal unattached to reality. Yet regrets proliferate about what has been left undone and the ways parents feel they have failed their children. Only a certain growth on the parents' part can balance honest assessments with unattainable expectations.

One divorced father, quoted earlier, openly admitted harsh judgment of himself relative to his daughters: "Their mother feels extremely guilty about going back to school and not giving them time. If men don't take on guilt, they put more burden on the mother to take it on; I've tried to be honest with myself and take my share. My withholding of emotions has affected, very clearly, my daughters' relationships with men. It's very evident that they have had difficulty establishing good relationships with men and I have to have some responsibility in that. It's an acute issue for me to face."

laissez-faire attitude While some parents are striving to be perfect, pushing their children to perfection, others assume a more *laissez-faire* attitude. One such parent reflected, amid a chuckle of laughter: "I really shy away from taking credit for my kids. No credit, no blame later, I guess." Echoed another, "I'm not keen on taking too much credit because that means you have to take the blame, too, right?" She laughed as well.

Coming out from behind the mask of parenthood is easier when the image of perfection has been knocked from its pedestal.

AGING AND THE BODY

children as a reflection of getting older Seeing children leave home serves as a milestone in the aging process. Parents are forced to admit, "My kids are leaving home...I'm getting older." Especially during the teenage years, children serve as a constant reminder of aging to parents who see firm bodies compared to sagging or flabby ones, who see huge quantities of calories consumed as they must subsist on what often seems like starvation diets by comparison, who see full youthful manes replaced by thinning or gray hair, who see the vitality of youth compared to a general slowing down. Parents feel a certain envy of their sons or daughters and perhaps an unconscious resentment. The person inside the middle-aged body can easily feel age thirty until a glance at the youthful teen brings the parent back to reality. Suddenly this parent may feel *over the hill*.

After the first child leaves, a parent may remark, "I don't really feel that old. Somehow I don't feel old enough to have a kid of my own in college. I can remember how old my folks seemed when I left for school. Now I realize that they weren't that old at all!" Parents often see their friends and peers aging more than they see it in themselves. Gradually, thought patterns are interrupted with self-admonitions about whether certain behavior is appropriate for "someone my age," whether "I'm too old to do this," or whether "I'll make a fool of myself."

By the time all the children are gone, the reality of aging is more concrete. Aches and pains don't disappear as quickly. Quickness and agility in sports are slackening and must be replaced by mental adeptness. Said one attractive mother who looked much younger than her forty-six years: "It bothers me to be getting older. My husband told me to go see a dermatologist and get specific advice on what I should do about my face to keep my wrinkles from getting worse. My daughter will say 'Oh, Mom, your wrinkles look so good.

What have you been doing?'" She chuckled as she spoke, but only to disguise her hurt.

Children's perceptions of their parents as old are very real. Children often see their parents' active lives as over because those lives no longer revolve around the child and her or his needs. In the child's mind, the parents' lives are frozen in time.

. . . yet feeling better The fortunate thing about the health craze which has permeated the country over the last two decades is that people do take better care of their bodies, they do stay in better shape. Some lose weight. Some start exercising, jogging, or walking. Some cut back on alcohol. Some stop smoking. The emphasis on controlling this aspect of life manifests itself in health foods, health clubs, and health books and videos by the rich and famous. By the time their children leave the nest, chances are that a lot of parents do look and feel younger and their bodies are healthier than their counterparts of a generation ago.

sexual worries While improvements in the sexual relationship are frequently experienced by many couples and they feel the relief of not having to worry about children overhearing noises from the bedroom, the big bugaboo of middle age still remains sex — cloaked in terms of female menopause and male climacteric. As mentioned earlier, menopause simply means the stopping of the menstrual cycle. Climacteric means a corresponding period in males when hormonal changes cause sexual activity and competence to lessen. This may manifest as impotence.

Men do worry about their continued ability to perform sexually at a time when women have more freedom to express themselves sexually, uncomplicated by the fear of pregnancy. As the pleasure in and quality of sex begins to improve, a man's inability to perform can be a crushing blow. Studies suggest that impotence can often be traced to the use of marijuana or alcohol or identified as a side effect, frequently unmentioned by doctors, of drugs treating diabetes or high blood pressure.[5] But, in many cases, the decline in the sex drive is due more to health concerns, levels of stress, loss of interest, performance anxiety, and other psychological reasons than to reasons of a biological nature, as shown by the surprising resurgence of sexual desire that can occur with a midlife remarriage.

Women worry about hot flashes, potentially upsetting hormonal changes, and the drying up of their vaginal fluids. They worry about being less sexually attractive in a society where the youthful female image still dominates magazine and television advertisements. Moreover, midlife aging in men is often viewed as physically and sexually enticing. Age does not bring this enhanced perception of women; perhaps that is why women sometimes feel middle-aged before men do.Our society has erected an unfortunate stereotypical image of the menopausal woman that is only now beginning to erode, thus freeing women of an enormous burden and guilt. In other cultures menopause does not necessarily have such a negative connotation.

While neither men nor women should relegate themselves to sexual unattractiveness or inactivity simply because of age, there are facts about *sexual aging* that couples need to know. Maggie Scarf in her book, *Intimate Partners*, examines some of the changes in sexual responses that midlife women and men face; she recommends *Human Sexual Inadequacy* by Masters and Johnson for further information. As another option, many couples seek counseling with a therapist specializing in sexual dysfunction. When such problems remain unresolved, the fiber of a marriage may be badly shaken.

redefinition of middle age   Parents forced to include themselves under the label of being *middle-aged* are causing a redefinition of what middle age is all about and what it really means. Middle age is not old — except to teenagers. Middle age does not mean shutting down, but rather gearing up. Gloria Steinem had a great response a number of years ago when told that she didn't *look* fifty years old. In effect she said, "*This* is what fifty looks like."

Parents of children leaving home are drawing conclusions along the same line. "If this is middle age, maybe it's not as bad as I thought. I'm not really that old. Besides, I have almost half my life ahead of me."

Some parents project themselves positively into old age. "I made up my mind a long time ago," said a woman in one of the helping professions. "I deal with a lot of beautiful, beautiful, elderly people and I've already taken a role model of who I want to be like and how I want to grow old. It's a slowing down of energy, but definitely positive. It's a confidence in social situations and an enjoying of things more.

"Society still has quite negative feelings about growing old and I'm going to have to forge my own way. The kids' leaving is the beginning of an era...of having to deal with my aging. I'm just not going to grow into a crotchety old person. Whatever I have to do to achieve that, I hope to have the stamina and enthusiasm. I look at the people who run the races when they're seventy and I think...there I go...there I go."

Mind over matter. The children's leaving home can transform from a liability into an asset — a benefit of growing older. Gradually, parents can begin to understand that the wisdom and sense of mellowness that they feel does support the notion that older is better. Being the parent of a grown, adult child can be okay.

MORTALITY

Few people look forward to death. Yet coming to grips with mortality is a phenomenon of middle age, often brought on by the death of one or both parents. Whereas that parent provided a buffer to the reality of death, now the middle-aged mother and father provide that buffer for their children. As children leave home, each parent becomes even more aware of her or his *aloneness* in the world. No person will necessarily be around forever.

"The death of a parent," said one woman, "brings forth all the scary feelings...you're at the top of the heap now. You face death in a way that I don't think you do until that happens. It suddenly comes zeroing in. Sometimes I deal with it reasonably well. Other times I start thinking about my age, how much longer I have to live, my body breaking down...and I get very depressed. I deal with it intellectually but how well I'm coping with it down here," she stopped and pointed to her heart, "I don't know."

For women, particularly, this issue may seem more complex. Knowing statistically that men have a shorter life span, women must deal not only with their own mortality, but face the reality of a life without a spouse. Single-parent mothers may confront the possibility of living much of the rest of their lives alone.

Men, on the other hand, may feel mortality as a closer reality. They may die first. They are more likely to see one of their peers die, perhaps unexpectedly. They also know that, the law of averages aside, they could be left alone without a spouse.

Perhaps the reason parents are concerned with hanging on to parenthood is that its passing marks the beginning of a final march toward death.

Physical life may indeed seem finite. "I think," said one mother, "that the loss of kids symbolizes...perhaps unconsciously for many parents...the fact that death is closer and more real. In a sense, I am also grieving for part of my life that will never come again. If you think about it, I am facing the end of a major biological function...one that in some species of the animal world brings death."

JOB/CAREER

men evaluating careers When children leave home, fathers begin to take stock of their careers and examine the efforts that they have expended to get where they are. Were the results worth it? Do they want to continue? Protecting the image of the powerful father gives way to dealing with unresolved dreams and admitting how much of life has been shaped by the expectations of others. An integral part of letting go of the unfulfilled dreams of youth involves the shelving of those demands that the father is still projecting onto his child's identity. If a father has feelings of personal failure in his career, then he may be able to acknowledge that he dreams of his children *making it* so that he can erase his own discontent with life. Some fathers may come face to face with the fact that they are jealous: they are afraid that they will be outperformed by their children.

An evaluation of job and career may yield traditional solutions rather than startling discoveries. Certain men will narrow their focus and make one final concerted push to the top before they are too old or before the younger movers-and-shakers pass them by. Other men, perhaps being more honest with themselves, critically evaluate their chances for a starring role in a corporation and revise their goals downward; some decide not to make the effort for further advancement — it is simply not worth it. Still others realize that their workaholic exteriors result from a desire to avoid going home; work is a substitute for marital fulfillment.

Those who have been extremely successful may see no motivation or incentive in forcing a change. When a career has been a pressing imperative in determining the substance of one's adult life and when a person's image of himself (or herself) has been largely defined in terms of career success, letting go of this compelling thought pattern may be traumatic indeed.

Many men decide that there is more to life than chasing an elusive rainbow and change is in order. If that change means readjusting the emphasis and amount of time spent on work, then energy is freed up and redirected toward personal growth and development. The possibility of exploring a new career based on a different interest depends substantially on how much a man likes what he has been doing or how much he feels bored by the same old thing. A move into a second or third career at this stage in life is not uncommon.

Tim, a very successful businessman who realized that his role as provider was winding down, reminisced about his career at midlife: "I'm not sorry about what the job did for me. But business is highly stressful, competitive, and aggressive, and I feel badly about what it has done to me in that respect. The stress can be terribly debilitating and impacts my wife and daughter. Do I think about a second career? Oh, sure. I know some people who are exceedingly happy with theirs. But it takes a lot of guts. I don't know if I could do it."

His daughter was gone and his wife worked, but releasing this role was not going to be easy.

introspection for career women Women who have had full-time careers experience a sense of self derived not only from the status of conforming to the *super-mom* myth but from the accolades of the work world, as well. They, too, face the career-evaluation issues men address. These issues may be especially charged for single-parent mothers who have been making it financially on their own.

As with men, forcing an introspection is not easy, particularly when it seems that a herculean effort has gone into establishing a career, getting to work every day, and raising the children that one is now losing. Said one mother, "My son's leaving forced me to deal with my lost hopes for my life and the successes I wanted...and still want." Also following in men's tracks, women may bury themselves in their work when the children leave, particularly if they made sacrifices along the way to put their family first or limit career involvement. Other women, who have seen work as a grind for years, may feel like the pressure is finally off—even though they continue to work. Still others may quit or investigate new opportunities.

homemakers facing more options While those in the work world evaluate careers, homemakers evaluate whether to enter (or reenter) the marketplace. Many homemakers already have part-time or very flexible jobs, or are preparing for more involvement in the work world. Women may go back to school. They may take a successful volunteer role and turn it into a paying position. Some join the family business. More than anything else, there seem to be numerous options available when women no longer feel restricted by the mother role.

Liz is a good example of a homemaker who began anticipating a career years in advance of the first of her six children leaving home. "I went back to school when I had my midlife crisis at age thirty-seven. The oldest was just starting high school and the youngest was only four. But I was approaching forty and I had all these children and I thought how am I ever going to find time to do anything else, prepare for anything. I'll be busy with them...and then suddenly they'll be gone and what will I have grounded myself in, what will I have prepared for?

"I had the sense that I had never really had a chance to do anything or be anything or accomplish anything. I had to prepare for another lifestyle...a different mode of being. It's all very classic and the only thing that went along with it was an absolute determination not to chintz on the kids. I couldn't feel like I was walking out on the family and just thinking about me. I've probably put more time in on our kids than some people...and probably with no greater success, either. I didn't have all that much time, but I had a glimmer of time...almost like the law of rising expectations...so I wanted to invest it the way I wanted to...to use my mind. It was a heavy compromise...my husband was very supportive emotionally but, like a lot of husbands, he didn't really have the time to support me in any substantive way.

"It took me six years to get my master's degree and I am just starting to help edit some historical papers as an assistant. I'm also trying to get an article published. My husband won't be a surgeon all his life. Once we get the children educated we won't need to make quite so much money and he may move over a notch and I'll have something to do that I like. I have these grandiose schemes that scare me and I say to myself I can't possibly do that...and then I say why not?...the kids are leaving home. Some of the *why not* is overcoming the image of the writer as august. Whether it's the woman saying, 'Oh I couldn't possibly do that,' or whether it's just that I have some of the wrong genes, I don't know. There is a sense of having gotten a second career...although that's too overblown a word for what I'm doing right now."

Some women feel that they have worked hard for many years, twenty-four hours a day, raising a family and ministering to its needs; and now is the time to enjoy the leisure, take frequent vacations, and go on the business trips which they couldn't share in the past because of the children. They may feel that volunteer work is more rewarding than a corporate job might be. Certainly this is a situation primarily connected with women near the top of the socioeconomic scale; thoughts of working come to mind, but not seriously. The majority of women do not have this luxury.

"I think about working," said Lucy, whose nest was finally empty, "but I also realize that now I have this absolutely delicious freedom and I don't want to tie it down to a nine to five routine. I'm free to travel, which we do a lot, and we do things I'm interested in. I am tempted...I would love to do something else but I think I like the freedom more. Furthermore, at age forty-seven, I'm not going to get any high-powered job and I wouldn't want to be full-time...and part-time is not very exciting."

Other women who accept this role of the unemployed homemaker may feel guilty, at risk, or angry because they know that the norm has become the woman who works. They may feel that they started marriage and family under one set of rules; now the rules are different, and they are caught in the middle. Psychologist Ann

Block comments:

> If women have not been in the work place for a long time, it is a very difficult situation, a great strain. It can cause serious mental illness sometimes. It brings out the very worst, every weakness that they ever thought they had—in addition to having to deal with age, divorce, kids leaving.
> My advice to women is to get a career, have a skill. Women have to make a big shift if they don't have a career. They may stay in very poor relationships because they feel that they can't make the adjustment, plus they can't make enough money. They can't get a job by showing pictures of their kids and saying, "I did a good job!" They're really very capable, but they don't always feel that way.

Feelings of ambivalence are not uncommon when a woman is faced with this career-choice dilemma. "I have to decide what I want to do: if I want the loose part-time relationship I have now with the company where I'm not making much money or if I want to work full-time and just get limited vacation. George and I take a week off every two months. I'm not making enough money to make it worthwhile, but I want to work. What I really want is my own business so I have the flexibility. I need to find something to do. Steve will be sixteen next year and that whole burden of driving him will be lifted. So many of my friends are working. I realize that I'm going to be left behind if I don't do that...but I just can't seem to make that commitment."

financial independence for women Women going to work for the first time may be encouraged and excited by the initial glimpse of financial independence that they feel. Money has the perceived ability to give a sense of worth in a way that the endless chores of motherhood and being a homemaker, rarely rewarded by society, do not.

Unfortunately, there are often negatives involved in this transition which seem to coexist with the new identity. Accepting an entry level position can seem demeaning after all the years of being in charge of and successfully running a household. Being on the low end of the earnings scale, as so many older women new to the job market are, can be financially trying and frustrating. For many women these factors are gradually offset by the sense of being in control of their lives and in control of a work situation.

This newfound power may give a woman the strength to deal with issues that have been ignored or make decisions that have been avoided, particularly about the marriage. Faced with the reality of being self-sufficient and on her own, growth is usually inevitable. A woman becomes her own person, a person of value, no longer just a person who must please and make everyone else happy.

While it may seem that women are being forced into the marketplace when the kids leave, in reality, some women respond positively to the fact that the decision has been made for them. They do not have to decide whether to work, but rather where. Men are not as lucky. While there may be a monotony to their lives, the decision or ability to make a change at all, much less which one, can be difficult.

One catalyst leading women into the job market is the fear of being too dependent upon their husbands, both financially and for a sense of identity. Society also places pressure on women to perform and achieve in a nonmaternal manner once the mother role is complete. Another impetus is that once the children have gone, feelings of guilt which have prevented a mother from working in the past no longer exist. But there are rewards for taking the plunge into the work world and research has shown that, once the children have left, the mental health of mothers who are employed outside the home surpasses that of mothers who are not.[6] Marital expectations become more realistic and center around rediscovering a mutual sharing, a partnership of equals.

husbands feeling threatened   While women discover some of the harsh realities of the business world and learn that coping with this stress takes effort, they may also discover that their husbands feel threatened, not only by their entry into the work force, but also by their gradual assumption of a more active and aggressive role in many aspects of the marital household, including sexual activities. Husbands may openly complain about wives with a commitment outside of the home — unless that commitment is within the volunteer arena. Volunteerism is still the most socially acceptable commitment for an upper-middle-class wife who wants her competency recognized in a field unrelated to homemaker chores. Husbands may complain when their wives are no longer available to go on business trips or handle the couple's entertainment.

Joining the work force is often more difficult for those women who lack the clear-cut economic need that working-class and other women have. The older a woman is, the more resistance she may face from not only her husband, but family members as well. Unless she is very determined to make outside employment a reality, she may eventually succumb to this pressure. Poor health on the part of the husband may also force her back home. Regardless of the reason given, the switch to an allegiance outside of the home is thwarted.

For some women the threat of jeopardizing the marriage is so real that they opt for a continuation of the homemaker role or, if they remain employed, opt for a more passive role in household decisions or the sexual relationship. Having made that choice, however, women are not necessarily immune from further emotional upheaval.

PERSONAL RELATIONSHIPS

relationship with the child Numerous relationships are affected in the midlife phase of parents: the ones with their children, with their parents, with their friends, and with each other. The most obvious, of course, is the changing relationship of the parent and child to one of adults. The dynamics of this change are discussed in the letting go chapters of this book.

relationship with the parents' parents Another is the shift that midlife parents may have with their own parents. Sometimes, only through seeing their own children leave home, can mothers and fathers gain a full understanding of what *their* parents experienced over two decades earlier. If those parents let go gracefully, midlife mothers and fathers may, for the first time in their lives, understand the depth of their parents' caring. This understanding may act as a catalyst for better communication and increased sharing; the adult child may feel more comfortable reaching out to the aging parent and more accepting when placed in a childlike role by that parent.

If, however, the apron strings with aging parents have not been cut, mothers and fathers may stymie their own self-development by seeking only familiar patterns that minimize risk. As a consequence, aging parent and adult child may never fully understand or know each other, or themselves.

Other mothers and fathers may realize that they have yet to resolve real or imagined grievances with their parents. The inability to do so may greatly affect whether a mother or father perpetuates the grievance with a son or daughter. If conflicts can be put aside, mothers and fathers have an easier time accepting their parents for what they are, letting go of what they are not.

While midlife parents still face responsibilities to their offspring, they may also have to provide increasing care — in the form of time, energy, and/or money — for their elderly parents. Sometimes called the *sandwich generation*, these mothers and fathers must parent in both directions. Ultimately, they become role models for the relationships that they will one day have with their offspring.

"I carry an active model of my relationship with my father into my relationship with my kids," said one father. "I want their relationship to be as positive as that with my father. There's a parallel. I must have respect for my father in order for my kids to respect me.

"In your old age you reap the seeds that you've sown in your relationship with your parents. I'm very much aware of this. With my dad, I am the parent and helping him let go so he's ready for the dying process. Parents are not loved for how nice they are to you."

relationship with friends As parents begin to reexamine their relationships with peers and other friends, old friendships may be renewed and those which developed primarily because of the children's activities may gradually fade away. When individuals make overt or subtle changes in their lifestyles, attitudes, or feelings, those changes become mirrored in the people with whom they choose to spend their time, gradually leading to a perceptible shift in their circle of friends. The relationships that survive this period of transition usually have an intense and lasting quality.

relationship within the marriage One of the biggest impacts of children leaving is on the midlife marriage relationship. A few general comments here will be explored more fully in Chapter 13. For most couples, by the time the children are all gone, so many years have elapsed that memories of time centered on each other are just that — faint memories. Couples may no longer seem to have much in common. Communication skills may have disappeared. Parents in blended families — that is, her children and/or his and/or theirs — may have never lived together without children.

The weaker a marital relationship, the more the problem areas may be exacerbated by the children's leaving; the more stable a relationship, the easier for parents to adapt to the children's separation, to work on realignment of the marriage relationship, and to value the uniqueness that they find in each other. When parents are strong in their relationship with each other, they may feel like they are having a second honeymoon.

Some people at middle age, whether married or single, may find it easier to admit that they don't want to be alone now that the children are gone. They understand the fullness that comes from loving and being loved. Other individuals may conclude the opposite: they want time alone. Although not a common experience, the situation can arise (as it did in one interview) where one partner decides to explore, or admit to, a change of sexual preference. While confronting homosexuality does not always lead to divorce, that can be the result.

increased tolerance in all relationships Throughout the many relational realignments that may occur during middle age, there is often a need to *set things right* and repair any damage, committed knowingly or unknowingly, against another human being, particularly a family member. Tolerance of others' differentness expands, often to the point of actual appreciation. Regardless of whether the person perceives this increased esteem for others as wisdom or maturity, the tolerance usually feels more comfortable and adds contentment to life.

realignment of importance of relationships This crucial assessment is addressed in the next chapter because it is an integral part of the midlife change which occurs in the setting of new directions.

PROFILE

All of Carol Bruce's children had left the nest. Compounded by the death of her mother, her adjustment to a life without children was more difficult than she imagined and she was far from completing this midlife transition in her life. She was still struggling.

"I don't feel unfulfilled in terms of my children at all. It's just that I find myself needing to work with myself more now (there's not that immediate demand of doing something for someone else). There's a shift from outward stuff to more inward stuff.

"Where I feel the crunch is having everybody leave and that really surprises me about myself because I've been very careful to keep my own personal interests going, my contacts, and my professional part-time job teaching art. I really do have to shift gears. When I think about it logically, I realize that for twenty-six years raising kids has been a major part of my energy, plus having my mother live with us. She definitely represented extra problems. She died a year ago so it was her death plus having everybody out of the house that changed my life.

"This next year with the kids all scattered miles away...that's a clean sweep and I think it's forced me to rethink my life even though I have tried to keep myself alive...keep my interests...keep my self. But I'm finding that you really do have to make a shift and I really am in transition more than I ever thought. My husband used to say, 'Oh, you're never going to have any problem with everybody out of the house,' because I have been interested in a lot of different things with just enough work, just enough income, to make me think that I am contributing something.

"But I think that women put so much of themselves into raising children and family that, even though we may not be particularly nurturing-type people in the beginning and may resent having all these people intrude on our own personal life, there's a void which I really didn't expect." Carol paused with some nervous laughter. "I'm still teaching...painting more for myself. I go to more plays and concerts. And I'm studying Jung. That is where I find my ongoing spiritual renewal...the nurturing side that I need for me. I like the Jungian idea of the journey toward wholeness.

"I've been scared...mostly by surprise. I thought I had myself all set up. Mother lived her life through me and I made a conscious effort not to hold on to our children in any way because I was so hurt by what she did. I'm still trying to work through my relationship with her. I'm doing a lot of reflective work. It's a starting over again, in a way. A lot of the stuff I was doing I want to continue doing, but emotionally it's still a starting over which I was not expecting."

1. pp. 62-74.
2. New York: W.W. Norton & Company, Inc., pp. 119-120.
3. Carole Klein, *Mothers and Sons* (Boston: Houghton Mifflin Company, 1984) p. 192.
4. As taken from the album, *Verities & Balderdash*, by Elecktra Records, 1974.
5. Scarf, p. 238.
6. Rubin, p. 230.

CHAPTER 12

SETTING NEW DIRECTIONS

Each day when I get up I pinch myself...to know that I can do exactly what I want for that day. Isn't it wonderful? I've waited a long time for this.

RELEASE

change of focus The essence of a successful midlife passage for many mothers and fathers seems to lie — as it did for Carol Bruce — in a change of focus: a shift from being outer-directed to that of being inner-directed. Most men derive an image of themselves from the investments that they have made in external forms of success: job, home, cars, wife, children, status in the community, and other material possessions. Most women derive an image of themselves from the investments that they have made in relationships and in helping others: children, husband, friends, and parents. Even women who work, particularly if they have children, place a great deal of emphasis on relationships for their self-concept.

a world unlocked As fathers and mothers look beyond the self-image that they have derived from their respective roles something wonderful can happen. The world, which had seemed locked in and full of a pattern of sameness, can be opened up anew and explored. Self-examination. Introspection. Discovery. Integration. Wholeness. Changing sense of self. Reassessment. Refocusing. Transition. Self-understanding. Moving forward. The children who have left home are going off into the world to explore a world without parents; simultaneously, parents are reformatting their lives without children. Both are growing. Both are breaking out and finding new meanings to life. Both are developing new selves.

The image evoked is that of a spherical shape moving through space. The sphere always occupies space, but as the placement of the sphere changes, the space inside the sphere also changes. If one thinks of life as being on a continuum, then the essence of the individual imperceptibly changes whenever there is movement. Of course, people do not always choose to move nor do they always move in the direction anticipated, and whether movement is forward, backward, or sideways is often highly conjectural. But through this gradual evolution people can enrich themselves and their relationships.

With the arrival of children in their lives, parents often become victims of behavioral expectations dictated by society, by themselves, and by their children. When the offspring leave home, there is a release from a great many of these expectations. Demands on the parent change and the role of being a parent shrinks dramatically. Long-standing habits, no longer necessary or relevant to daily living, can be discarded. Decisions made long ago can be reversed.

Restructuring a life without children can be welcomed in a way that parents are embarrassed to admit, yet the transition is often less traumatic than anticipated. "It's a real watershed," said one father. "I told my wife...we have to stop and think. What do we want to do? We can go into the Peace Corps; we can open a boutique. In the end, I love what I do so I didn't change...but I did take the time to do some real soul searching."

time to think If a road map exists to the redefinition process, an important step is for parents to take time for themselves — private time to relax and think. The sooner that parents let loose of the status quo and accept this freedom to explore and change, the more momentum they will have to find new directions, set new priorities, and discover different facets to their inner spirit. As they dig around in their memories, they can rediscover ideas or parts of themselves which have been repressed for years. Fresh thoughts and activities can become part of the individual as old ones fade away.

Each parent needs to face this personal crossroads with just the right amount of challenge, not expecting too much or accepting too little — that proper balance of discomfort and comfort. For those prepared, or already in transition, the process can be exciting. For those resisting change, life can become terribly frightening. For those who have used children as an escape or coverup for their own problems, exacerbated behavior can result — as illustrated by excesses of food, alcohol, or drugs. (Although, interestingly enough, sometimes the kids' leaving will trigger a cessation of previous abuses in these areas.) And for those who hide behind other facades — such as physical appearance, material possessions, job, volunteer work, friends and family, prayer, or humor — self-knowledge can remain as elusive as ever.

A woman may realize that part of her independent self did not mature; long ago she simply went from being under her father's wing to being taken care of by her husband — a husband who has come to represent her as he might a dependent child. As arresting as that is to a woman's development, it can also hinder a man in his self-examination.

the self without children In rediscovering themselves, parents must examine those aspects that were filled up by the children. If there is a gap in the *self* of a parent, then the parent must now look closely at that gap and do something: discard it, change it, or renew it. Filling a loneliness or void may not be easy, nor is recognizing a specific cause for general feelings of discontent. If parenthood itself has been a core ingredient of the person's identity, this must gradually be put aside so that the person's own individuality can take precedence. No longer do mothers have to be the selfless caretakers or fathers the selfless providers. And where a parent has assumed both functions in their children's lives, the task at hand may seem doubly difficult.

With the children gone, a parent may suddenly feel uncertain about this new identity. When parents have spent so many years centering on children and developing patterns and perhaps unhealthy games that play to the needs of either themselves or the child, the recentering on oneself can seem awkward, especially for parents who feel pangs of guilt. And the paradoxical consequence is, of course, that having put so much energy into children, women can have a hard time finding something equally satisfying — even if they are dedicated to a career. A new commitment at midlife may not appear out of the clear blue.

key to redefining self The key to redefining the self seems to be whether or not a person's identity is tied too closely to a single aspect of life. When parents have invested in numerous facets— career, family, marriage, other relationships, physical fitness and health, spiritual awareness, community service, and personal development — and have meaningful commitments apart from raising children, then the loss of one of these roles is not overwhelming to the mother's or father's identity and self-exploration may seem easier. When, however, that identity is closely linked to only one source, then the potential for having a personal crisis is greater.

Those fathers or mothers who have difficulty with this redefinition of self or who feel they are in a life cycle crisis may wisely seek professional counseling.

NEW PATHWAYS

androgynous shift   If anything, though, the midlife years often represent an androgynous shift within the person. A man may begin to discover those nurturing, emotional, and feminine aspects of his inner self that he has so long suppressed and expected a woman to provide. Too often, a man has no intimate relationships, no sense of trust in others. A woman, who has placed family at her center of reference and who has constantly been the one to adjust her life to the lives of others, may begin to discover those independent, powerful, and masculine parts of her being which can take her in another direction to a better sense of self. While a woman often pursues her quest in the work world, a man may explore his undeveloped self through creative forms of expression and more meaningful, open relationships. Energy put into a career may diminish as the emotional sharing with other individuals intensifies.

Perhaps the chart below will be helpful in graphically depicting the midlife transition that often occurs as men and women work to achieve a balance in their lives and explore the center of their being. Men seek intimacy; women, autonomy. They both seek inner peace.

Midlife Transition

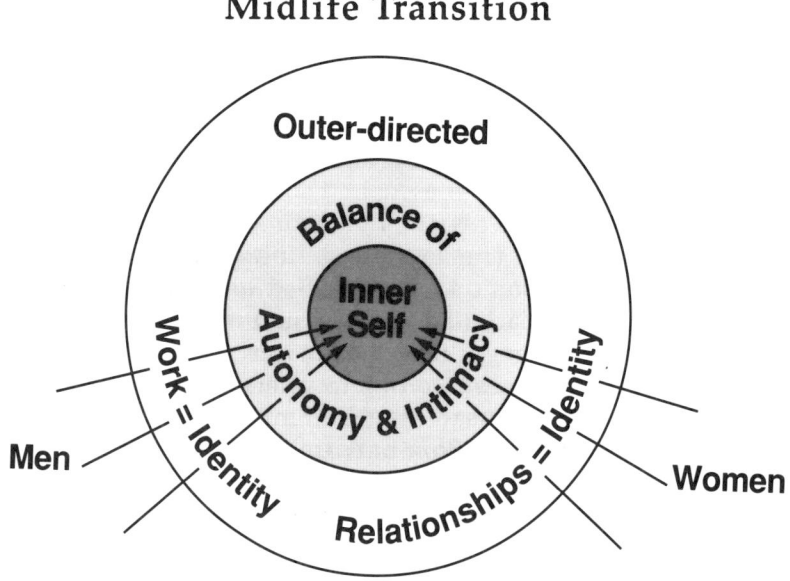

What a switch that, after all the years of molding a career and denying the nurturing, gentle, and vulnerable aspects of his identity, a man may now see a value in what has seemed natural to so many women for years. A man, who has for years tried to escape emotional attachments and the attendant highs and lows that could make him feel uncomfortable or out of control, may gradually view life with a new perspective. With practice, a man may no longer need a woman to fill this gap or give him what he lacks or does not want to acknowledge in himself. He can begin to love a woman for who she is, not for what she brings to him.

For the first time a husband may be aware that he has not acknowledged his wife's needs or responded to a sense of interdependency between them; he can begin to nurture her. Conversely, a woman can begin to love a man for who he is, not for the feelings of power, independence, and security he brings to fill her missing parts. Each can begin to develop in themselves those traits so long sought in the partner.

difficulties As a woman becomes more in touch with herself, she may feel guilty at first to discover that she likes being alone, that the drain of children and other relationships has been exhausting. Slowly she may become more comfortable with her feelings and begin to understand one of the basic underlying truths of life that is often repressed: each person is alone — no one else is ultimately responsible for providing anything in a person's life. The difficulty is that she must simultaneously overcome the notion that some male will always be accountable and take care of her.

When the woman's attention focuses on developing her independent self, a husband may be upset to discover that he is no longer the center of his wife's world. Many of his reactions may parallel those experienced when a wife gets a midlife job: he may become sick, sullen, and irritable or depressed in a subsconscious desire to force her back into a dependency role ministering to his needs. Subtly he may be playing the favored-good-child role in an effort to get her back; he may be saying, "See what a good boy I am." Overtly he may use other attempts to win her back, showering her with time, attention, and gifts — endeavors that once might have won her over but no longer hold that power.

If a man's attention shifts away from his career, a wife, on the other hand, may also become fearful or suspicious. A new career could mean a change of lifestyle financially; new relationships may seem threatening. Difficulties are minimized when both partners welcome change and lines of communication remain open.

generativity people during middle age often reach out to help others, balancing their personal needs with this outside commitment which brings a new sense of purpose. Erik Erikson uses the term *generativity* in his book, *Childhood and Society*, to describe a time when adults seek to make lasting contributions through the guidance of the next generation. Although this need is often fulfilled during the child-rearing process, itself, the term has more commonly become identified as a middle-aged phenomenon, particularly for males. Encouragement of others frequently occurs when one becomes a mentor — a role popularized by the media.

freedoms of new life Freedom is the most noticeable and spontaneous result of *life after kids*, as one parent phrased it. For the first time in years parents can act without reference to the effect something will have on their children. They no longer experience a teen's rejection; no longer feel a victim of the teen's self-centered insensitivities. A huge responsibility and weight have been lifted from the parents' shoulders. Mother and father are free to become new people with a revived zest for living. A rejuvenation takes place.

Parents are free to travel, to pick up and go, and to have a little adventure in their lives. They're free to learn new skills, go back to school, start new careers, or explore new ideas. They're free to take a year off. They're free to move — from a large, expensive, and time-consuming house to a smaller house or a maintenance-free apartment; from the suburbs to the city or a summer place; or from the cold to a warmer climate. Exercising any of these choices may forever change *home* as everyone has known it — physically, emotionally, and geographically — so moving is a big step even if necessitated for financial reasons.

Parents are free, not only to choose where to live, but with whom to live — if anyone at all. They're free to convert a now-empty room into a separate bedroom for one of the spouses. They're free to make new friends that go with their new life or spend more time with the old ones. They're free to explore new sports and hobbies. They're free of, or at least see the end in sight, the overwhelming financial responsibility that children represent and have more money to spend on themselves; they can *feather their nest*, to coin a cliché. They can decide that it's okay to earn less or take early retirement. They're relieved of housework, cooking, and other chores that accompany children.

"I couldn't believe it," said one teen after leaving home. "They were buying everything! Suddenly they had all this money and they were so funny about it. I opened the refrigerator and I said, 'We never had this food when I lived here!' They teased me about that.

It's their whole attitude. Dad's really changed. He's excited because they're starting their lives all over...it's just them."

Delightfully, parents suddenly feel free to say what they think or be less than perfect, knowing that their children are not around to get embarrassed or criticize them. They're free to act on impulse, to go where their inclination takes them, to do what they always wanted to do. They're free to change their lifestyles. They're free to have fun — alone, together, or with someone else. They're free to act like kids and get in touch with those childlike qualities of life that are so easily submerged when parents must constantly play the mature parent role for their children. They're free to laugh at life and enjoy it more.

Said one spunky mother, "I started taking piano lessons when my daughter left. She wasn't there to correct me! It was a real role reversal. I play golf and just leave money for my son to go eat...with a see-you-later note."

Another mother, reminiscing about her and her husband's experiences, said, "I was missing the children, but I was also loving having my own life. We've had a wonderful time actually. We were young when the children were born. We really didn't have a life together. We can go on trips at the drop of a hat and we can do exactly what we want. I was afraid to travel when the kids were young and leave them at home because my dad died when I was age three. I didn't want my kids to know that feeling of abandonment that I lived with so much of my life. Now I like not having to make arrangements for them...not having to worry. We eat when we like...at nine or ten at night. It's so much easier arranging for just the two of us instead of the four of us."

If parents feel that they have lived their lives according to society's rules, they are now free to make their own rules for the future. The *shoulds, oughts,* and *have tos* can be thrown out or revised. To some, the time may seem like a second chance; to others, a last chance to do as they want before old age sets in. Different people have different perspectives. To those who see their life in broad terms, this is only one part of the evolutionary process: changes have occurred in the past and they will continue to happen.

Said one father, "As a couple we spend a lot of time on what we want to do and not what society wants us to do. We write our own script. We don't let other people do it much at all. We realize that one half of life on earth is spent without kids."

inner spiritual growth Life on one's own terms, then, is the excitement and the challenge of midlife. Carl Jung, the renowned psychologist, theorized that individual growth does not truly begin until age forty when people place an emphasis on spiritual development. At this point, individuals discover a new puzzle — one where the key rests with inner peace.

Whether this peace evolves from the study of Jungian concepts, a spiritual path oriented in either Western or Eastern philosophies, or a return to organized religion, the journey is often firmly rooted in God or a Higher Being. The more committed an individual becomes to seeking this inner contentment, the higher the probability that the individual will stop looking for personal satisfaction in the external world.

Midlife adults successful in making this multifaceted transition have a revitalized sense of well-being, cultivate a cheerful, positive attitude, and no longer carry (if they ever did) seeds of disappointment with life. Their inner cores radiate newfound strength to others.

PROFILE

Not one woman but two share their thoughts in this Profile. Their circumstances are different and the words that they use to describe their midlife transitions vary, but both are struggling with the unknown. Neither has a conclusion yet; each life is in a state of transition.

"I have tried to make myself more open, more accepting...not only of myself, but of others. This path of being a full-time artist actually began two years ago. Sometimes I am scared to death. But always I am excited.

"It's been hard to change my concept of time after years in the working world, but it's happening. I've had the time to explore new ideas, explore myself. My children (when they're around) approach me more; I have more time for them...I'm more relaxed. Stress happens without us always knowing the form it takes and without as much of it I've seen my menstruation cycle problems disappear, my alcohol consumption go down, and my headaches diminish.

"In December I bought all new paints. In January I made a snowman for the first time in years. In February I sat on the beach and sketched for a week. In March I saw parts of the U.S. that I didn't know existed. I painted the desert and the mountains. I visited friends. I've worked very hard at letting go...releasing that worry and need to always be in control...and it seems to be working. And interestingly, my biggest growth...that as a spiritual being...has been totally unexpected. I meditate all the time now.

"I'm still not sure where it will all lead...if I can support myself with my art and waitressing or if I'll have to go back to a regular-type job. When the right day comes, I'll know the answer."

* * * * *

"I've been working three years. I don't want to teach the rest of my life. I've been spending more time with Sandy (my youngest) and am looking at him as an only child. I'm doing things for him that I never had time to do with the others. I nourish his needs and wants. I'm scared about my career because I'm so old. I'd feel guilty if I worked five days a week because I probably wouldn't feel like running him here and there.

"I've definitely had a midlife crisis. You realize that you're getting older and that there are a lot of things that you haven't done and wonder if you'll have time to do. You wonder how well you've done the things that have been so important to you.

"I have a lot of regrets...I think routine took over an awful lot which it shouldn't have. The sports the kids played...I wonder if the value to them outweighed the unity that our family could have had. We very rarely sat down as a family for dinner. Sunday was the only day. The oldest boy...I think I was too hard on him. I regret that my husband and I haven't done more as far as trips go. I can see now that we could have...and your kids grow up anyway, let's face it.

"I've resolved to just keep busy and active. It hit at forty-five. The empty nest means a big chapter in your life is coming to a close...and it has been your whole life. I've had other interests, but I've done the same things every day for years. And how are you going to adjust when you don't have that any more? Teaching has definitely helped or I would have been a basket case because I'm not that domestic. Some women isolate themselves when the kids leave and they start drinking and doing these awful things. They're still at home and say they're busy but you know it can't be. And I've always had a fear about that.

"I tell my husband, 'There's life after your children have gone...believe it or not.' You realize that to keep friendships going...and my personal friends have become more important....takes more working at it as the kids leave. I'm happier to just stay home and read a book. It's easier to get in a rut now than ten years ago. We always went out to get a break from the family. We looked forward to going out. I can see why old people...it's really very easy to get wrapped up in your own self and home, and call your children and let them entertain you. Unless you have a life through your friends and your job, you're going to be that same boring person. A lot of friends are made through your kids, so when they leave you have to make the effort."

All of midlife introspection takes effort.

CHAPTER 13

ALONE AT LAST ...
BUT ARE WE HAPPY?

Did you hear the joke about when life begins?
Well, the priest says that life begins at the moment of conception. The minister says that life begins at the moment of birth. But the rabbi...well, he says that life begins when the kids leave home and the dog dies.

ROADBLOCKS TO RENEWING THE MARRIAGE

difficulty of marital renegotiation   The period following the children's departure is a new phase — one with the potential to be the best years of a married couple's life together. Both partners usually have their health, they are alone without other family distractions, and they have time to share together. Sounds like the ideal situation.

But readjustment is often not that easy. The *we* which represents the couple must be redefined, as must *home* without the children. While some couples may have made adjustments in anticipation of children leaving, usually the separation itself acts as the catalyst for transition.

The empty nest issue for a couple may not be dealing with the child's separation, per se, so much as it is dealing with each other. Pointing to this issue, a therapist describes a female patient's situation:

> She came to see me because her last child was leaving. She and her husband were frozen in fear about dealing with each other. They had never dealt with each other. They'd

always had one crisis after another with the children to contend with — a game, a meet, Brownies — always something. They'd never really known each other through the years. And this was a very sophisticated woman; she worked and led a very involved life. We think sometimes it's the children leaving which causes the problem, but I would look at the relationship, if one exists, with the spouse.

Not surprisingly, the numerous roles that children have played within the dynamics of the family setting — and this chapter will examine a number of them — often impede this transition. Husband and wife must relate to and communicate with each other; no one else is around to run interference. They must appreciate what they still have in common or seek out new avenues to explore which will infuse the marriage with intimacy. Gradually they will renegotiate the marital relationship, perhaps even significantly redesign the implied marital contract. If this renegotiation is not successful, the fiber of the marriage can be seriously shaken.

"There wasn't a replacement when my son left. The hardest part has been renewing my marriage. A third energy force was always a factor in how we related. In his absence we have to depend on each other. It's been very difficult because we're eighteen years out of practice. I recognize and appreciate the fact that Fran is involved in her career development, and now that our son has left, we're getting used to dual careers in the household. I expect more of her time but her work has accelerated...and she works evenings. We tried meeting for lunch but it was such a transparent thing. So there's no replacement for Bruce. Our careers are out of sync. We're both highly competitive and our son diluted it...we're without that force to soften the competition.

"We have contemplated a separation...we need space, some time away to re-sort where we're going and what we're going to do. Before our son's departure we always had an excuse not to deal with it. We are seeing a counselor. All these forces are far greater than we can handle ourselves. And those are not easy sessions. It's so difficult to try to make the transition."

Interestingly, his wife had been working for years, but as long as Larry could focus attention on his son, Fran's unavailability was not a cause for concern. Only when Bruce left home was the enormity of the gap between husband and wife evident. Some months later they separated.

marriage at all-time low There are a number of reasons why the readjustment to couplehood is so difficult. Studies have shown that, prior to the children leaving, the marriage is frequently at an unprededented low.[1] Marital satisfaction is highest following marriage and drops off sharply after the first child is born. Preoccupation with raising a family and supplying its economic needs tends to affect adversely the quality of both sexual relations and caring companionship.

Although sometimes there is an increase in satisfaction prior to the children's leaving, it is usually not until the couple is alone once again that marital happiness has the potential to equal or surpass the level experienced early in the marriage. Intimacy may be possible for the first time in years. If the marriage is to survive, it will often get better.

weak parental self-esteem The key to meeting the love needs of someone else is largely dependent upon the ability one has to feel good about and love oneself. This is the reason that outside interests, confidence in one's own abilities, and healthy solutions to one's own problems influence so strongly the prospects of successfully rejuvenating a marriage. When parents — particularly mothers — are afraid to explore the postparent self and fill the gap left by children, or home fails to assume an identity unrelated to the children, then readjustments are blocked. When parents cannot resolve the personal issues of midlife mentioned in the previous chapters, the marriage is jeopardized by additional stress.

no emotional support from spouse Another difficulty in readjustment between spouses arises when offspring have been the focal point of a parent's life and provide more emotional support for that parent than does the spouse. If marital problems arose early in the marriage, then affection for a spouse may have gradually been displaced by affection for the children — children who eventually become the target of almost all emotional investment. Over a period of time the parent comes to rely heavily on the psychological reinforcement from the offspring. Eventually the parent may get all love, tenderness, and nurturing support from the children, rather than from the spouse.

When children who have met these psychological needs for so many years leave home and can no longer fulfill that role, not only is the separation a severe blow but there is scant emotional framework for the marital partner to fall back on. Typically this phenomenon happens to mothers; even those with careers are not immune if their emotional needs have not been aligned with the spouse. But children can also provide fathers with the same emotional escape. In fact, children may represent the only emotional closeness or intimacy that some fathers have ever known.

spouse needing to be parented A husband or wife may welcome the departure of the children because he or she can once again become the focus of the spouse's attentions. Unfortunately, for some couples this reorientation is emotionally unhealthy — a dependent spouse is expecting to be parented. In other words, the offending spouse wants to be treated as a child, and an only child at that, with the parenting spouse attending to all needs and desires. One spouse turns into the surrogate parent for the other or infuses an already existing role with renewed effort.

A dependent wife may seek to perpetuate this childlike role, but, more typically, the husband is the spouse seeking the subordinate role. The wife (or husband) is left not with an adult seeking recommitment but rather with an ongoing parenting responsibility. In some cases, the wife wants and needs this mothering role. In other cases, she mourns not only the loss of the children but the loss of the potential of an adult relationship. The parenting spouse may not want to put up with this tedious and wearisome role, and unless the marriage relationship is restructured, pressure mounts to end it or contrive to have the children return, thus regressing to the previous status quo.

child as buffer Frequently children act as a buffer to the friction that might otherwise erupt between husband and wife. In a sense, the couple hides behind the kids. Arguments are muted. Differences are overlooked and idiosyncrasies tolerated. Demands or needs are ignored and feelings stifled. Alert couples are aware of these dynamics.

Commenting about the departure of her children, one mother reflected, "The first thing that happens is that there's no buffer. Husband and wife are alone and, in our case (being we married very young), we had scarcely a memory of life without a family. When you have kids you don't argue in front of them, you don't fight, and it gets to be a habit. You muffle yourself. At least we did."

When the buffer disappears and children no longer drown out reality, differences between the spouses may be noticeably acute. Yet because one person cannot really change another, efforts to resolve such differences face stiff resistance, often thwarting readjustment.

child as barrier to intimacy For many parents the very presence of children proves an acceptable interruption to intimacy and sex. The erratic or late hours of teenagers and their frequent comings and goings are ready excuses for restraint or abstinence in otherwise-private activities. Parents who have hidden behind the shield of their children to avoid sexual or intimate encounters lose this barrier when the kids depart, thus complicating the readjustment process.

child as source of manipulation Complicating the readjustment issue even further are family dynamics which center on manipulative interactions. Usually these situations are reflective of deep-seated instability in the marriage. For example, one parent may play a child against the other parent to keep that parent on the outside of activities and child-rearing experiences. By shutting the secondary parent out, the primary parent and the child can then act as a unit to exert power and influence. Recognizing the unspoken conspiracy, the secondary parent may learn to manipulate one person of that unit to gain control over the other. Thus, interaction between family members frequently appears to have ulterior motives. When the child who is involved in this manipulation leaves, the parents are faced with major problems.

child as communication link Other parents may have become so used to communicating with each other through a specific child that they no longer deal with each other directly. The departure of that child brings about the threat of divorce or separation because the couple cannot function together without the child's intervention. The child may respond to this need for stabilization by returning home and/or developing a problem so severe (for example, hospitalization for psychological reasons) that the parents must once again focus on the child. In this manner, the family unit is reconstituted and the marriage can continue.[2]

Sometimes this child is the *problem child* who provokes endless fights between the parents. All of their attention focuses on the child and her or his difficulties. Fights may intensify prior to the separation as parents desperately seek to avoid confronting critical issues within the marriage. Only when parents are able to break the cycle and begin examining those problems which have been deflected for so long does the marriage have a chance of improving.

child as cause of jealousy Jealousy can also play a role in family dynamics, getting in the way of the marriage relationship. Jealousy can arise when one parent gradually substitutes one of the children for the spouse. Such replacement may happen unintentionally or be the direct result of overt gestures of seduction by the parent. In other cases, the son or daughter may take the initiative to attract the attention of the opposite-sex parent.

Regardless of who arouses the jealousy, a hotbed of sexual tension, guilt, and rivalry can erupt. Spouses on the receiving end of a child's attention may experience relief from a monotonous marriage; spouses being left out may find it hard to understand why they are no longer the object of affection and sensual overtures. Obviously relishing his daughter's attention, one father related, "My wife is jealous of the time my daughter takes from me. My daughter plays up to me. Meanwhile my wife is climbing up the walls because she can't get a word in edgewise." He had no motivation to initiate a change.

A different type of jealousy can be experienced by one or both parents when they observe the romantic involvements of their child. Parents may feel jealous of the youthful enthusiasm of love that so many teenage couples display. Theirs may not be a relationship of commitment, but the teen couple's exuberance and passion can cruelly point out the emptiness of the parents' marriage.

No matter how the jealousy arises, the bad patterns developed when children are at home can be difficult for parents to undo once the offspring are gone.

child as "perfect mate" Perhaps the most unexpected readjustment that parents may encounter results from the realization that the child of the opposite sex embodies the qualities of a *perfect mate*. This is not an easy issue to resolve. A husband may see a daughter as a reincarnation of the shy, innocent, and loving woman that he married years earlier, a person who now exists in memory only. Corresponding feelings of women are investigated in Carole Klein's book, *Mothers and Sons*. She comments that mothers may feel that their sons understand them better, appreciate them more, show more concern, and have become their "emotional and intellectual mates....Mother may have to acknowledge that her son, not her husband, is the man she would have liked to marry."[3] The son may represent the only male that she has ever fully understood.

child as scapegoat Scapegoating is another family dynamic which impedes marital readjustment. By using a child as a scapegoat, parents gain a target for their hostility — hostility essentially unrelated to the child.[4] The targeted child (there may be more than one) takes on traits which reflect areas of contention within one of the parents or between the marital partners. Mother and father are then free to displace their anger at themselves or at their spouses onto the child without dealing directly with the issue — thus diminishing tension or diverting a potential showdown.

By implicitly agreeing to play this role and acting out undesirable parental characteristics, the child shoulders full responsibility, allowing the parent(s) to avoid it. In the heat of a confrontation, a parent may yell exasperatingly, "You're acting just like your mother!" or "Why do you always have to remind me of your father?" Having avoided for years focusing attention on the true nature of the conflict, the parents' reaction to the loss of the scapegoated child inevitably alters the marital relationship.

child as resolution to parental identity Somewhat related to the process of scapegoating is the phenomenon whereby a parent encourages certain behavior within a child in order to resolve the parent's own internal conflict. This can be seen when parents want a child to attend a particular college or select a certain career. For example, fathers may want a son to achieve job successes which always seemed out of reach for the father.

Alternatively, behavior may be openly criticized when, in actuality, the child is acting as a conduit for growth within the parent. Such an example might be the awakening stages of a mother's need for independence. She may berate her daughter for not wanting to get married or for acting too independently within the family setting. Secretly, however, the mother admires the courage her daughter exhibits — courage that the mother is lacking. In other subtle ways the mother may actually encourage her daughter's independence.

If these longings by either mother or father act as a catalyst for resolving struggle, then the parent benefits; if not, then the departure of the child leaves a void in the psyche of the parent that may hinder the reestablishment of the marital relationship.

a couple in confusion Children definitely impinged on the relationship of Lucinda and her husband. Understanding of the dynamics between the two of them was, perhaps, evolving. Two children had left home; two remained — both in their mid-twenties. Lucinda had a full-time career — a fact not necessarily apparent from her comments.

"At one point Fred seemed to change so much after the kids left that he was not content with anything. He couldn't sit still. He had to be out on the street with the guys. He had never done that before. When the kids were at home, his duty was to be home.

"I made more demands on him than I had. I would zero in on him because the kids were gone. I just wanted him here whether I had anything for him to do, or we were going to do anything or not. I focused attention on him and he didn't want it. He wanted to get out and see what everybody else was doing. I'm adjusting.

"Missing the kids has affected me differently. It's just me and the checkbook. I don't give it a thought...if I see something I want...there's no obligation to the children. And my tastes have changed to more expensive things. My weight has gone up since the kids left. I eat junk...late at night...ice cream, cake. At this size I have to buy more expensive things to look nice. Fred used to buy clothes for me but he doesn't like it now; he can't tell what my size is. I never had a weight problem before. When the kids say something about it, I get mad.

"When Beth talks about leaving I get very upset...visibly so. I will miss her most of all. There is something comforting about her, in knowing that she is going to come home or in what she says. When I am going through a change or Fred is, she is the one I talk to.

"Do we do something to keep the other two kids here? Apparently we do because nobody's interested in leaving. We make it too easy. They don't know how to cook! They do pay rent, but often it's late. I buy the food. I do my son's laundry. Why make it uncomfortable for them? I could never ask them to leave. They don't bother me that much.

"Could I be avoiding intimacy? It could very well be. I know that things are not like they used to be...it could be because it's a house full of adults. Maybe Fred and I don't have that much to talk about. I often wonder what we had to talk about before the children. Maybe I'm scared to find out. What did we do before the children, I ask myself. I think I'm pretty boring. I like staying at home. If everybody's gone and it's just the two of us, then what? We're good friends. We like each other as individuals...but finding that common ground between us may take some creative doing, I guess.

"Maybe I am subconsciously trying to hold on to the kids. Even the two that moved out...I'm never really out of contact with them, so I've not had the chance to miss them. I've never really separated from them.

"I have felt the separation more in my relationship with my husband than I have felt it with my children. It has bothered me more than the kids leaving. I think the distance between Fred and me was there before but I didn't know it. I noticed it when the first two left and I didn't have to concentrate on them and I could concentrate on him. I had fewer and fewer things to focus in on...like he was the only thing left. He said, 'I've always gone out,' but I didn't notice it until I was not busy with the kids. Seems like I'm not ever busy any more. I zero in on him: Where is he? What is he doing? When he's here I don't have anything for him to do. It's just that I'm here so he's supposed to be here, too."

THE MARRIAGE CONTINUES

less marital strain While these family-dynamic situations often act as roadblocks to renewing the marriage, the opposite can hold true. Parents often get along better simply because the absence of kids means fewer issues to disagree about.

In some families the child leaving is a welcome release: the child and one of the parents have not gotten along, and this constant tension produced a strain on the marriage. In spite of guilt feelings that the parents may experience, the child's parting is actually crucial to the survival of the marriage. This type of conflict is especially seen in blended families where a child and stepparent never reach a level of understanding or comraderie.

Often parents of large or blended families move to a smaller place so they don't have room for children to come and go so freely or settle in permanently. The goal is to create an environment where talk between mates can be nonthreatening, constructive, and uninterrupted. During an interview with one blended couple, the wife brought out a number of points dealing with the need to protect this environment. "Life is wonderful but basically none of them can come back. They chose not to go to school so they're in and out too much. I can't handle it any more. Our life is so wonderful when they're gone. They just create a whirlwind; they're big kids, and when they leave I'm a basket case.

"It would be a problem if his daughter comes to live with us. I feel jealous when she's intruding on my female territory. We vie for my husband's affections. Jack and I are set in our ways, our routine. Lots of times we don't come home after work. Kids are disruptive...a hullabaloo. Then, if we're out of sorts with the kids, it spills over into our sexual desires.

"We do a lot of traveling. Maybe we'll move to Florida after our parents die. The kids seem to be moving back...so we'll have to move to Florida to get away from them. Maybe we'll get a one bedroom apartment so they can't come back with us!" Both husband and wife laughed as if in jest, but it was obvious that the idea had already been discussed.

personal growth Seen as challenges, family-dynamic situations can also lead individual parents to healthy introspection. If areas of prior conflict (where a child's presence caused unhealthy patterns to develop) can be effectively resolved and set on a positive course, then growth for the parent results.

Interestingly, positive changes for the self, pursuit of autonomous interests, and accommodation of new needs and demands within the changing marriage relationship often precipitate a redistribution of power between the partners. If not viewed as a threat, this transformation actually focuses concentrated commitment to the marriage, and emphasis on parental roles recedes.

sexual freedom One of the most exciting aspects of having the house all to themselves is that parents can return to being lovers with an air of sexual freedom, intensity, and closeness perhaps reminiscent of having an exciting affair or a second honeymoon. Parents who felt intimidated by the knowledge that their teens were sexually active may feel an additional release. Couples can make love whenever the mood strikes, wherever it strikes. They can walk around the house in seductive teddies or jockey shorts — or in nothing at all.

As each spouse responds favorably to this new twist, letting go of the reserve and inhibitions of the past may become easier. Suddenly there are many things that have renewed meaning because they are shared: participating in new activities together, spending significant amounts of time talking directly to each other as confidants, discovering thoughts and feelings in the other person which were somehow hidden over the years, laughing and having fun, enjoying getaway weekends, buying surprise presents for each other, having dinners by candlelight, indulging in tender backrubs, exploring new sexual pleasures or fantasies, allowing a childlike playfulness to erupt — all designed to let the other know that she or he is special.

increased intimacy Renewed intimacy takes time — time which may be measured in years, rather than months. The stronger the marriage, the less time needed for readjustment. If there is a solid marriage and each parent has multiple interests and commitments, then separation from the children does not cause severe marital strain. All couples though, including dual-career couples, must make an investment of time to restore intimacy and become indulgent in each other. Fortunately, there are numerous benefits to be gained from putting forth this effort.

"The empty nest is a particularly important time for a couple to reaffirm their commitment," said one husband, "so we took time to be together. We knew that this was the way life was going to be for us. We looked forward to it and enjoyed the heck out of it. It was a good fall."

Intimacy may be easier for those couples who spent their early married years without children. "We were married for some time before we adopted," said one wife, "so we had a close relationship.

Even after the kids came along we did things together and enjoyed each other. When they left, there wasn't a gap that needed to be filled. We already knew how satisfying it would be with just the two of us."

Many marriages improve during the middle-aged years because spouses are more accepting and tolerant of their mates. Accommodation within oneself and with the spouse is easier. With increased sharing, the comfort of having known someone for years cements the marital bond. Quite simply put, these couples are happier.

status quo Sometimes the marriage does not improve. Those couples who feel exceptionally strong about their responsibility to the marriage as a lifetime commitment will stay together in spite of the fact that the children are gone and early marital expectations remain unfulfilled. Some couples will recognize that their marriage has become a maintenance of the status quo primarily for reasons of expediency. Superficial compromises may be negotiated, but the fear and risk of challenging the fabric of the marriage relationship outweigh any potential benefits. Both partners feel that the issue at stake is so integral to their general mental health and life satisfaction that the threat of disrupting this way of life cannot be justified.

Men and women may approach the status quo from slightly different viewpoints. Marriage may represent for men the only intimate relationship available so that even if it falls far short of the ideal, living without it is unimaginable. Research has shown that a man's overall feelings about life happiness are often closely tied to his marriage[5]; if the marriage dissolves, well-being and satisfaction would likely plummet. Women, on the other hand, may come to a similar conclusion but for a different reason. They fear that if the relationship is put to a test they will be found wanting by their husbands who may decide to leave; they fear that their husbands will not place enough value on the marriage to keep it together if *the boat is rocked*; or they fear being left economically on their own. Each partner may decide that coexistence as the price of security is a compromise worth making.

deteriorating marriage In other instances, the status quo deteriorates and the marriage becomes nothing more than a shallow, hollow union where the parties share little in common. Yet, neither wife nor husband has the courage to terminate the relationship in spite of the fact that the children were their excuse for staying together over the years. Without the children around, they stay together out of habit and the consequences of that decision become painfully obvious.

"My parents' relationship has always been very stormy...a love/hate thing," reflected Bob, a thirty-seven-year-old whose relationship with his parents was strained. "Their world revolves around the three kids (even though we're all adults)...her world especially. They should have gotten divorced twenty-five years ago but didn't because of us kids. They used to be very social, but over a period of time they desocialized themselves so that now they have no social life. They just have the children.

"I don't think Dad had the courage to stand up to her. He never told her to grow up. He never told her, 'I'm going this way, you can go that way.' I fault him for not leaving her. He would have had a happier life but he was afraid to start over. Now they're both locked in and unhappy." Bob shook his head.

marital counseling Sometimes steps have to be taken to save a marriage. Marital counseling may be needed to rekindle awareness of the partner's needs and to develop communication skills which allow expression of feelings. Lingering patterns of criticism and judgment can be difficult to put aside but with professional help and concentrated effort, couples can survive. Also available are intense one-on-one weekends called marriage encounters, usually sponsored by religious groups, which use heightened communication to guide spouses in becoming reacquainted.

THE AFFAIR

experimentation and upheaval Midlife is a time for experimentation and the sexual arena is oftentimes no exception. The freedom to be different and challenge the habit of marriage may be unleashed as the children leave. Diminished responsibility for the children leads to diminished responsibility to the marriage. As a relief to boredom with one's mate, affairs represent real opportunities for excitement.

Fantasies of an affair may be real or imagined: real if they result in an affair with another person, real if they are enacted through the spouse in a burst of sexual activity, but imagined if flirtations with another person lead only to daydreams of infidelity. Often the extramarital affair is the direct result of conflict in the lives of the couple and serves as a punishment or warning to the other spouse. A husband may have an affair because he feels threatened and neglected by his wife's dedication to a job or involvement in an activity which excludes him. A wife may have an affair to assert her need for and feelings of independence. One partner may do it to get back at the other, or the partner may simply no longer be attracted by the other.

In some instances, the affair results from a close look at the sacrifices that a spouse has made to stay in the marriage. It represents "a confrontation with what has been given up in order to be in the relationship — with those lost aspects of the self which are perceived as having been surrendered to the relationship and to the partner who turned out to be so dismayingly different from the golden dream."[6] Instead of the contentment the spouses expected in middle age, they are faced with upheaval.

aging and sexual tensions The affair may be a manifestation of the tensions which result from growing older. Such infidelities arise from a desire to bolster self-confidence in sexual abilities or attractiveness: menopause in women and the inability to perform in men may send both looking for affirmation from someone else. Complicating matters still further may be a wife's growing confidence in her love-making ability at a time when her husband's fear or performance anxiety leads him to avoid sex.

By having an affair with a younger woman, a man may actually substitute someone who will allow him to continue in the father role because he knows his wife and children no longer need him. A younger woman's financial dependence may revive his provider image; her adoration may restore his masculine prowess and youthful zest.

opportunity for new understanding Not only does an affair present opportunities for meeting unfulfilled sexual and emotional needs, it may also provide a chance to establish a more open, communicative relationship. A new person may offer more understanding, more sharing, and more acceptance than the spouse does. An affair often allows a person to break out of a rut, to get in touch with new parts of the self, or to write a different script—the very things that a spouse seems to stifle. If the new relationship only repeats the patterns of the marriage, then little change or self-exploration arises. When the growth arising from the affair is incorporated into the marriage, then the couple may stay together. Otherwise, affairs frequently lead to divorce.

an unsettling experience Although two of her three boys were still at home when Laura's husband had an affair, their presence prevented him from leaving. She had seen some of the experiences of her friends first hand and felt very wary of the perils that might befall a middle-aged couple. "Children stand in the way of a clear-cut relationship," she said. "They complicate it. Maybe it will be better when they're all gone...although thinking about the last one leaving seems scary. Then there's only the two of you and you don't have anybody running interference. I would hope that it would be good but I don't know. I have a friend in San Francisco and when her kids left she looked forward to the change and expected things to get better. She wanted to spend time together — maybe go out for romantic dinners — and thought that they would get closer. But it didn't work out that way for her. Things are still the same and he spends just as much time with his job. I think that would be real disappointing. Maybe it's just a fantasy.

"Frank had an affair two years ago with someone he met on a business trip. I didn't know about it. He told her that he was going to get divorced, leave his job, marry her...the whole thing. He didn't tell me, but he told her on the phone everyday, practically. He was getting meaner and meaner to me and he'd never been that way. I was really devastated, horrified because I could see me doing that — and I did have a brief affair once — but I could never see him doing that. I was really surprised. Through all this I never told him about my escapade...he would never have gotten over it. I thought he was going to leave; I told him to leave. But he couldn't stand to leave the children. Finally it just passed. He called and told her he was not leaving. He made his mind up and that was the end of it...I think.

"I was pretty scared. Frank and I don't talk much. He's really closed. Now that I know that she's married and left the country, it's totally gone. He also wanted to quit his job. I said okay, let's go live out West. I could have done it. When it came down to brass tacks, he couldn't do it. And then whatever it was came to a head and it just dissolved. He doesn't think about it anymore.

"Sometimes I worry that it will flair up again, come back to him, because he never really resolved it. Everything is still the same. But the next time it happens, I'll get divorced because I am never going to let that happen to me...that total devastation. That's one reason that I'd like to have a good job...so that I wouldn't feel scared, because I was scared. I was shocked. I felt bad about myself. I'm forty-eight and I keep thinking to myself if he's ever going to do it...that's the bad result of the whole thing...that I'm never really sure that he won't someday do it again...I wish he'd do it now rather than wait five or ten years like a couple I know. She's in really bad shape. They were fifty-five and now he's got someone twenty years younger. She's very upset. Financially, she's in bad shape."

Laura has good reason to wonder if this situation will arise again after the kids leave; midlife divorce is a common occurrence.

DIVORCE

couples who stayed together for the sake of the kids When children have been the only focus of a couple, the greater the likelihood that the marriage may dissolve. Wives, feeling an enormous investment in raising the children, may have stayed in the relationship because of the kids; husbands, feeling a keen sense of financial commitment, may have done the same. Now, both are free.

Wife and husband may have withdrawn into themselves and have difficulty relating to each other. Because children are not around to act as a buffer or the glue that binds, spouses may be forced to face problems previously ignored; they may be forced to accept the partner as she or he really is or forced to decide realistically whether or not the marriage should continue.

Spouses may come face to face with the fact that the marriage was flawed from the beginning, that the reasons for getting married were not anchored in a sturdy foundation of love, and that the situation will never get any better. This particularly holds true if, not only have the children been the reason that the relationship endured, but pregancy was the reason the couple got married in the first place. Failure to take action now may only lead to divorce later when it might be even harder to pick up with a new life.

spillover from other midlife issues The many other issues surrounding midlife often influence how a wife and husband feel about each other. The issues become so clouded that whether the marriage is suffering from incompatability or from something else — such as career reassessment or worries about mortality — may not be easily determined. One study did yield some insight, however: divorce was more prevalent among men who were suffering a midlife crisis as a result of the empty nest than as a result of any other factor.[7]

double whammy for women In her book, *Women: Psychology's Puzzle*, Joanna B. Rohrbaugh speaks of the threat of the midlife divorce in terms of the "Dominant Goal" and the "Dominant Other" (i.e., the mate). As they grow, she says, males are rewarded for their independence and aspirations to attain a goal; females are basically rewarded for their dependence and reliance on another person as expressed through love and marriage. Thus, failure for men is measured in terms of career disappointments and failure for women in terms of loss of attachments. Complicating matters still further, "if the couple separates, the wife has lost everything: her Dominant Other, his (and her) Dominant Goal defined in terms of his career, and her Dominant Goal defined in terms of the marital relationship itself."[8] It's as though she has no separate identity apart from the marriage; its loss becomes a severe blow.

A very real concern for women, of course, is that they won't be able to manage financially once divorced. This fear is not ungrounded: statistics indicate that a drop in income of sixty to seventy percent is not unusual for divorced mothers to experience.[9] To face such a financial disruption at midlife cannot be taken lightly.

paradoxes The broken marriage at midlife reads like a litany of paradoxes and opposites. The wife may feel threatened by the direction that the husband is taking or the husband may feel that the wife has gained the upper hand. The status quo may be challenged by a juggling for power. The husband may seek change of the status quo and the wife resist, or the other way around. Either may be tired of the unrelenting compromises or dreary repetition that they find instead of the excitement and rejeuvenation that was expected.

Just when they should be getting closer, they begin to pull away. Just when they should know each other best, one may not like what the other has become. Each may feel criticized or attacked by the other through direct statement or inference — for being themselves, for their weaknesses, for their lack of achievement. One may seek a mutual sharing while the other reverts to childlike dependency or, its opposite, a controlling, bossy behavior. One or the other may feel trapped.

In spite of the bleakness within the marriage, either spouse may be terrified of a lonely life without the other and that now-familiar emotional grounding — no matter how unsatisfactory life together is. Thoughts of divorce may preoccupy daily life and discussions, and yet neither spouse is able to follow through. Eventually one may escape when life seems unbearable.

surprise at frequency There are some preconceived notions of what is normal in marriage. One is that couples who have been together for twenty years will stay together and uphold an unwritten tenet of social responsibility. Yet more and more one sees long-term marriages fall apart as husband or wife, or both, gradually come to the realization that happiness and self-fulfillment outside of marriage are acceptable goals. A changing society has given its approval: a couple does not have to stay in a poor relationship.

Statistics indicate that the rate of divorce climbs during midlife as compared to the early-thirties age group. "One quarter of the marriages that have lasted fifteen years or more now end in divorce."[10] Such deterioration of the marriage mentality in middle-aged adults has become a fact of life, and yet, understandably, people still express surprise and confusion.

"Some of the couples that I thought were going to be together forever because they were all-American, super-special people doing all the right things have gotten divorced and it has usually been around the time that children leave the nest. When I was younger and heard about a couple age fifty-five getting a divorce I would wonder why in the world that was happening. But now I can see exactly what happens: the two individuals are facing their own selves and each other without any external demands. We get so caught up in the sheer demand of carpooling or doing what so-and-so needs or taking trips...but you end up being faced with yourself and with your partner. For people who don't wish to do that I can see how they would split.

"I know one couple where the wife was terribly organized, terribly responsible...the *super-mom* type...but her husband just did not want a marriage relationship any more. The oldest child is twenty-five. It's been sheer agony for her. I almost have to think that it's some kind of a quality of spirit that seems to be able to help people through this time of transition or crisis...that helps some people and not others. The husband was so tired of being programmed by his wife that he didn't want to be married anymore, didn't want to deal with it. That seems to happen more with men...they fulfill their responsibilities and then get out. They seem to be saying, 'I've been a good provider and I've been a good father and the children are on their own.' A lot of men are not able to even talk about their feelings. The only way they can cope is to just get out and start life over again."

effect on children The thought of their parents getting divorced can be quite traumatic for teenagers and young adults, even to the point that they feel personally responsible for holding the marriage together. Not only have they left home but home, as they know it, may disappear. Once the marriage dissolves and that burden is lifted, children may experience feelings of relief and actively pursue the opportunity of getting to know their parents as two separate, unique individuals. Parents, on the other hand, finally released from feelings of resentment against the children who seemingly kept them trapped within the marriage, may seize the chance to strengthen and revitalize the parent-child relationship.

other positive aspects Generally though, after the initial shock and pain of reestablishing a life alone, both men and women manage pretty well — much to the surprise of friends and relatives. (In fact, part of the scare that others experience when they see a midlife couple divorce is acknowledging the reality or tenuousness of their own marital relationship.) Few want the old marriage back. They find the newness of life stimulating and rewarding in unexpected ways.

PROFILE

Sally James, while still married, could be described as being in a state of indecision and flux. She had two children, Noelle who attended a private college a couple of hours from home and Ted who attended the local university. Ted still lived at home. The marriage had survived for the sake of the children; but because they were now pretty much on their own, Sally was prepared to leave if she and her husband, Mike, could not resolve their problems.

"Sometimes Noelle shows up unannounced at home on the weekend and we have plans. I get irritated because I feel guilty going off and leaving her and yet I think...we didn't know she was coming...and we have things planned, too. My husband's the type to drop everything if she's coming home and cancel all the plans. He goes overboard.

"The negative feeling I have about her when she is home is that sometimes, to be honest, I get a little jealous of the extra attention that is showered upon her by my husband and the grandparents. I have my particular place and status and I don't want her in my territory and I don't want to invade hers, either. Last summer she spent a lot of time with us because her friends were not around. We couldn't go anywhere without having her along and I kind of resented that. I felt like saying, 'Hey, you get to party all year down at school and this is my time to go out. I don't always want you there.' My husband wants her to go with us. Possibly it's a way for him to escape from one-on-one with me. We're in marriage counseling but we still work hard at avoiding each other. Having her there is a buffer.

"The last five or six years the marriage has been rocky. The biggest part of not leaving while the kids were still at home was the financial picture. Because of his job they would live with me; that was a given. I didn't see how I could support two kids. For a lot of years I used the same old excuse...when the kids are gone...in fact, I think I told him one time, 'The minute they both leave, I'm leaving, too; I won't have any other reason to stay.' So that kind of posed a deadline.

"Now that Noelle's gone, I wonder...is this the time? I started thinking about it more seriously...as opposed to just one of those comments you make knowing you don't have to act on it. I have thought about it a lot. Knowing that I was thinking about it has finally forced Mike to take some actions on his own to rectify the problems that have been there all these years...so some good has come out of that. Plus, he sees that soon it's just going to be the two of us, so if it's going to work, we've got to get it working now.

"I've figured up how I can afford it and how the assets can be divided. I've got the whole thing worked out. He knows that I can pick up and go at a moment's notice. He felt threatened initially, but now he's realized how serious I really am and that the ball's in his court. He's really working on it.

"Will we make it? It's still too soon." She gave a little laugh. "He will have to reevaluate how much time he spends away at work. Also, he feels guilty about the time he spent on the job when the kids were growing up. Now he's overcompensating for it by being so upset that she's gone and, when she is home, he just showers her with anything she wants...trying to make up for what he didn't do. She doesn't take advantage of it...she could.

"I think Mike's had a midlife crisis. He's very depressed looking at his life and thinking nothing's the way he wanted it. It's just a bag of junk. He's tearing his whole being...pulling away from some very basic things that he always believed in...testing a new lifestyle. He's really suffered." Not until later did Sally reveal that this "new lifestyle" was actually an affair with another woman.

"My husband may have felt left out because Noelle and I did all the college stuff together — writing for information, going to interviews, etc. I assumed it was because he didn't want to face the issue...maybe we did that to him.

"Her leaving meant this part of our lives is over. Now there's a new part. And I want to approach it right...from the beginning...not like the last ten years. I want to get rid of all the bad stuff of the past, which may include my spouse. Noelle's leaving brought those things into focus.

"I remember when I was younger looking at couples married twenty, thirty years who were getting a divorce and it never made any sense to me. I thought after twenty years you've either worked out your problems or you haven't. You wouldn't still be together, surely, if you haven't. It seemed like the dumbest thing in the world to me. Now, I can see. At that age I thought of a marriage as being static, but it isn't! My husband can't communicate feelings at all. He can just analyze and tell me what he thinks, not feels. He says, 'Women always have to know how you feel.' He thinks that men who do that are wimpy and soft.

"When I found out about his affair last year I cried and carried on and couldn't eat...the whole routine. He said he would give her up. But he didn't, and this year when I found out, it didn't really bother me. I started thinking about where I was going to live...making all these plans...ahhh neat, now a whole new life's going to start. I was excited about it. It may have been a mental way of protecting myself and avoiding the issue. I just told him I was leaving, period. He absolutely fell apart. He was very, very upset. He couldn't do his job, couldn't do anything, couldn't function. If I leave, also, he's like the child losing his parent...he loses the parent role I play for him...so he is now addressing some things head on.

"He said that it started because of that comment I mentioned to him a few years ago that when the kids left, I was leaving, too. Apparently he never forgot it and felt totally abandoned. He felt forced into this situation. The other woman was a friend. I'm not angry at her. I feel a little bit responsible so I'm sticking around for counseling to give it one more shot. I made a list and he agreed to the points: counseling, restructuring work hours, finding a church for both of us, doing projects around the house, getting along with my family. He says the affair is over but I don't really know.

"Noelle said to me once, 'Mom, why do you put up with that crap from him? I've watched you put up with that for years. Why do you do that?' If I left, she would understand.

"I figure if it's not going to work, let's decide it's not going to work so I can get on with it. The years are going by so rapidly. I don't want to wake up one day and feel like I've been caught short. I don't want to have any regrets about what I should have done. I've got to make the most of this life...now, not later."

1. Michael P. Farrell and Stanley D. Rosenberg, *Men at Midlife* (Boston: Auburn House Publishing Company, 1981) p. 121.
2. Jay Haley, *Leaving Home* (New York: McGraw-Hill Book Company, 1980) p. 30.
3. p. 130.
4. Farrell, p. 153.
5. Lois M. Tamir, *Men in Their Forties The Transition to Middle Age* (New York: Springer Publishing Company, 1982) p. 18.
6. Scarf, p. 21.
7. McGill, p. 163.
8. New York: Basic Books, Inc., Publishers, 1979, p. 409. Rohrbaugh's primary reference for Dominant Goal/Dominant Other concept is S. Arieti and J. Bempora, *Severe and mild depression: The psychotherapeutic approach* (New York: Basic Books, 1978).
9. Rubin, p. 132.
10. Nancy Mayer, *The Male Mid-Life Crisis* (Garden City, New York: Doubleday & Company, Inc., 1978) p. 117.

CHAPTER 14

WHEN THE NEST FILLS...AGAIN

I have never seen such great smiles on the faces of people who are going forth...and, in the words of my father, "Forth is not back home."[1]

THE WHYS OF THE UNEMPTY NEST

no laughing matter Of course, everyone laughed at the joke. But in some respects, the issue is no laughing matter. Much has been written about college graduates who can't make it on their own and return home to live. They seem to be unwilling or unable to face life head-on and embrace adulthood. They move back home because they need a job or to save on expenses or to be protected from life's viscissitudes. They often seem immature. Somehow, they don't understand what it means to struggle. When one reads these stories, there is frequently an underlying current of what might be called the *spoiled-child syndrome* — the story of a child emotionally crippled when it comes to dealing with things that don't work out the way she or he expects. These young adults find it easier to go home to a cocoon which fosters financial and emotional dependence.

Sometimes young adults are returning home in failure. They may have flunked out of college or have been rejected by graduate schools. With this loss of self-esteem comes an ego in need of buttressing.

Parents have to fight the urge to make things right for these emerging adults in the same way that parents gradually let go when the child is growing up. Parents often want to insulate their offspring from the harsh realities of the world by protecting them from the unpleasant or by assuming their problems. In the end, that may not be fair to the children.

economics and expectations There are a number of factors leading to this returning-home phenomenon. Certainly, the economy is a major one. Jobs are not as easy to find. For those that do exist, competition can be intense. Additionally, in spite of their education, these young adults are often unprepared for the jobs that are available.

This generation of children recognizes that, in material terms, they will not necessarily be better off than their parents. Yet, they are used to the good life and have a difficult time scaling down their expectations. One way that young adults can launch themselves into financial stability is to live with their folks and begin saving for a down payment on a house. Recognizing the high cost of housing, parents often lend or give additional funds to help out with a home mortgage. Other parents may encourage the young adult to live on his or her own by helping with monthly living expenses.

the changing norm Another factor is the changing value in society of what the *norm* is. In spite of the implication, the norm is not static; it is continually evolving. For some the norm used to be getting married out of high school or after working a few years. Later, the norm was getting married and settling down after college. More recently, there has been a delay in the settling-down process; young people often wait to marry or have children.

The norm is still changing. Undoubtably, today's increased life span gives each person more time in which to grow up and become a functioning adult. Why should a young person rush into the responsibilities of life when a few years' delay still leaves decades during which to be an adult? The modern-day realignment of male/female roles also affects the norm. Young males do not have to assume the responsibility of provider for a wife and family; young females do not have to assume the responsibilities of children while foregoing a career. Nothing is automatic.

With this delayed approach to life's responsibilities, young adults also take longer to figure out what career they want to pursue. Upon reaching a decision, they may return home to take additional college courses and thus qualify for graduate programs. Sometimes they live at home throughout their graduate study. One mother described her feelings when her son returned to take courses in preparation for medical school and she and her husband were no longer alone.

"When he came back it was bittersweet. He's a nice person to have around...he and I have a lot in common...but it had been awfully nice to have just the two of us here. There's a sense of having lost a little freedom. There's a sense of having a boarder so that life needs to have a routine to it. We're not as free to eat out spur of the moment. He got into med school and will probably live here another year before he gets an apartment. It's not easy to come home...he's made a real effort to make it work. There are no frustrations on my part because we know that there's an end to it. If he just stayed, we'd kick him out. That would be the best for him."

The parental norm has also changed: many parents try to stay out of their kids' way once they return and let them *do their own thing*. Ironically, this more relaxed environment is the very ingredient which lessens the young adult's need to leave home.

Perhaps the norm will continue to shift and expected behavior on the part of both parents and children will be a return home after college. The media will no longer comment about it; people will not express surprise when it happens. Returning home will be the norm.

Comments by numerous parents pointed up that this is not yet the case for many; they clearly felt the ambiguousness of the departure issue. "Sure I missed them when they left...but then they came back." Said another, "What I'd like to know is when do they really leave...for the last time?" And another, "You only think it's the end when they leave for college; it's not."

sexual freedom One of the compelling reasons that young adults used to leave home and settle down was sex. Today, the pill and other methods of birth control, as well as more lenient attitudes about sex on the part of many parents, frequently make it unnecessary for children to escape home to enjoy this fruit of life. Parents may cramp the child's activities some, but chastity is rarely required. Children are often free to come and go as they wish; curfews usually disappear. These young adults can act as independently or dependently as they want. They can test their wings without leaving the nest to do so.

emotional dependence A major contributing factor to a young adult's return home appears to be her or his emotional dependence or immaturity. Whether due to affluence, emotional coddling, or problems in the family's letting go process, the young adult is unable to cope with the emotional business of growing up. In short, the child is psychologically unprepared with parents unwilling to relinquish control over the child's life.

Parents, if they are honest with themselves, may admit that they are accomplices in their child's inability to be independent. Unfortunately, breaking the dependency pattern is complicated: parents can become guilt-ridden when they don't acquiesce to the child's apparent needs.

parental persuasion Not surprisingly, those parents who need to acknowledge that a child is returning home to stabilize a deteriorating family situation (by refocusing attention on the child) are the least able psychologically to do so. Subtle messages from parent to child may initiate the return home as the child falls victim to a pattern of profound illness, academic misfortunes, or employment-related failures. Other parents may succeed at talking the teenager into living at home for a year or two before making the break. When parents thoroughly enjoy that feeling of being needed again or of being a part of a more youthful scene, subsequent departure may be discouraged entirely.

ISSUES...THE NEXT TIME AROUND

parental right to say "no" Certainly parents have to decide what is right in each potential returning-home situation. They have the right to decide yes or no.

If the lack of responsibility shown by the young adult so severely clashes with the parents' values that everyday living might become unbearable, then parents need to say no. If a young adult has a drinking or drug problem and steps toward rehabilitation have failed, parents are sometimes forced into insisting that no return be allowed. If offspring simply want to take from the situation and are not willing to accommodate or compromise, then the discrepancy in expectations bodes a poor working relationship that might be better left alone, in spite of a short-term hardship for the child. If both parents and children cannot approach renewed living together in a spirit of cooperation, then damage may be done to the lifetime adult-adult relationship which cannot be easily repaired. In the end, parents have a right to call a halt to their parenting responsibilities and tell their kids to stand on their own. The question is often *when*.

impact on parents When dependent young adults come back into their parents' lives by reentering the nest, parents have often settled into a child-free existence. New patterns and routines have been established; life no longer centers on the children. Young adults who move back home or are frequently in and out can cause discomfort, resentment, shock, or outright anger; for married parents, the marital relationship may be subjected to significant stress. If the family home turns into a revolving door subject to the child's whim, too many readjustments are required of the parents. Matters are further complicated if a child wants to move back home with a parent who has remarried since the child left home. This exciting marriage at midlife may have no room for the intrusion of an extra person.

Assuming a young adult does move back home, the family dynamics truly change: before, only the husband-wife relationship existed; after, there are three relationships — husband-wife, mother-child, and father-child. The number of relationships operating under one roof has tripled. The peace and quiet that parents expect and are used to may disappear. They may experience difficulty getting along with each other. Children once again impinge on the parents' time, their relationship, and probably their finances. Parents should not feel forced into moving to a smaller place to avoid the returning children problem but, as already suggested, some do.

impact on kids Parents are not the only ones to suffer; there are also readjustment problems for the children who return. Young adults are significantly different from the teenagers who previously left home, yet their new role within the family structure may be undefined. They may not want to be told what to do, yet they're not really on their own. They may not enjoy feeling like a guest in their own home, yet in some ways they are — for the parents have reclaimed the home as their own. Home has become a way-station for the kids, yet often they want to fit back in and feel that they permanently belong. Children, as well as their parents, feel the loss of privacy and constrictions on lifestyle.

tips for parents Are their any tips for parents in dealing with the returning child? Perhaps most important is for parents to be in agreement about how to handle situations so that the young adult does not start manipulating either parent. Mothers and fathers should not wait on their children, do their laundry, cook their meals, pay their bills, and so forth (refer to comprehensive lists in Chapter 9) even if, "It's no bother."

If the parents are making more concessions than the child, they need to remember that the child's needs should no longer always come first nor should those needs act as a wedge between the parents and *their* needs. Having set a new direction to their lives, parents should not let children completely disrupt it. After all, the home is the parents'; if the young adult wants absolute freedom, she or he must get a separate place.

When young adults return home, ground rules and a specific timetable for leaving are helpful and perhaps necessary. For the easiest return to handle is a temporary one. This prevents the lingering effect: the child who never leaves, the student who never finishes, the person who refuses to grow up. *Dear Abby* letters periodically deal with the child who has overstayed his or her welcome — by a few years. Parents can be forced into literally throwing their child out and changing the locks — not unlike the mother bird pushing her young out of the nest so they can fly on their own.

unexpected benefits Sometimes there are unexpected benefits to be gained from the child returned home. Different family dynamics, fewer siblings, or personal growth on the part of the young adult and the parent can mean improved relationships and a chance to become reacquainted. If older siblings negatively influenced a younger child's behavior, this emerging adult may now have the space to be on his or her own terms. The strengthening of adult-adult relationships may ensue.

One mother told the story of her friend's second daughter, Annie, moving back home. Because she had always thought that her older sister was favored, Annie had acted out and been a problem child. After she returned home and lived alone with her parents, she explained that this behavior was not her *true* self. Finally able to discuss grievances on both sides, parents and child were making strides to develop a whole new relationship. The move back home had been the catalyst.

Another parent spoke of the joy she felt living with her twenty-two-year-old daughter for five months. "It was such fun having her around again and getting to know her as an adult. It was a real high. She's a wonderful person and we get along well together. We were able to share funny experiences, her romance entanglements...all the stuff that makes a mother and daughter close. Sometimes we would go to a nearby restaurant for dinner and just sit and talk. She helped me through the ups and downs and final dissolution of my long-term relationship. How I cried when she left...even though I knew she needed to be out on her own dealing with the added responsibility. I really missed her."

facing reality More than anything, the returning child forces parents to face reality squarely. What kind of a relationship do they really have with their child? Lack of distance may erase those illusions of perfection which creep into the parent-child bond. Parents realize that they are not as free of their parenting responsibilities as they once thought. Parenthood may linger because they care.

Leave-taking is gradual: children rarely leave for good the first time around. Growing up and getting settled seem to take longer now as the norm shifts; it may include floating around, dropping out, or going from mindless job to mindless job.

Ultimately, becoming an adult is a task that the child must do; a parent cannot do it by proxy. For some families, the issue may evolve from one of *cutting the apron strings* to one of *cutting the kid's strings*.

PROFILE

Lou Stern and her husband had one daughter, Stacy. They had adjusted fairly easily when she went off to college in New England, but after graduation Stacy returned home to live. This adjustment was more difficult. It took her almost a year to find a job and, at times, her parents felt that they worked harder at trying to find her a job than she did. When employment finally materialized and Stacy moved out, everyone was relieved.

"When our daughter came back it was because of her inability to get a job. What I saw was the deterioration of her...someone who had majored in economics and read *The Wall Street Journal* and who was now staying in bed until eleven in the morning, not reading the paper, and watching the soap operas...regressing in a terrible fashion. That was totally alien to my kind of routine. Anybody sitting around the house was not very welcome to me. I wanted her to get on with her life. Yet I realized that it was difficult for her.

"There was a sense of having a *child* home again and I felt some responsibility for her just when I thought that the long period of schooling was at an end. We were almost starting over again without knowing where we were going. She had no direction. She's always done things at her own speed and no amount of prodding was going to hurry her along.

"I don't know why she regressed so. She'd always worked summers and yet she had been scared to look for work in Boston or New York so she came home to nest. Coming back to these surroundings made her regress more than if she had lived somewhere else. She could play the child again.

"I think that there's a difference between this generation and mine," Lou reflected. "I would never have thought about going home to live. I didn't really know my parents very well...the relationship was rather stiff. But my children feel so much more close to us and know that they have a comfortable house to come home to. We're more open as parents, and we have done more with them.

"She's not a dependent child and yet she wanted a lot from us. Stacy gets her wants and her needs mixed up. I guess kids' dependence on their parents meets some need.

"Basic personalities played an important role in our testy relationship. She and I are very different and I can't see us ever living very comfortably under the same roof. She is very slow...she eats slowly, she moves slowly...and I am not. In a daily living situation, people who are slow bug me. It's bad enough when it's the mother giving orders to the child but when the relationship gets on an adult status and there's this clash of personalities, it causes problems.

"She's a social animal; she likes to talk. My husband and I like to read, especially at night. She demanded conversation. I went through this in the daytime but the conversation was not terribly stimulating: soap operas, dates, who was at the bars. It was like going back to teenage conversation, in a sense. I was busy and wanted to be peacefully existing without all this chatter. And at night, if she didn't go out, it was the same thing all over again.

"Stacy could not come to grips with my house rules which were very simple. Her meal patterns were erratic and unpredictable. She's a very messy individual and her things were strewn all over the house. Her room was horrible, although it had always been that way. She did her laundry but then she'd leave it in the washer for three days. I didn't want her living that way here.

"Once she decided what to do, she attacked it with gusto and is doing a great job. She loves the world of finance. But you can't push kids. They have to find their own direction."

---

1. As told at the commencement ceremony of the Class of 1985, Brown University, by Bill Cosby after he received an honorary degree.

CHAPTER 15

VARIATIONS OF THE THEME: MARRIAGE, MILITARY, AND MOVING OUT

I think that growing up is a bitch...and they make kids do it...who've had no experience.

ALTERNATIVES

the stay-at-home kids Finding the common threads among those going off to college is easier than categorizing the similarities of those left behind. By and large, this latter group does not leave home until they are older. While at home, some will get jobs. Some may do nothing for a while. Many attend a local university and do not leave home for another four years or more.

the noncollege route Of those who do leave after high school, some will join one of the military services — often leaving within a couple months of graduation. Others will get married. Still others will seek independence and move out, frequently with a boyfriend or girlfriend. Those joining the military may be stationed hundreds of miles from home, perhaps overseas. But many of those who go out on their own will live nearby or within a one-hundred-mile radius.

parental feelings In spite of the different variations in the separation process, the reactions of parents appear to be universal. (This should come as no surprise: sprinkled throughout this book are quotes from parents whose children left for noncollege reasons.) For each parent who significantly grieves the loss of a college student, so also may a parent grieve the loss of a child to the military, particularly during times of military unrest. For each parent who takes in stride the departure of a freshman, so also may a parent take in stride the marriage of a child. The range of emotions appears to bear more correlation to the parents' individual emotional makeup than to the type of separation involved.

What may complicate a parent's reaction to a separation is that when middle- or upper-class children do not go to college, their parents may experience a sense of disappointment or even anger. Parents may feel that their child is not living up to his or her potential. They may wonder if their child will make it financially.

Young adults going the noncollege route are often more quickly emancipated from their parents' control because the financial strings attached to tuition bills do not exist. Therefore, parental feelings of disappointment at the noncollege path may actually arise from the desire to delay separation.

If there is going to be real upheaval in a family over a separation, a noncollege departure appears to have a greater likelihood of being the cause. Of the many interview requests made during the course of writing this book, only a very few parents refused — in each case to avoid reliving the pain associated with a child's leaving for the military or the estrangement created by an unapproved marriage. No parents of college-bound children needed that protection, although that is not to say that such parents do not exist. But rather, the author suspects, it was the unexpectedness and disappointment at the marriage or military commitment that caused the heartbreak — for heartbreak was indeed the result. In these situations there existed a greater air of finality and permanence to leaving the nest; parents of college-bound children more likely felt that they had *loaned* their child to the university for a while.

age and distance There do appear to be two significant factors which may influence a parent's reaction to a child's leaving: distance and age. How far away from home will the child be? How old is the child when she or he leaves? If the child gets his own apartment a few miles from home, the impact of leaving is lessened. If a daughter gets married but not until age twenty-three, the impact is also less. However, if either moves a few hundred miles across the country then, regardless of age, the separation may not be taken as lightly by the parents. The farther away from home a young adult moves, the greater the chances that parents will worry or be upset by the separation.

The older the child, the more the separation is expected as part of the life process. As each year passes, parents have more time to get used to the notion of separation. They usually see their children's lives grow more distant and apart from the family. They see their friends' children leave. Parents see their child mature. Gradually, they come to know that *it is time* for the young adult to go.

the kids' reaction One of the biggest sources of anxiety for eighteen-year-olds is a compelling issue: "What is going to happen when I get out into the world? Will I make it?" Parents often are not aware of this worry. When students go to college, whether at home or away, the issue is basically deferred. For the noncollege group, however, this issue is often much more real and troublesome, as the quote at the beginning of the chapter suggests.

MARRIAGE

tying the knot uncommon at eighteen Getting married right after high school is not today's trend; a couple moving in together is more likely. So when kids do get married, parents may be apprehensive and feel like their son or daughter is not ready, especially if a pregnancy is involved. Said one parent of getting married so young, "They seem like babies...even though we did it, we seemed older. I hope that they put off having kids for a while."

"The wedding was so fast that I questioned the decision," commented Karen, whose daughter had been living at home before she got married. "It was disturbing that they got married after knowing each other only four months, but there was no changing her mind. She was too young...I didn't feel like I had finished raising her yet. The marriage may have been an excuse to leave home. I even asked her if home was that bad, although she said no.

"I would have felt better if she had spent some time living on her own...facing groceries, rent, all those things. It's hard realizing that she's a full-fledged woman...a married lady. She shouldn't even be married yet!" Karen laughed.

An early, unapproved marriage can be traumatic indeed. One couple whose daughter ran away to marry a boy they disapproved of refused to see or speak to her, their son-in-law, or their eventual grandchild for a number of years. Only through the aid of a church was the family eventually reconciled.

less worry or more? The younger kids are when they marry, the less chance that they have faced life on their own. If parents feel unsure about their child's ability to cope with life or to manage financially, then they often worry. Parents may also worry because they know that such an early marriage probably has no more than a fifty percent chance of surviving. "When my son got married," said Diane, a mother of three, "I worried about his being happy...whether he had picked the right person...whether they would be happy together. I was not at ease with his marriage...and they did get divorced."

However, when parents feel confident of their child's decision and ability to cope, worry may be nonexistent. "If you feel like they're secure in where they are, then you don't miss them and you don't worry about them," Diane continued. "You feel like they're mature enough to handle it — financially, mentally, or whatever.

"When our daughter got married, that was just wonderful. She was ready and everybody felt like it was the right thing to do and we had the best time. It was a very happy wedding...we really enjoyed it. She had chosen the right one. She was going on with her life."

Marriage may also help to eliminate worry for those parents who have a more traditional, paternalistic attitude. Said one recently married daughter, "I think that my parents feel that they don't have to worry as much about me now that I have a husband." Showing obvious displeasure with their approach, she went on to add, "I feel that they should have treated me more like an adult when I was home."

parental adjustment When kids live at home until they get married, there is a greater likelihood that the newly-wed couple will not move out of town, thus making adjustment for the parents easier. "I don't really think that I missed my children," said Marsha, a mother whose children lived at home until each got married. "I see them quite a bit...maybe once a week. They're just around, or I talk to them. By the time the last one left, I had grandchildren. When I might have been missing one thing, something else was replacing it...so I didn't feel that emptiness."

Because grandchildren often do fill up an empty place in the parent's life, a more profound adjustment can be required should they move away. Marsha went on to describe her situation. "My daughter and her husband may be transferred. I would be very lonesome. I sit for the kids three days a week...they're an important part of my life."

Dee also had an easy time adjusting when her daughters got married. "My one daughter just moved two miles away so I see her or talk to her almost every day. I thought I was going to miss them when they left but surprisingly, I've kind of enjoyed it. It was harder on my husband. She's still like a baby to him."

Once young adults have resided out of town, they often continue to live out of town after a marriage. Yet their parents will probably experience only minor adjustments because they are already used to a long-distance separation. However, when a young person simultaneously marries and moves away, the end result can be fairly upsetting.

a sudden separation Louise described how she felt when her daughter married at eighteen and immediately left town. "She was on the wild side and I was always scared that she would get into trouble. I was on vacation in January and when I called she said that they were going to get married and move to California. He had a get-rich-quick scheme. I said, 'You're what?' It shocked the daylights out of me. They were talking about a June wedding. I got home on Saturday and they had gotten married on Thursday. No family was there...a couple of friends stood up for them. They left on Sunday.

"They had an old car that I did not even trust to make the trip and they couldn't take a lot of things with them...and me not knowing where they were, how they were doing...nothing. She had never been out on her own.

"It was three days before she called and I was on edge...shaky and nervous all the time." Louise threw her hands into the air to convey feelings of frustration, almost desperation. "I couldn't keep my mind on my work. It was so hard not to worry. The uncertainty...that's what drove me crazy. Her husband was not good to her. He'd get on drugs and hit her. Finally she left him and moved back. Now it's going to cost her quite a bit to get divorced. They owe the credit union, credit cards, and a car loan.

"But California's in her blood; she went back there to live. I'm not as worried about her this time because she's older and has been out working. She knows how to take care of herself."

a child's perspective The thoughts of young married adults are not necessarily that different than those who leave for college. Marilyn, who had recently gotten married, talked about her feelings of leaving home.

"Going through my room before I left was strange...throwing away most of my things...things that reminded me of different times and different boyfriends. I really realized...this is it. You're not a kid anymore. You've got to get rid of all this stuff. It was kind of scary in a way.

"I was happy to get out of the house so I don't miss it. But, in some ways, it does seem weird. Nobody is around to pick up behind me. I'm picking up behind somebody else. I see my folks about twice a week and we talk even more often. I do feel like they're interfering in some things...butting in. I can tell when Mom's biting her lip because she's just dying to tell me something...but I like having my own life and not talking to them about everything.

"They treat me as an adult a lot more. When I think Dad's going to criticize, he's giving encouragement instead. He'll say, 'I know, I've been there,' or 'You're going to learn from your mistakes.' He's surprised me a lot...he's mellowing out. He understands when we don't want to come over. He just takes it in stride. Mom's taking it a lot worse; she gets real sad. But I'm just not her baby anymore. If I don't call her for a while, she makes me feel bad. She's putting pressure on. I know she's trying not to, but she's still trying to hang on."

father of the bride When daughters marry and leave home, fathers often seem to have a special emotional reaction. Many cry on wedding day. They seem to feel a personal loss. They may miss the attention and affection they get from a daughter. Said one mother of her husband, "He seems lonely without the girls clamoring over him. He seems to need that. Now his granddaughter is the highlight of his life. He is like a changed man when she comes over."

A grown daughter herself, Gwen spoke of her father's reaction to her early marriage. "When I was fifteen, I got married and moved away. I was so homesick. Dad called me every day from work. 'Don't tell your mother,' he said. 'She thinks I'm bothering you.' Then on Sunday, when Mother would get to talk he'd say, 'Come on, we're running up the bill. We've got to get off the phone.'" Gwen giggled at the memory of her unsuspecting mother. "She didn't know that he and I had been talking all week." Clearly, the calls from Gwen's father helped her to make a major transition in her life at such a young age and she was grateful to him.

MILITARY

no place else to go Often the military is chosen, particularly by males, when options seem limited. Life appears to be in a state of upheaval. Home and family structure may be weak or nonexistent. The teen may have had academic problems or dislike the idea of continuing with a formal education. Some young adults can't, or won't, find a job. Some have been in trouble, often because of a wild streak. To many parents, this is a *problem child*. The child may lack motivation or simply have too much time on his hands and may need to *grow up*. Ironically, this may fulfill a pattern of failure set up by the parents.

"He quit high school three months before graduation," related one mother. "We decided that since nothing else had worked for him...he never completed anything...we'd signed the papers. I cried. I wanted him to go and I didn't want him to go. I was worried about him, yet I was excited for him. I had a lot of mixed emotions. I felt guilty that I was so glad he was going. But he had a terrible driving record...he'd wrecked four cars. He was very expensive."

Because the teen's life seems to hold little direction, parents often feel that the decision to go into the military is a good one, whether the choice is regular enlistment or reserve training and duty. Often the child's father was in the military and feels comfortable with this course of action. Some parents feel totally relieved to be rid of the problems and frustration that arose from seeing their child flounder. Lacking self-discipline, the child looks to the military to provide it.

When Meg left for the Marines, that was exactly what she was seeking. "I was a little wild. Even though it sounds strange to admit it, I really thought that I needed the discipline. My friends said, 'Are you crazy? Why do you want somebody telling you what to do?' But deep down I felt that I needed to respect something. The Marines are like family now. Besides," she added, "where else can you do something you like for twenty years and then retire?"

Mary's comments reflected a frequently-heard parent's point of view. Her oldest son had given her and her husband many headaches. "We were totally relieved when Tony left. He had been such a problem his last year of high school. He wanted to run all the time and party. He was very expensive. He was also very smart and I worried that he was going to throw his life away. He was working almost full-time at nights and loved it. He was drinking and running. I was afraid that he was going to be a waiter the rest of his life.

"Drugs really led to Tony's obnoxiousness. He wrecked three cars before he left. He totaled out a couple, one by hitting a tree...he was speeding. Finally they cancelled his insurance and he had to buy a bicycle to get to work. It was a blessing that he went into the Army. He's definitely changed. He's a lot more conscientious."

Generally parents don't worry excessively when the child leaves, regardless of the distance involved. They feel that the military will keep a tight rein on their child; the perils of drugs and alcohol and late nights will, in all likelihood, be more closely monitored than they could be at home.

"I would worry more if he had moved into an apartment," Mary continued, "because his life would be so unstructured. He'd run a lot more, be a lot wilder. Now I know he's on a schedule. The military is ideal...I didn't think he'd ever go. I tried to talk him into it...and then breathed a sigh of relief. He likes it. He's really gung ho."

opportunities Enlisting is, for many young women and men, a stepping stone to get ahead in life. A sizeable contribution toward college can accumulate: by contributing a few hundred dollars, the young person can become the recipient of many thousands earmarked for college. With education expenses enormously high and parents unwilling or, as often the case, unable to meet these rising costs single-handedly, the only chance some kids have at further education is through the military.

Skilled training is another opportunity afforded those who enlist. In the military, young people are quickly put in positions which tap their potentials and abilities. Schooling plus leadership skills result in marketable job experience. Independence and self-confidence are strengthened. Some may join to satisfy a need for new experiences, adventure, or travel. Some may seize the opportunity to get away from home or perhaps an overprotective parent.

Until he enlisted, life seemed to hold little opportunity for Nat. "He joined the service for the money," said his mother. "He couldn't get a job after he failed his junior year of high school. He was not motivated and he was in with a bad crowd. He was wasting his time and his life...and I couldn't go on supporting him. It was sad to see him do this to himself because he's very bright. I was about ready to pull my hair out. His going was such a relief. What else was he going to do? I was elated.

"Now he's really trying hard. He's studying and is tops in his class. He went in with the attitude that he was going to be the best soldier that the United States Army had ever had. This is really what he wants to do. In twenty years he'll have a pension and he can start something else. It's really nice to know he's making something out of his life."

In general, the lower the family on the socioeconomic scale, the more the military holds out the prospect of opportunity. For parents accustomed to punching a timeclock, the military often represents a good avenue for the kids to improve their lives. It also holds out for the kids a chance to help their parents, to alleviate some of the household financial burden.

Upper-class families tend to have mixed emotions about enlistment. They would rather see their kids go to school first. Even though many of these parents are able to afford college, their children may choose the military specifically to establish independence from home.

drawbacks Although the military may look like the right choice, parents can have legitimate concerns. "When you sign up for four years, that's a long time," said one parent. "You're not signing up for four years when you go to college; you have options. You don't have the option to get out in the military. He went in to try to find something better and if it wasn't, he was in for four years...and that's awful." The finality of the decision was echoed by another parent: "With the Navy, it was like the ultimate gone."

There is also the safety factor. For the first time in many years, 1991 meant declared war and casualties. Even during times of relative peace, troops can be sent to troubled *hot spots* or used for *minor* invasions; accidents can happen at boot camp. Regardless of the maneuvers, peaceful or warlike, the effects can be lethal. Parents can easily feel frightened and wish that their son or daughter had not enlisted.

The fact that kids in the service seem so young to be alone and on their own is also a concern of many parents. Betty spoke of her twins. "They both were really homesick. Sonny's called every day this week. The telephone bill was almost one hundred and fifty dollars last month...and one hundred and eighty this month. I hide them in the drawer. I can't tell my husband. I don't know how I'm going to pay. But they're homesick. They're kids...so when they get afraid or they get bored...they call each other and bill us...or they call us. Sure you worry. They're babies...they're only eighteen."

Some parents are upset about the conditions surrounding the decision. One father and mother alternated comments and feelings about their son, Greg. "I didn't think that he really wanted to go," said Greg's father. "He was unhappy in love. I felt that it was a rebound and he didn't really know what he was doing...he was reluctant. He had lost his volunteer ambulance job with EMS for insurance reasons. He had also lost his regular job and was stuck with a part-time job he didn't like. He was spinning his wheels. He felt that he needed to get his life together...and he did.

"There were just too many emotional things going on," continued his mother, "and we could see all his frustration. We didn't think Greg was excited about it. I don't think that you base a life decision or a career decision on unhappiness. I felt strongly that he was doing that, and he probably was...but it worked out okay."

The tension surrounding the situation was reflected by the father's personal reaction. "It was hard on me. I remember the first night that he was gone. I cried in bed that night. It was tough, but it's just growing up. It's hard...but you get used to it."

emotional strain Not all parents can take military parting philosophically; some suffer intense emotions. Partly the loss of the child and partly the surprise or disappointment at the decision seem to cause these heightened feelings. The phone was not able to disguise the tears of one mother as she said, "We just live each day one at a time and pray for the best. Each time he comes home we have to go through his leaving all over again. I just can't talk about it. It's too painful. I can't go through it again in an interview." It had been seven months since her son first left.

Another mother told a similar story through her tears, but with an added note of hope because her crisis had eventually passed. "All you had to do was look at me, and I'd cry. I was wondering what John was doing all the time...until the letter finally came. When I got that first letter, it was legible and articulate. I couldn't believe it. I was so excited that I called and read it to Eddie, the friend who had influenced John's decision to join up. John was on a diet. He wished his sister a happy birthday. He told his brother to wear a seat belt and not to drink and drive. He even had the commas in the right place...all those things that are important to a mom, but don't mean anything.

"My friend jested, 'They've done more for him in two weeks than you were able to do in twenty years!' In a way, Eddie was right."

Because John had created such havoc in her life, she had the tendency to avoid him. In spite of the tears at his leaving, she found that she was able to recapture an intimacy with her own home. "I stay home a lot more now that John is gone. I'd like to play house for a while and see if I like it! Isn't that the way? There's always the good news and the bad news to things."

a father's story Brad, a father of four, spoke matter-of-factly when discussing his second child's departure into the service. "I was kind of relieved for him, really. Everybody wants to go to college, I guess, but he never would have made it in college the way he was. He needed something to stiffen him up a little bit. He was wild...too flitty to attempt college. I was sorry to see him go...I miss him. He said he was kind of homesick...I was, too, when I went. But he's adjusted now.

"You miss them but you don't lose sleep about them. You know they're fairly safe when they're in the service; the military has pretty tight reins. They're safer than they are around home, what with driving and drugs and not knowing what they're doing at night.

"He joined before he got out of high school and then got cold feet. He thought that he had made a bad decision...but he went the week he graduated. It was his own decision. I had been in the Army so I don't know if he was trying to impress me or what. I thought it was a good thing.

"I'm always glad to see young people stiffen up and try to make something of themselves rather than depend on somebody else to do it for them. When you get to be eighteen it's time to get out and do it. When you leave, you're gone. That's it."

a mother's story Patsy's story of her son, Red, was a little longer. "I knew he would not do well at college; he was not academically inclined. We had pushed him through school since kindergarten so it was a relief that he graduated! He didn't have enough self-discipline or desire for college.

"He was a regular troublemaker. We didn't even think he was going to make it through school. He drank. He lost his driver's license. He had a lot of problems. The military seemed to be an alternative. For men, what type work is available if you don't go to college?

"He was a very difficult child to raise so I thought: he's going to be out of my hair at last!" Patsy paused to laugh. "The day came and we went to airport. It broke my heart. I just cried and cried. It really hurt to see him leave. I was worried about the training...it's so hard and brutal. They try to wear you down.

"He wrote every week...which surprised me. I wrote and sent cards to keep his morale up. In basic training you can't call them and they can't call you. I never heard his voice for eleven weeks. That was the hardest part.

"My husband missed Red more than I thought he would. He's usually not very emotional but he wrote more than I ever expected he would...every week. I was surprised and pleased. When we went to the graduation it was so emotional. We were so proud to see him. He had really trimmed down.

"He's having money taken out of his paycheck for college. He says he plans to go after four years. Then he'll go back into the service as an officer and become a pilot. That's what he really wants to do.

"I'll tell you, those Marines...whatever they say or do, it works. He's even studying and is second out of fifty. He wants to do so well. He gets upset if he misses one answer on a test...and that has never happened before, I can tell you. Just goes to show that if you're really doing what you want, you can succeed."

MOVING OUT

many different reasons The reasons for moving out are many, not all of them happy. "When my Josh left," said one mother, "he was gone for four months before I heard from him. We'd gotten into a big fight and he just left. I didn't even know where he was. I felt completely hurt and sick and not sure if he'd ever come back. It was awful."

A father told a different story. "My daughter left her mother's home at sixteen because she couldn't get along with her stepfather. I thought it was terrible. She lived in an apartment by herself for a while and then she married at eighteen. She's pretty wild.

"I know of a neighbor kid who had a bad family situation...the dad drinks. Finally, the parents got a divorce. Then his mom let the dad move back home again so the son moved out...he just couldn't take it."

As these cases illustrate, the reasons for leaving home may involve an *escape from* rather than a *going toward*. Some kids do not get along with one or both of their parents and need to get away; some may have a blowup over a particular issue and decide to move out. Others are motivated by a parental divorce, a remarriage, or conflicts with a stepparent. In some cases, teen pregnancy is the motivator. Unfortunately, nowadays, too many young adults leave home for the first time because they need help in a residential treatment center for drug or alcohol abuse. Finally taking control of their lives, a few will not return to the family setting.

Similar to some military departures, parents may feel a keen disappointment when the young adult moves out for other reasons. "I tried to keep him from feeling like a failure," said one parent whose son left home a few months before high school graduation. "Eventually he got his GED. I tried to help him feel good about structuring his own life. I helped him move and from that day forward he's supported himself. He's done very well...but I've been disappointed. He's not tapping any of his intellectual potential. I don't care what he does...if it's a challenge for him."

moving out by degrees "All my children have left in degrees," said one mother. "The ache comes when they walk out and say, 'Well, I won't be home for nine months or a year...until I get a vacation.' That's kind of final. If you know that they'll be home in six weeks or two months then it's not so bad."

Some kids move out to live with a friend while they go to school part-time and hold down a job — or the other way around. But their parents' home is still very much a part of their routine. A father explained his son's ongoing relationship with the family dwelling. "He came here to do his laundry. He was always here to eat supper. He worked down the street so his leaving was not as major as it might have seemed. It was natural...but he had his parties somewhere else! Then he got married and things changed."

independence "My daughter left home to gain her independence!" Ellen laughs. "But we work together so it wasn't so much of a loss. She usually comes to see me on Saturday or Sunday. If she moved out of town, I would feel a terrible loss."

Once again, the threat of an out-of-town departure causes parents to reflect on the empty space that would arise in their lives. So long as the thread of continuity exists through visits or the telephone, a child's need for independence can be accepted more easily by parents.

"I knew it was going to be a wonderful learning experience...a positive growth experience," said Jan. She was talking about her daughter. "I did not worry about her; she lived in a good area and had a roommate. The main thrust was that she wanted to establish her independence.

"Now that she was free, she was more able to come back home. Even though she enjoyed her independence, she liked being close with us...especially when we weren't always in conflict. The funny part about it was that, in moving out, I think she found that she really did like us. We weren't such horrible ogres. She was over here every two days or so and she'd join her dad for lunch downtown."

Experts say that mothers often don't worry as much when daughters leave home. Mothers have more confidence in the ability of daughters to manage the daily chores of life. A son's self-sufficiency can be in question, as the next example illustrates.

false starts "I didn't realize Mickey was considering moving out with a friend. As far as I was concerned, he was not ready." Gerry talked about his son. "He did make the discovery that it was such a hassle trying to keep up with his laundry, getting groceries. Living on minimum wage was hard. All that came into focus for him.

"They moved to a cabin that was not finished. There were wasps and bugs but he and his friend thought it had a lot of possibilities so they tried it out. Mickey found out the responsibilities of living by yourself. They had no hot water and he really missed it. One thing after another he started missing. Then he didn't get along living with the friend...so in four months he moved back home. Now he pays rent."

At such a young age, kids can easily underestimate the responsibility and expense of living on one's own. They can fail to assess adequately the many complications which may arise. In short, their lack of maturity may emerge, as it had with Mickey. Fortunately, most young adults are able to take such falterings in stride — even if their parents cannot.

Sometimes parents supplement the income of children who want to move out and be on their own. This help may allow them to survive at some minimum level or, for the more affluent, to maintain a lifestyle similar to that left behind. This help may be contingent on certain conditions, such as going to school or having a job; often there is a time limit — a phasing in of full independence. If the child is not able to make this transition within the alloted time then financial support is withdrawn, forcing the child to seek a different rooming situation or return home.

This is exactly what happened to Jan's daughter. "When her roommate moved out, I was worried. Then she took in another friend who left her with a bunch of bills. Finally, she had to move back home because we withdrew financial support; we stopped supporting her in that lifestyle.

"From the beginning, we were concerned that she had bitten off more than she could financially absorb. In the end she had, but it was good that she found that out on her own rather than our telling her. She did not really feel that she had failed."

Major illness, serious car-related injury, or industrial accident also can cause a false start. They may delay a child's leaving or cause a return home. Said one mother whose son had been on his own for a while, "He got that yeast syndrome and couldn't hold down his job. It's been about six months now and he's finally doing okay. But what a shock for my system to have him back home. Now I'm wondering when the nest will stay empty." For some accidents and illnesses, recovery can take years; for a few, independent living never happens.

posslq (persons of the opposite sex sharing living quarters) Because kids usually cannot make it financially living alone, they often find a roommate. A nonromantic roommate usually means that the family remains the center of the child's emotional commitment. A romantic roommate, however, often means that the young adult's emotional allegiance shifts away from the family and focuses on the new relationship — a marriage of sorts.

Parental reaction to this rooming situation varies. Some parents may feel that their children are simply too young. Others may breathe a sigh of relief, grateful that marriage is not part of the picture. Still other parents may have more difficulty with its acceptance because of moral issues. (And, sometimes, parents have to deal with the acknowledgment or suspicion of homosexuality: the *romantic* roommate is not of the opposite sex but rather the same sex.)

Therese was afraid that her daughter was not in touch with

herself as a person when she began living with her boyfriend at age seventeen. "I was happy that she finished high school," said Therese, "but I wanted her to get some insight into what she wanted to do with herself and not depend on someone else for her happiness. She's going to have to stand on her own two feet regardless of whether she's married or living on her own. Today you have about a fifty-fifty chance of any relationship being permanent. And even if you do have a permanent one it takes two incomes to maintain a household.

"My main objective was for her to stop and think about what she wanted to do as a person...to be whole within herself. She's not ready for that; she's got this rescuer kind of mentality. But she'll overcome it eventually."

Another woman described the situation of a friend whose daughter left town right after graduation. "She moved to California to be with her boyfriend and work there. It was hard for the parents to realize that their daughter would choose to be with someone else far away. It was especially hard for the mother. She was depressed for a couple of weeks. She cried a lot. When she took her daughter to the airport she was really upset. Deep down she knew that it was the daughter's decision and that she had to adjust...and she did. But it was awesome."

parents who jump the gun Sometimes parents move out first. Said one West Coast mother, "I'm the one who left the nest!" She was dating an out-of-town man so when her mothering responsibilities seemed to be winding down and her rent was about to escalate, she went to live with her *significant other*. "I beat them to it...but they were practically gone anyway. They led very busy lives."

Other parents jump the gun, so to speak, by calling an end to a child's self-indulgent lifestyle. "It got to the point where I said, 'Hey, I'm giving you an ultimatum. You either get a job or you go somewhere else to live. It's as simple as that. My child support has stopped and my pay doesn't amount to beans.'

"It was a tight crunch for me and here he was...lounging at home and watching TV all day or else bumming around with friends. It drove me crazy. Hell, he was able to work. I didn't mean to be hard...but those were the facts of life. Within two weeks he was working. He met his to-be wife and shortly after that he moved in with her. I missed him."

job relocation Even at very young ages, job relocation can be a possibility. Young adults are single and often willing to move without being reimbursed for expenses. Chain-type enterprises may take advantage of this situation, as they did in the case of Lenny.

"When Lenny left, it was upsetting. He was very young. He was going to run a store alone. It was difficult. He moved to a city where he knew no one. We worried about his safety. It was all very sudden. He had a week to get a whole apartment of furniture ready.

"He found a nice apartment and had a nice job so we had to feel good about that. He was old at nineteen, more mature...but he came home every other weekend. We would have felt more disturbed if he was so tied to home that he wouldn't go.

"We worried about whether he'd eat, lots of things. He'd also just been dumped by his girlfriend so he was devastated. We worried because he was unhappy. We worried about his making friends.

"We worried about his finances. He was there on a shoestring, and we really couldn't help him that much. He really shouldn't have gone, but he was single so it was cheaper for the company to take a chance with him." Lenny's father paused to laugh. "The only good thing about it was that he met a sweet girl...she worked for him. They got married and we love her."

As an afterthought, his mother added, "I just never dreamed that any of our children would be in another city. It never entered my mind."

"a free agent" Mother and father spoke of their son, Jason. "He had plans to be in Florida for three months," said his mother. "The day he was leaving I realized that he was not going to come back. He told us he was coming back, but just to make us feel better. He had packed everything into the attic. I accepted it. I couldn't do anything about it...but what a letdown. He would never discuss things. Out there in the driveway, everything started coming together as he was pulling out.

"If that's what he wanted to do, I can let go and say fine...because I left home at a very early age. I was seventeen when I got my own apartment and job."

Jason's father continued. "I didn't realize it for a while but when he left I was very, very sad. He had just broken his arm so I worried about his physical condition. And then he got sick down there. That was the hardest part...his being away and being sick.

"I worried about him...putting too much trust in people he barely knew. There he was, just a young boy. Sometimes, you don't have as much confidence in your own children. I worried a lot. The night that I realized that he wasn't coming home, I went back in my bedroom and cried.

"College is a real necessity as far as I'm concerned, so I can accept that kind of leaving a whole lot easier...even though there are a lot of things that can lead them astray...drugs, peer pressure. When they're gone from home you can't monitor them the way you can if they're home. Knowing that Jason was over a thousand miles away was very hard...very hard. It's hard when they're so far that you can't see them.

"In a way, though, we were ready for him to leave; he was so active." They both laughed. "We constantly worried about him because he did all these crazy things. From the time he was fifteen we did not make any out-of-town plans because one time he had a party and we came home early. It took our neighbors years to get over the whole situation. I wish that he were closer so we could see him now and then...not just once a year.

"Jason had fifty dollars left in his pocket when he finally decided where he wanted to settle. We didn't jump in and say, 'Okay, we'll send you a couple of hundred to keep surviving.' We'd send him money to come back home, but we didn't want him settling so far away. He got work day to day. He said he had to prove he could do it. And, of course, he did...he's been very successful.

"I had a feeling that Jason left to show us that he could take care of himself." Jason's father suddenly became very nostalgic. "But last Christmas as he went down the ramp to get on the plane, he stopped and turned around and looked at us. Even after he was on the plane and made the turn back to the seats he stood there. He kept peeking around the corner at us. He wanted to see us longer...he was homesick. I could see that he would have liked to stay if he could, but he had to go. He has to be a free agent. He could not be the same person if he were here."

CONCLUSION

If parents see themselves in the role of coach, they'll see themselves as working on the same team. To stand on the sidelines and watch closely is often the very best thing that a parent can do for a child. A parent ideally should take as much pleasure in the child's independence as the child does.

IRONIC TWIST

When I started this book, the underlying reasons were those of sadness, confusion, and emptiness. After two years of work, the book was nearly finished and my son came home to live for a few months. Glenn had hiked one thousand miles of the Appalachian Trail and was taking the rest of the year to work between his sophomore and junior years. My daughter, Tiffany, had also decided to take a year off from her schooling by delaying entrance into college for one year.

Despite intentions to get apartments of their own during this period, both were living at home. Financial reality had proven too big an obstacle to overcome. At the exact point in my life when I had expected to be completely on my own, the opposite had occurred.

Two rather humorous incidents pointed out the irony of this turn of events.

> At Christmastime I visited my next door neighbor — a mother of five and experienced grandmother. She asked me how things were going.
>
> "Well," I said, "Glenn's driving me crazy. He doesn't have a job yet and he's home all the time. He just takes up so much space. It's certainly not my first choice." I shook my head.
>
> "See," she said, "what did I tell you? They keep coming back. You just think they're gone. I told you this would

happen, didn't I?" She looked at me and laughed, clearly reveling in the wisdom that I had discounted a mere two years earlier. She had warned me.

*****

A couple of months later Tiffany and I had occasion to visit a friend in Atlanta — who asked how the book was coming and when it would be done. Suddenly she looked at me and laughed.

"Here you are writing a book about kids leaving home and you've got both of yours back." She continued laughing with real delight — perhaps inspired by the fact that she had never had children to contend with. I, too, joined in the laughter. The joke was clearly on me.

"You thought you had to worry about being alone and here they are home again. I see it happening to a lot of my friends. They think their kids are gone...and then they're not."

But those were brief snapshots of an interim stage — a period during which I continued to change and began to look forward to their next departure. By the time they left, it was clear to me how much I had grown and let go: I was ready to "stand on the sidelines and watch," as one mother had put it. I couldn't wait to be alone.

PERSONAL GROWTH

In researching and writing this book I learned a great deal more than I bargained for — about myself and about my relationships with other people. I learned that all relationships require a letting go and a dropping of expectations, not just those with maturing young adults. For me this meant with male companions, cohorts at work, my parents and other members of the family, friends, and even casual acquaintances. Mostly, I realized that I wasn't nearly as good at letting go as I thought. I needed more practice.

I understood that the main shift from parent to child is, in a sense, that of power — power over the young adult's life. As children grow and mature, they take that power and begin to parent themselves. Those who fail to make that transition continue to seek approval and parenting from others; those who are successful generally become self-confident adults.

I also came to understand the process as a gradual one. Relationships do not change and grow on a straight-line basis: the *two-steps-*

forward, one-step-back rule definitely applies to letting go. These young adults often do return for short, and sometimes longer, stays. The separation break is not as final as it first appears.

Children who separate successfully stop seeing their parents in that role and begin relating to them as people. The end of the parent role, however, does not mean an end to caring and love and, sometimes, need — for either the child or the parent. As one mother succinctly told her children when they left the nest: "I won't be around to parent you, but I'll always be your mother." If a mutual interdependency can develop, the emerging adult-adult relationship is enhanced, and both can learn from each other.

Parents who let go gain respect for their children as separate individuals. These parents find pleasure and satisfaction from a free-thinking young adult; they understand that perpetual dependence only thwarts a child's development. They know that, in all likelihood, they will relate to their offspring longer as adults than as children.

Although there is a wide range and diversity of what might constitute *normal* in the letting go process, those parents who appear to be most successful cultivate a certain detachment from their offspring: while they may *feel* for their child in a particular situation, they don't take on the child's problems and moods as their own. They don't live the child's life. They understand that parenthood is not a life-long occupation. If they haven't completely worked themselves out of a job by the time the young adult leaves home, they are close.

As parents we have trouble letting go because we resist change. We often don't want to face the many issues that a child's leaving triggers. Not only do realignments in relationships become necessary, but priorities need reevaluation. The effort to change one's focus from that of *doing* to that of *being* can be confusing and exhausting.

Naturally, as a result of my interviews, I drew some general conclusions. I discovered that many parents do not do a very good job of letting go; they do not adequately prepare themselves — or their children — for the next stage. Too many children have difficulty assuming responsibility for their own lives. Our affluent society contributes more to this situation than parents care to admit.

So much complexity is wrapped up in the leave-taking. There is the actual physical separation. There are the numerous underlying issues, both conscious and unconscious, and the fact that parents are often hesitant to look directly at their feelings or discuss those feelings with others. I did hear of a church that sponsors a *postparenthood* support group, but I couldn't help wishing that our society had a *leave-taking rite* or ceremony — a time of acknowledging the transition that both parent and young adult face.

The existence of such a ritual, I concluded, might have made it easier for me to anticipate the separation issues. I would not have been so hesitant to express my feelings of loss — to myself or to my child. I would not have been so surprised that I missed the physical contact that had been there for eighteen years. Of course, I probably would not have written a book, either.

The empty nest inexorably arrives. Those parents who view its arrival as a natural, positive experience are better able to let go. Not surprisingly, there are no easy answers to letting go, no one magic way to make it work smoothly. When parents see letting go as cathartic, however, the separation acts as a catalyst for life introspection and understanding. The empty nest becomes part of life's flow and signals the time for moving on.

* * * * *

One day, as I went out on my front porch, I noticed a young bird cowering in the corner. It was struggling for first flight. I couldn't resist the temptation to watch. Quietly, I retreated into the house. Lying down on the floor behind the lower portion of the screen door, I propped up on one elbow and viewed independence in the making, wing flap by wing flap.

Fledge, as I nicknamed this young bird, was not having an easy time. Its first attempts at locomotion brought zero lift and simply drove its body onto the concrete in a hopeless semicircle. I wondered if one wing was broken. Even though I knew that interference in the life of a wild animal was taboo, my initial reaction was to provide a rescue. And where was Fledge's mother, I wondered, just when she was needed? Was she concerned?

Gradually Fledge flapped over to the top step and caromed down — truly a nose dive. At this point Momma Bird flew down to bring eats — either (I presumed) as reward or sustenance — and (I imagined) words of encouragement. Finishing the snack, Fledge flapped around while she waited and watched. When no real progress was made, she flew away. Did she know that her presence perpetuated a dependence of sorts?

Eventually Fledge semiflew to the next lower step. Things seemed to be making progress and I wondered if Momma Bird chirped a note of congratulations. Sometime later Fledge dove off the side of the steps into the flower bed — perhaps the most flightlike yet of its attempts but, alas, no longer within my viewing range.

Slowly I arose, feeling a little stiff. So far the process had easily consumed forty minutes of my time — and I had a book to finish. After checking to make sure Fledge was okay I retreated to my desk. I kept a lookout for cats in the yard but essentially Fledge was on its own. Somehow, though, I couldn't resist a periodic peek from the porch to see if flight had yet been achieved. Finally, after about two hours, Fledge was gone.

I felt relieved and happy. Fledge had made it. I wanted to make obvious analogies about me and my kids, about all parents and their children. Momma Bird clearly knew that less was better.

And I now understood that she was right.

BIBLIOGRAPHY

Abdul-Jabbar, Kareem. *Giant Steps*. New York: Bantam Books, 1983.

Anderson, Christopher P. *Father The Figure and the Force*. New York: Warner Books, 1983.

Baruch, Grace and Jeanne Brooks-Gunn (ed.). *Women in Midlife*. New York: Plenum Press, 1984.

Berardo, Felix M. (ed.). *The Annals of The American Academy of Political and Social Science, Middle and Late Life Transitions*. Beverly Hills: Sage Publications, 1982.

Bettelheim, Bruno. *The Children of the Dream*. Toronto: The Macmillan Company, 1969.

Block, Marilyn R., Janice L. Davidson and Jean D. Grambs. *Women Over Forty*. New York: Springer Publishing Company, Inc., 1981.

Bodin, Jeanne and Bonnie Mitelman. *Mothers Who Work*. New York: Ballantine Books, 1983.

Bowlby, John. *Attachment and Loss, Vol.II: Separation*. New York: Basic Books, Inc., Publishers, 1973.

Brewi, Janice and Anne Brennan. *Mid-life Psychological and Spiritual Perspectives*. New York: The Crossroad Publishing Company, 1982.

Buscaglia, Leo. *Loving Each Other*. Thorofare, New Jersey: SLACK Incorporated, 1984.

Caine, Lynn. *What Did I Do Wrong? Mothers, Children, Guilt*. New York: Arbor House, 1985.

Cohen, Joan Z., Karen L. Coburn and Joan C. Pearlman. *Hitting Our Stride*. New York: Delacorte Press, 1980.

Coles, Robert. *Privileged Ones. (Children of Crisis, Volume V)* Boston: Little, Brown and Company, 1977.

Crichton, Jennifer. "Who shall I be?" *Ms.*, October 1984, pp. 59-61.

De Beauvoir, Simone. *The Second Sex*. New York: Alfred A. Knopf, 1971.

Ehrenreich, Barbara. *The Hearts of Men*. Garden City, New York: Anchor Press, 1983.

Eichenbaum, Luise and Susie Orbach. *Understanding Women*. New York: Basic Books, Inc., Publishers, 1983.

Erickson, Erik H. *Childhood and Society*. New York: W.W. Norton & Company, Inc., 1963.

Farrell, Michael P. and Stanley D. Rosenberg. *Men at Midlife*. Boston: Auburn House Publishing Company, 1981.

Feinberg, Mortimer R., Gloria Feinberg and John J. Tarrant. *Leavetaking*. NY: Simon and Schuster, 1978.

Feuerstein, Phyllis and Carol Roberts. *The Not-So-Empty Nest*. Chicago: Follett Publishing Company, 1981.

Galinsky, Ellen. *Between Generations: The Six Stages of Parenthood*. New York: Times Books, a division of Quadrangle/The New York Times Book Co., Inc., 1981.

Gibran, Kahlil. *The Prophet*. New York: Alfred A. Knopf, 1955.

Gilligan, Carol. *In A Different Voice*. Cambridge, Massachusetts: Harvard University Press, 1982.

Goodman, Ellen. "Apron Strings." *The Courier-Journal*, September 16, 1986, p.A7

Gross, Jane. "Single Women: Coping With a Void." *The New York Times*, April 28, 1987, p.1.

Gross, Zenith Henkin. *And You Thought It Was All Over!* New York: St. Martin's/Marek, 1985.

Haley, Jay. *Leaving Home*. New York: McGraw-Hill Book Company, 1980.

Halpern, Howard. *Cutting Loose*. New York: Simon and Schuster, 1976.

Klein, Carole. *Mothers and Sons*. Boston: Houghton Mifflin Company, 1984.

Kotre, John and Elizabeth Hall. *Seasons of Life*. Boston: Little, Brown and Company, 1990.

Leonard, Linda S. *The Wounded Woman*. Athens, Ohio: Ohio University Press, 1982.

Levinson, Daniel J. *The Seasons of a Man's Life*. New York: Alfred A. Knopf, 1978.

Littwin, Susan. *The Postponed Generation*. New York: William Morrow and Company, Inc., 1986.

London, Mel. *Second Spring*. Emmaus, Pennsylvania: Rondale Press, 1982.

Mankowitz, Ann. *Change of Life*. Toronto: Inner City Books, 1984.

May, Rollo. *Love and Will*. New York: W.W.Norton & Company, Inc., 1969.

Mayer, Nancy. *The Male Mid-Life Crisis*. Garden City, New York: Doubleday & Company, Inc., 1978.

McGill, Michael E. *The 40- to 60-Year-Old Male*. New York: Simon and Schuster, 1980.

Nichols, Michael P. *Turning Forty In The Eighties*. New York: W.W. Norton & Company, 1986.

Peck, M.Scott. *The Road Less Traveled*. New York: Simon and Schuster, 1978.

Porcino, Jane. *Growing Older Getting Better*. Reading, Massachusetts: Addison-Wesley Publishing Company, 1983.

Reese, Deboral F. "The Children Are Gone." *The New York Times*, December 11, 1985, p.C13.

Rohrbaugh, Joanna B. *Women: Psychology's Puzzle*. New York: Basic Books, Inc., Publishers, 1979.

Rubin, Lillian B. *Women of a Certain Age*. New York: Harper & Row, 1979.

Sanford, Linda T. and Mary Ellen Donovan. *Women and Self-Esteem*. Garden City, New York: Anchor Press/Doubleday, 1984.

Scarf, Maggie. *Intimate Partners*. New York: Random House, 1987.

Sheehy, Gail. *Passages*. New York: E.P. Dutton & Co., Inc., 1976.

Sheehy, Gail. *Pathfinders*. New York: William Morrow and Company, Inc., 1981.

Simmons, Ira. "Marsha Norman hopes to stay on top of Wheel of Fortune with her first novel." *The Courier-Journal*, May 3, 1987. p.I9.

Stein, Murray. *In Midlife: A Jungian Perspective*. Dallas: Spring Publications, Inc., 1983.

Still, Henry. *Surviving the Male Mid-life Crisis*. New York: Thomas Y. Crowell Company, 1977.

Tamir, Lois M. *Men in Their Forties The Transition to Middle Age*. New York: Springer Publishing Company, 1982.

U.S. Bureau of the Census: Historical Statistics of the United States Colonial Times to 1970, Bicentennial Edition, Part 2. Washington, D.C., 1975.

U.S. Bureau of the Census: Statistical Abstract of the United States 1986 (106th Edition). Washington, D.C., 1986.

Van Hoose, William H. *Midlife Myths and Realities*. Atlanta: Humanics Limited, 1985.

Viorst, Judith. *Necessary Losses*. New York: Simon and Schuster, 1986.

INDEX

A

affair 193-95
affluence 83-4, 124-25, 134, 223, 229
agenda 103-104
aging 160-63, 194
ambivalence 15, 36, 42-45, 53-55, 104, 167
androgyny 71, 176
anger 15, 24, 66-67, 75, 107, 143, 156, 166-67, 205
apron strings 65-66, 169
autonomy 102, 126-27, 190
avoidance 24

B

birth 101
bond 50, 67, 69-71, 85, 152
breaking away 35-36, 108
buffer 40-41, 55, 163, 183, 185, 196

C

career 163-69, 177
career women 95-99
challenge 22, 30, 104, 107
change 38, 68, 106-107, 115-19, 135-36, 148-51, 164, 173-80, 228-29
child 2
child as spouse 78-79, 184, 187
child-bearing years 17
children of choice 152-54
children, single-parent 40, 81-87
climacteric 140, 143, 161, 194
college 2, 28-45, 202, 226
confidence 9-10, 125-28
conflict 103, 123
consequences 123-24
control 35, 40-41, 104, 118, 156, 177
coping strategies 15

D

decisions 126-28
demographics 142, 203-204
departure 5, 159
dependence 42-43, 78-79, 119, 129-30, 168, 185, 197, 204
depression 66-67
distancing 125-29
divorce 40, 196-99
Dominant Goal/Other 196-97

E

education 134-35
eighteen-year-olds 2, 6, 28
emotions 5, 42-43, 62-71, 78, 218-20
empty nest 13, 16, 44, 67, 74-75, 87, 94, 158, 182, 191, 196, 202-208, 224, 229-31
empty nest syndrome 140, 144-46
excitement 5, 7, 28
expectation 5, 10, 105-106, 228

F

failure 22, 155-56
families, large 55-57, 155, 190
family dynamics 7-9, 22-23, 40, 44, 48-61, 182-89, 206-207, 221
fathers 62-71, 113, 158-59, 168, 215-16
fear 21-25, 36-37, 124, 143, 168, 192
feelings 5-25, 28-44, 62-71, 74-77, 152-54, 177
finances 24, 31, 66, 79, 83-84, 104-105, 130, 167-68, 196, 202-203, 227
first born 51-52
freedom 5, 11, 28, 40-41, 52, 82, 87-89, 122, 153, 178-79, 191, 204
friendship 114-15, 126
friendship, college 38-39
frustration 37

G

generativity 178
growing up 6-7, 36-38
growth 115-16, 151, 190-91
guilt 44-45, 70, 78, 116-17, 153, 168, 177, 190, 204

H

holidays 40, 77
homemaker 95, 165-68
homesickness 29, 117
hormones 143, 161-62
hostility 103
humor 113-14

I

independence 28-36, 42, 52-53, 82-84, 104, 107-108, 128-29, 132-34, 159, 167, 177, 193, 222, 227
individuation 103, 117
in loco parentis 120
investment 118, 196
isolation 30

J

jealousy 186-87
job relocation 224
judgment 155-57
Jung 96, 179-80

K

kids 2

L

labeling 141
last child 55, 130, 155
leave-taking 1, 3, 5-13, 21, 28-29, 45, 117-18, 207, 229
leave-taking, noncollege 210-26
letters from dad 69-70
letting go 3, 6, 9-10, 100-36, 169-70, 229-31
listening 110-12
lists 120-22, 131-34
loss 13-20, 44, 64, 75, 78-80, 147, 196-97, 206
love 108, 112, 115, 132-33

M

macho image 62
manipulation 41, 116-17, 124, 130, 158, 186, 206
marriage 2, 144, 170-71 182-99
marriage at eighteen 212-25
maturity 34, 49, 67, 101, 107, 117-18, 122, 204
menopause 140, 143, 161-62, 194
mental click 29
middle age, definition of 162-63
midlife 96, 140-80, 196-97
midlife crisis 145-46
midlife issues 148-72, 196-97
midlife myths 140-47
midlife passage 145-46, 149-51, 173-80
military 215-20
missing home 39-42
mistakes 118
mortality 163
mothers 15-17, 62-71, 76, 144-47, 154-58, 167-68, 184-85
mourning 17-20, 38
moving out 220-26
"myth of independence" 96
"myth of motherhood" 144-45
"myth of the family" 23

N

new person 31-36
nostalgia 17-18, 77
nurturer 64, 68, 70-71, 146, 154-55, 176-77

O

openness 114-15, 128
options 87-89
overprotection 24, 78-79

P

pain 13, 15, 24, 33, 107
parent, concerns 3, 21-22
parent, noncustodial 79-80

parenthood, goal of 3, 6, 20, 107, 117, 229
parenthood, negative 98, 153-54
parenting 9-10, 14, 19, 23, 101-102, 106-107, 117, 124, 156, 159, 205-207, 228
parents' weekend 33, 77
perfect parent 34, 78, 118, 133, 159, 179
person, separate 9, 19, 48, 86, 148, 198
physical contact 112-13, 230
pipe dream 99
polarization 105
positive attitude 112
posslq 223-24
power 30, 228
praise 112
preparation 120-29, 135
pride 5-7, 84
privacy 113, 206
privileges 122
problem child 186, 215
psychological aspects 3, 14-17, 193

R

rejection 23-24, 80
relationships 1, 57-59, 86, 119, 169-71, 228-29
relationships, parent-child 1, 6-10, 15-25, 32-36, 100-36, 147, 198, 207, 228-31
relief 5, 10, 50-53, 152
respect 113, 115, 132
responsibilities, lists 120-22, 131-34
responsibility 55
returning home 134-35, 202-208, 227-28
role 16, 20, 81, 99, 104, 115, 117-19, 123, 152-60, 196-97, 229
room left behind 43-44
rules 122-23

S

sandwich generation 169-70
scapegoat 187-88
security 50, 192
self-discipline 108

self-examination 148-72
self-reliance 131
self-worth 108-109
separation 1, 3, 5-17, 20, 24, 49, 59, 74-75, 105, 107-108, 128-30, 210-25, 229-31
separation gap 97-99
sexual differences 84, 125, 222
sexual relationships 87-89, 161-62, 169, 185-86, 191-94, 204
siblings 48-61
single parents 2, 68, 74-93, 136, 157, 165
socioeconomic groups 1, 166, 168, 211, 217
space 113
spirituality 96, 179-80
spoiled child 202
stepparents/stepchildren 67-68, 190, 221
straitjacket, emotional 68-71
stress 11, 21-24, 77-81
super mom 78, 165, 198
support 112
surprise 39, 97-98, 197-98

T

television 136
time 110, 174-75
"top dog" 53
transition 23, 149-51, 167-68, 173-80, 190-91, 228
trust 112-13

U

unconditional love 16-17

V

values 110
vindication 87

W

women's movement 94-99, 144
working mothers 2, 95-99, 156-57, 165-68
worry 21-22

To order copies of *And Suddenly They're Gone* for yourself or friends, please complete the order form below and mail to:

> Tiffany Press
> P. O. Box 62, Department A
> Jamestown, CO 80455-0062

along with your check or money order made payable to Tiffany Press. (For a volume discount, contact the above address.)

ORDER FORM

Qty	Item	Price	Amount
	And Suddenly They're Gone	$14.00	
	Colorado Residents add $.53 per book Sales Tax		
	Shipping and handling: add $2.75 per book		
	☐ Check ☐ Money Order	TOTAL	

Would you like this book autographed? _____ Yes _____ No

Name _____

Address _____

City _____ State _____ Zip _____

Daytime phone (___) _____

Ship To (if different from above):

Name _____

Address _____

City _____ State _____ Zip _____